SHIMMERING IMAGES

SHIMMERING IMAGES

Trans Cinema, Embodiment, and the Aesthetics of Change

ELIZA STEINBOCK

DUKE UNIVERSITY PRESS
Durham and London 2019

Designed by Jennifer Hill
Typeset in Minion Pro by Copperline Books

Library of Congress
Cataloging-in-Publication Data
Names: Steinbock, Eliza, [date] author.
Title: Shimmering images : trans cinema,
embodiment, and the aesthetics of change /
Eliza Steinbock.
Description: Durham : Duke University
Press, 2019. | Includes bibliographical
references and index.
Identifiers: LCCN 2018037349 (print) |
LCCN 2018047135 (ebook)
ISBN 9781478004509 (ebook)
ISBN 9781478003243 (hardcover : alk. paper)
ISBN 9781478003885 (pbk. : alk. paper)
Subjects: LCSH: Transgender people in
motion pictures. | Transsexuals in motion
pictures. | Gender identity in motion
pictures. | Motion pictures—Social aspects. |
Motion pictures—Aesthetics.
Classification: LCC PN1995.9.S47 (ebook) |
LCC PN1995.9.S47 S74 2019 (print) |
DDC 791.43/65267—dc23
LC record available at
https://lccn.loc.gov/2018037349

Cover art: Older Dandy Dust returns to
fly through the void (screen capture,
Dandy Dust, 1998, [Ashley] Hans Scheirl,
Millivres Multimedia).

CONTENTS

PREFACE   CALL ME THEY

I've been called a lot of things. And I've called myself a few—a female transvestite, a butch oma, someone who believes in nonbinary trans love like others refer to the Old Testament (something open to interpretation). In the course of researching this book, I've been fully guilty of that most perverse, and common, knowledge-seeking pleasure: me-search. The versions of "me," however, have been morphing, accumulating under the aegis of changes in name, body shape, clothing style, country, job, and interest groups of all kinds. I can remember learning, as an undergraduate amateur drag king (Danny Illdoya), Leslie Feinberg's pronouns *ze* and *hir* and thinking how cool it would be if we really could get some gender-neutral pronouns recognized. If nothing else, then to hush those twittering naysayers who claim that those who fantasize about abolishing the gender system were all a bunch of elitists, or freaks, or elitist freaks; "yeah, like that'll ever happen," they snigger. It felt certainly possible to me, if only enough people would use them in languages where gendered pronouns are relevant. But I never actually thought some version of personal pronouns for genderqueer people, namely "they," would become incorporated into *Merriam-Webster's Dictionary* only some fifteen years later. A dictionary!

The singular use of the pronoun *they* to refer to someone whose gender is unknown—as in, "Ask your friend if they want to come along"—is an old phenomenon that has lasted continuously since around 1300. The use of *they* as a nonbinary pronoun, however, is relatively new, which is why it is one of the "words we're watching" for Merriam-Webster and has been included since 2013 in their historicizing catalog of word uses. This is but one indicator for Anglophone users that the implicit binary basis for understanding trans embodiment and identity, cited in the descriptors *male-to-female transsexual* and *female-to-male transsexual*, is under pressure as the sole conceptual world for transitioning. Another route is to highlight trans terminology as jargon, such as by capitalizing *Transsexual* to indicate the term's status as psycho-medical nomenclature, rather than a social identity. The language and related possibilities for understanding trans have wonderfully ballooned to include so many more than medical trajectories. My point is that people should have access to the categories to which they want to belong, and those categories must include so-called binary and nonbinary versions of being female/woman/she or male/man/he.

Though I prefer to be called they, this does not detract from my overarching commitment to categorical inclusivity. Including transsexual in the realm of trans categories, along with intersex and queer, results in certain unresolvable tensions among the vectors of sex/gender/sexuality. These tensions become compounded through how discourses, images, and sound markers supersede one another, creating a palimpsest of trans forms. At the heart of this book, then, is this inevitable historicity of being made in the years spanning a robust transsexual attachment to gender categories through mushrooming genderqueer detachment from such figurations.

Needless to say, this me-search has evolved from within an enormously engulfing wave of change. For example, when I began writing about trans representations, C. Jacob Hale's "Suggested Rules for Non-Transsexuals Writing about Transsexuals, Transsexuality, Transsexualism, or Trans ____," first published on Sandy Stone's website January 5, 1997 (and still available), was the only guideline for how, by following fifteen rules, to respectfully orient oneself toward transsexual culture and positions. It might seem unimaginable to some trans-whatevers today that *transsexuality* or *transgendered* would be proper, acceptable terms. In accordance with rule 1, "Approach your topic with a sense of humility," I have tried in my writing about trans cinema and theories to honor their historical specificity, and not to presume that I might "know better" from my vantage point now. The way I use the prefix *trans* to refer to cinema, embodiment, and identities borrows from Hale's openness to any and all future uses of trans___. I also at times cluster trans___ identities under the holey umbrella of *transgender* (it doesn't catch all the possibilities) in order to better stress the gendered elements of subjective identity formation.

This me-search arose from wanting to find images that resonated with my affective relation to trans___, and I close the chapters here literally not being able to watch all the new media with trans characters, narratives, thematics, and aesthetics, or produced by trans creatives. The tipping point of a wholly *new* sea change for articulating transness might not be pronounceable yet, but along the way the drip, drip of trans characterizations has puddled into the reality of bigger bodies of trans waters than one person could swim across.

The volatility around burgeoning senses of trans behaves according to market trends, in part, but also in response to, capacious desires for a gender vocabulary that feels adequate to one's lived experience, that does justice to it. With this in mind, the cinematic examples I draw from open up a rich field of how trans subjectivities, lives, experiences, and embodiments have been expressed in, if not pressed into, cinematic forms; accordingly, they demonstrate how cinematic forms have been investigated for their trans aesthetic dimensions. I see my deliberate chunking of materials across the chapters—from pre-transsexual to trans-entity to postgender—as a historical fact of development. It also is to show the wealth of discontinuity in what is today casually called transgender identities and politics.

Culturally, trans has a privileged relation to an aesthetics of change, particularly in comparison to the often negative framework for change emerging in relation to aging or illness. What filmmakers and cultural productions do with this imposition on trans to "stand for" change is what I'm interested in, both representationally and in terms of political agitation. The historical record I excavate demonstrates the superdiversity of trans experiences that resists wholesale appropriation, or collapse into a singular story, form, or ontology. Truly, the singular plural *they* is an incredibly accurate means to describe the singularities present within the plurality of trans. I offer the concept of shimmering images to describe this persistent vision of trans as change, and as a force that continues to achieve change through varying means and ways.

ACKNOWLEDGMENTS

This me-search was greatly enriched by companionship and camaraderie along the way that gifted me with the questions and language that shaped this book. My gratitude goes to my fellow wayfarers, whose words and warmth suffuse these pages (in a somewhat chronological order): Sebastian De Line, Kam Wai Kui, Susan Stryker, Tobaron Waxman, Mauro Cabral Grinspan, Vreer Verkerke, Del LaGrace Volcano, Lena Eckert, Zowie Davy, Iris van der Tuin, Stephen Whittle, Jack Halberstam, Trish Salah, Helen Hok-Sze Leung, Jules Rosskam, Aren Aizura, Jonathan Williams, Heather Love, Dean Spade, Alexis Shotwell, Nikki Sullivan, Cressida Heyes, Marije Jansen, Jennifer Lyon Bell, Charles Lofton, Christina Schäfer and Chris Regn of Bildwechsel, Skadi Loist, Mel Pritchard, Louis Baily, Nora Koller, Jack Waters and Peter Kramer, Jürgen Brüning, Anke Engel, Gert Hekma, Katrien Jacobs, Mario Caro, Greg Mullins, Griselda Pollock, Marianna Szczygielska, Anthony Wagner, Laura Horak, Cáel Keegan, Jasbir Puar, Ingrid Ryberg, Ulrika Dahl, Alanna Thain, Eugenie Brinkema, C. Riley Snorton, Che Gossett, Chase Joynt, Pamela Caughie and Sabine Meyer, and especially to three pillars of intellect and friendship who transitioned to death during these intervening years: Tim Stüttgen, Barbara DeGenevieve, and Doran George.

I also thank the directors who created the work that inspired this book's thinking, who kindly dialogued with me, and who generously shared their images: Mirha-Soleil Ross, Annie Sprinkle, Buck Angel, Morty Diamond, Barbara DeGenevieve, Ashley Hans Scheirl, Shu-Lea Cheang, and Cassils. I'm grateful for the invitations to speak about their works and with audiences at the following conferences: PostpostTranssexual: Transgender Studies & Feminism (Indiana University), Cinema, Embodiment and the Aesthetics of Pornography (University of Kent), The Politics of

Performance and Play. Feminist Matters (Leiden University), Queer Film Culture: Queer Cinema and Film Festivals (University of Hamburg); and at the lecture series *Jenseits der Geschletergrenzen* [Beyond Sex/Gender Borders] (Hamburg University), Mosse Lecture Series (University of Amsterdam), F*ck My Brain: Queer Theory, Culture, and Politics Seminar (*l'École des hautes études en sciences sociales*), *Geesteswetenschappen/* Humanities Presents (University of Amsterdam), Film Forum Spring School, Porn Studies: Cartography of the Pornographic Audiovisual (University of Udine), and Violence and Agency: Feminist Perspectives Series (University of Vienna).

I have also had the invaluable support of colleagues at many Dutch Universities, including Ernst van Alphen, Peter Verstraten, Astrid van Weyenberg, Pepita Hesselberth, Maria Boletsi, Liesbeth Minnaard, Isabel Hoving, Yasco Horsman, Frans-Willem Korsten, Madeleine Kasten, Eric de Bruyn, Janna Houwen, Looi van Kessel, Bram Ieven, Marijke de Valck, Rob Zwijnenberg, Kitty Zijlmans, Renée van der Vall, Aagje Swinnen, Lies Wesseling, Sally Wyatt, Rosi Braidotti, Kathrin Thiele, Rebecca Lindner, Janna Schoenberger, Noa Roei, Erin La Cour, Paulina Aroch-Fugellie, Jeroen de Kloet, Jaap Kooijman, Esther Peeren, and Eloe Kingma, and of my doctoral supervisors, Maaike Bleeker and Murat Aydemir, who amazingly trusted me with this project from day 1. I also have had the pleasure to learn from Mieke Bal, who continues to inspire my dedication to the field of cultural analysis and demonstrates what bold, gutsy scholarship looks like.

The time to research and complete this book was made possible through a PhD scholarship at the University of Amsterdam awarded by the Amsterdam School for Cultural Analysis, and a Veni postdoctorate research fellowship awarded by the Netherlands Organization for Scientific Research. I'm so happy that the initial interest and encouragement from Ken Wissoker at Duke University Press led to my working with the extraordinarily talented Courtney Berger and her editorial associate Sandra Korn, who together with the staff at Duke University Press has made my first book a dream come true. The two anonymous reviewers offered astute, generous readings that shed new light on myself as a researcher and writer while also concretely aiding me to amend the book's argumentation. I'm deeply grateful for their scholarly mentorship that enabled this book to come to a conclusion, literally in that they helped me to figure out how it would or should end.

For lifelong and lifesaving friendship, I thank my first feminist comrades, Brooke Skinner and Laura Scheutze. My parents, Allen and Sherry Steinbock, have been my true champions and, together with the guidance of Ed and Louise Steinbock, have shown me the value of hard work and trusting myself. I'm so glad to share them with Stuart, Stacie, Katherine, and their darlings; you have put so much sparkle into my life! From my "Dutch parents," Fred and Alie Copier, I have received the gifts of curiosity and a home away from home. I cherish every day that I have with my love, Laura Copier (and our Jackey Loulou), to whom I dedicate this book.

INTRODUCTION
Disjunction and Conjunction
Thinking Trans through the Cinematic

In one continuous motion, my idea of myself and who I am turns inside out, like a pond that flips upside down in the spring, when the cold winter water slides under, and the earth-warmed bottom water rises. The underlife comes to the surface. All those years I was no obedient asexual girl, but a restless lover searching for the lost garden, that place of male woman and female man. The mythic place before the Fall, before Adam was shaped from clay by Lilith, and Lilith chased out and forgotten, before Eve was torn from Adam's side and forced to lie down under him. From the beginning I have wanted you. I have wanted to sit beside you on our bed, touch you, feed you the jewels of pomegranate torn from the flesh of our lives. I have wanted to walk with you in that place where we are both at once, to lie down with you under the trees that have not yet begun to flame with the dividing sword, by the water that shimmers with heat rising, risen to the light.

MINNIE BRUCE PRATT, *S/He* (1995)

Cinema's greatest power may be its ability to evacuate meanings and identities, to proliferate resemblances without sense or origin. [...] There is no structuring lack, no primordial division, but a continuity between the physiological and affective responses of my own body and the appearances and disappearances, the mutations and perdurances, of the bodies and images on screen. The important distinction is not the hierarchical, binary one between bodies and images, or between the real and its representations. It is rather a question of discerning multiple and continually varying interactions among what can be defined indifferently as bodies and as images: degrees of stillness and motion, of action and passion, of clutter and emptiness, of light and dark.

STEVEN SHAVIRO, *The Cinematic Body* (1993)

t started when I tried out the words "trans lover" in my mouth, feeling them roll around, and hoping they would dissolve and absolve. I wondered whether this phrase would be a solution, perhaps not permanent, but would at least neutralize becoming caught between the sexual identity labels that rely on stabilizing the gender of myself and my intimate. As Minnie Bruce Pratt in *S/He* and many others attest, I was not the first, and surely will not be the last, to come up against desire's constricted grammar, or the "dividing sword."[1] I sought out film images that conveyed what I was experiencing in aesthetic terms, and in doing so, reveled in what Steven Shaviro sees as cinema's greatest power to give pleasure despite—and even in the evacuation of—meanings and identities.[2] Of course cinema tells moving stories in documentary and fiction about people I projected to be like myself, yet something else can be at play, which I seized upon. Gilles Deleuze expressed it thus: "the most complete examples of the disjunction between seeing and speaking are to be found in the cinema."[3] Cinema as a discrete aesthetic form presents a golden opportunity for staging disjunction, for experimenting with how bodies and images are seen and articulated, often in startling ways. Cinephiles might be defined by their desire to seek out novel ways of perceiving the world, intimately attached to cinema's world-making power.[4] In this way, cinephilia models an intensified mode of trans-loving and trans-becoming.

With *Shimmering Images: Trans Cinema, Embodiment, and the Aesthetics of Change*, I venture that the cinematic cuts and sutures between the visual and the spoken, between frames, and between genres are de-linking and relinking practices of transfiguration. I offer a cinematic philosophy of transgender embodiment through deep consideration of the ways that film constitutes a medium for transitioning, thereby eliciting modes of perceiving disjunctions that are advantageous to trans studies. *Transgender* need not refer to one particular identity or way of being embodied, Susan Stryker asserts, but rather offers "an umbrella term for a wide variety of *bodily effects*" that disconnect a series of "normative linkages."[5] Strung together, these linkages are the assumed coincidence of one's anatomy at birth with an assigned gender category, the psychical identifications with sexed body images and/or gendered subject positions, and the performance of gendered social, sexual, or kinship functions. Like in the cinema, one's perception of seeing and speaking can become disrupted by the disjunction between what one thinks they see (on a body) and how that body speaks (its subjective identification). And, in both cases, the resulting bodily effects can register in a range of affects. Engaging with cinematic aesthetics brings into my frame of analysis how transgender embodiment, whether on-screen or off, takes shape in the proliferating interchanges of seeing and speaking that, for some, create a shimmer of heat rising.

If I was a trans lover, then, this relation would not just speak to my own sense of transness, or deep affinity with people who might provoke delinking bodily effects, but also extend to loving how cinema engenders similarly novel transversals of sensory perception. In this regard, I examine the striking similarities within the aesthetic forms of cinema and transgender embodiment to understand their force of expression, forming and differing the body. The analogical thinking I engage in here is a trans studies strategy to explicate the potential—what if—relations between film and trans embodiment. This book's argument is built, therefore, upon an ampersand, first hypothetically conjectured but then pursued in great, literal detail through the corpus I've collected here. I concede that by pushing beyond simple comparisons, and inevitably invoking the generalization of change as trans aesthetics, I risk rendering trans or the cinema a mere rhetorical device for the sake of producing a metaphoric comparison of each in relation to the other.[6] To avoid this figure of speech, my method involves following parallel tracks between individual films and trans embodiments, between sound and image, form and content as they intersect in each of my cases. I do so to identify how their complex relationships inspire a shimmering specific to the context in which they appear, whether conjoined, tangential, or adjacent to each other. It is my hope that readers invested in the discipline of cinema studies will find their own ampersand constructions in which affective shimmering and cinematic shimmers can be excavated to bring new conceptualizations to form-content relations. Although my stake in transgender studies pushes a particular political agenda to defend an inclusive understanding of trans-and-cinema, I can imagine other projects developing with many other audiovisual image examples attuned to the ways the form and content of differentiated bodies are made to shimmer.

I intervene polemically in the rich history of feminist film theory to suggest a correction to its foundational claim of the sex/gender binary structuration: film's potential for thinking/feeling in a nonbinary way in shimmers recasts the assumptions of a strict male or female grammar for subjects on-screen and off. Contrary to Laura Mulvey, who considers the female spectator as a psychically cross-dressing woman in her spurious concept of "trans-sex identification" detached from any real understanding of transvestism or transsexuality, I see that a "cross-identification" is less uncommon, possibly open to anyone.[7] Even at the heart of psychoanalysis, *sex* is an unsettled marker: Mulvey's concept of identification is taken from Lacan's discussion of the mirror stage in which it is developed as a bodily transformation occurring on the threshold of the visible world.[8] In fact, should we want to continue down the path of psychoanalysis (which I mainly won't throughout the course of the book), Kaja Silverman and others demonstrate how multiple and complex forms of identification are just the normal course of (un)becoming a visible, sexing subject.[9] The difference I wish to make in the field of transgender studies is that a theory of shimmering images renders viable more, if not all, possibilities of threshold embodiments groping their way toward social identities. Regrounding the world-making practice of film in the transfeminist perspective of shimmering opens a line of escape from thinking in set binary oppositions by grasping the ongoing event of differential becomings.

Anybodys

One of this book project's crucial moments of theoretical and corpus formation occurred during the heat of August 2004, inside a dusty studio in Brooklyn. I sat with multimedia artist Tobaron Waxman, poring over his personally assembled video and film collection. We were preparing a presentation of clips from the female-to-male transsexual (FtM) erotic archive called "GenderfluXXXors Uncoded: A FtM Su*porn*ova." The title was a mouthful, but we sought to raise awareness of the breadth of imagery that spoke of, or struggled with, trans eroticism. The emphasis on FtM or trans men characters was to counter the common assumptions that trans people are mainly trans women and that trans eroticism is limited to the sexual niche of commercial "she-male" porn. Also, it was familiar territory, as both of us had created videos about transmasculinity and desire.

We looked outside of what might constitute a trans cinema canon, such as *The Crying Game* (1992), *Ma Vie en Rose* (1997), and *Boys Don't Cry* (1999). I wanted to show films that avoided the cinematic shock device known as "the reveal," which Danielle M. Seid describes generally as a moment "when the trans person is subjected to the pressures of a pervasive gender/sex system that seeks to make public the 'truth' of the trans person's gendered and sexed body."[10] In the dominant "natural attitude about gender," this bodily truth is that genitalia are the essential determinants of sex, which in turn determine gender.[11] Though naïve, this genital epistemology plays a structuring role in the film audience's reductive knowledge of a transgender life. The device of exposure goes beyond use as a plot twist in film and literature to frame news headlines and potentially to erupt anytime the trans body becomes subject to discovery, as with a doctor visit, a police arrest, a border crossing, or playing sports. The harmful stereotype of trans people as "evil deceivers and make-believers" stems from this kind of pretheoretical common sense about the anatomical reality of gender, as Talia Mae Bettcher powerfully argues. Bettcher explains the double bind of a conflated gender presentation (appearance) and sexed body (reality) as locking a trans person in to being either visible as a pretender, or invisible and risk forced disclosure; either way, she states, "we are fundamentally viewed as illusory."[12]

Though the filmic reveal is often played for comedic laughs or light drama, it actually stages a forced, violent moment of physical disclosure that undermines a trans character's understanding of themselves. The reveal enacts a struggle over the body's meaning, but one the trans person always loses. As a reparative narrative technique for this losing battle, Jack Halberstam's "transgender gaze" describes the cinematic structure in which a presumably cisgender spectator's identification aligns with the doubled trans figure; they are shown looking at each other in shot and reverse-shot in this moment of crisis.[13] Using *Boys Don't Cry* as his prime example, in a scene of abject dismissal of Brandon Teena's masculine presentation by stripping their clothes off, the cisgender spectator is made aware most of all of how the reveal feels, rather than how it feels to be trans.[14] In addition to this limited version of transgender looking that hinges on experiencing secondhand debasement, I find it restricting to assess trans cinema on the basis of how films that figure a trans protagonist or character deal with the reveal and the logic of being illusory. Given the groundwork laid already in this research area, it is not compelling—nor necessary—for me to write a history of the changing or static representation of trans* people in visual media.[15] The corpus of trans cinema might instead be circumscribed by the challenge of understanding trans forms of life as truth outside of the visual reveal (trans-cinema epistemologies) alongside describing trans lived experience outside of the dualist terms of mind/body, man/woman, true/false, and so on (trans-cinema ontologies). The sheer popularity and volume of trans cinema begs a fresh take on its appeal to a wide-ranging audience and as material for film-makers; consider the mushrooming trans film festivals from Amsterdam to Beirut, Seattle, Sydney, Los Angeles, Bologna, Toronto, London, Quito, Munich, and so on.[16]

Shimmering Images offers the perspective that transgender and cine-matic aesthetics alike operate through the bodily practice and technolog-ical principle of disjunction. More radically, within practices of filmmak-ing delinking and relinking across the cuts, gaps, fissures take place in the normal course of cinematography, rather than being exceptions. This makes it the art form most suited to a politically advantageous compari-son with transgender forms of embodiment. Moreover, approaching em-bodiment through film reroutes the emphasis on sex/gender difference through aesthetics. What if trans embodiment is not primarily about sex or gender, but about experimenting with the aesthetics of corporeality in terms of efficacy and political purchase? My formal inquiry of how dis-junction and conjunction occur is deeply interwoven with the political urgency of how degrees of difference, incoherence, and oscillation are ex-pressed as viable. As an example, the 1961 film version of the musical *West Side Story* negotiates how normative linkages limit gendered and erotic visibility both specific to and beyond transgender bodies.[17]

West Side Story features the character Anybodys, who wants to be in the Jets gang composed of white youth, the fierce rivals of the Sharks, who are all Puerto Rican. Gangs are made up of boys and their girls. Anybodys wants to be accepted as one of the (white) boys, but is rejected throughout the film and told to "put on a skirt." The phrase tells Anybodys that s/he can only be a Jet if s/he tries to be one of the girls. The script describes Anybodys as a tomboy, a girl who refuses to express female identification through girl gender presentation. For this refusal, and for expressing a gender-nonconforming identification, Anybodys is called a freak. In the character of Anybodys we can find anybody and nobody: everyone and no one. Any and all bodies are subject to the enforcement of a norma-tive gender presentation in alignment with their raced sex. Any body that cannot or does not have a recognizable gender expression as a boy or a girl becomes a *no body*, a presumably inconsequential body within this highly segregated social scene.[18] Moreover, this social scene of gangs organizes around a heterosexual scheme of boys and their girls. Where might a transmasculine body fit into this erotic script?

At a crucial point in the film, the character Anybodys is consequential because of what s/he knows. The gang's fighting has escalated and Tony, the leader of the Jets, has disappeared to hide from his crime. Everyone wants to find him and find out what he will do next, but he could be anywhere in the boroughs of New York City—a needle in a haystack. The Jets gang walks through the dark streets trying to figure out how to locate their leader. Lacking a socially normative body, Anybodys says that s/he slips in and out of the shadows, "like wind through a fence." Only this trans character can move between the barriers erected between the racial and geographic territories of the rival gangs to see and hear things others cannot. Stretching back to the Greek character Tiresias, gender-ambiguous and gender-changing figures are often the "knowers" of special secrets. Anybodys might be understood as another one of these fictional invocations connecting gender-variant embodiment with special knowledge. When a gang member says, "Ah, what's the freak know," Anybodys retorts, "plenty."

As a special agent for the Jets, Anybodys becomes more important to them, as indicated in one scene by becoming more visible, moving from the darkness behind the gang, yelling, "hey buddy boys!" to the side, hissing "listen, *listen!*" Finally, Anybodys arrives at the center of the group, and under the bright studio lights delivers the news that Chino of the Sharks has a gun. The gang takes in this vital knowledge and searches for Tony, while the new leader Ice tells Anybodys to go back to darting in and out of the shadows. From start to finish, this scene associates Anybodys with shadows. Living in an undetectable space, however, does not mean Anybodys is invisible to all. Ice alone seems to be able to acknowledge Anybodys: he says, "you done good, buddy boy," rhetorically making Anybodys one of the buddy boys s/he wants to be. This validation includes Anybodys in the Jets gang and, perhaps more importantly, in the social gang of boys. Anybodys wistfully responds, "Thanks Daddio." A quiet exchange that speaks volumes, this is the only point in the script that Anybodys is not denigrated, the one time that s/he is acknowledged with a grateful smile.

This fragment about the seemingly inconsequential character of Anybodys in *West Side Story*, and, moreover, his/her cinematographic rendering, is emblematic of my project. Anybodys, slipping in and out of shadows, moves into and out of the light, becoming a shimmer of a body, difficult to grasp perceptually. And, as the film suggests through dialogue, plot, and style, shimmers are difficult to grasp as knowable entities. We might also say that in general, like Anybodys's darting movements, the image is in fact constantly changing: the flickering of frames with black space between, or of pixels, generates a sense of movement. Yet, these changing forms of the image can appear consistent due to the viewer's persistence of vision that maps onto an acculturated perceptual schema. At issue is not why impressions shimmer, for they do so continuously, but rather how the identity of emergent or in-flux entities becomes stilled into a unit and fixed with meaning. This is to say that shimmering directs me to think about the patterning of light. Patterns emerge not just from regulated practices of looking, but from what Sean Cubitt calls "practices of light" that become modulated via visual technologies.[19] Light falls on a surface, but light is also captured, distributed, controlled. Prisms, kaleidoscopes, phantasmagoria, Chromoscope, and the "Shirley" card for white skin tones all represent proto-cinematic visual technologies for controlling light. In stressing the movement of shimmering, I pressure those stultified historical optics for perceiving gender *like this*, race *like that*, beauty *here*, desire *in situ*. Shimmering images come with components, requiring at least surface, light, a lens apparatus. I argue that cultural makers, like trans people, and certainly like the trans* cultural producers whose work I study in this book, have experimented with changing around the components to literally create new images that reintroduce shimmering into our line of vision.

Shimmering is my concept for change in its emergent, flickering form. What might this insight from cinema studies offer to transgender studies: that film consists in formal possibilities for grasping change within degrees of stillness and motion, of action and passion, of clutter and emptiness, of light and dark? In these pages I articulate a theory of the shimmering image that Anybodys forms in the stylized aesthetic of light and shadows and erotic script of longing in *West Side Story*. Any body becomes somebody to those like myself who desire to see across the disjunction, who trace the wavering oscillation. Our carnal vision affirmatively perceives what to others is a blind spot, seems inscrutable, or, worse, seems simply illusory. Drawing on cinephilic practices of looking to build new a conceptual model for trans desire—for transition and for those in transition— I make my way across the water that shimmers with heat rising.

Counting Past Two:
An Inventory of Shimmers

From 1997 to 1999 and again in 2002 in Toronto, Canada, Mirha-Soleil Ross co-organized the "Counting Past 2" trans film and art festival that winked at the necessity for learning more genders and genres.[20] Taking inspiration from her approach to trans as multiplicity, I collect and collate the promiscuous notion of shimmering. Iterations of the shimmer in the writings of philosophers and of trans and film scholars, including Michel Foucault, Gilles Deleuze, Susan Stryker, and Steven Shaviro, employ *shimmer* as a noun akin to sparkle or flash, the verb *to shimmer* sometimes translated as scintillate or glimmer, or *shimmering* as a modifier to describe change in its alluring, twinkling, flickering form. The various expressions of a shimmering quality confound distinctions in their writing between subject/object, thinking/feeling, and sight/touch. In due course I will discuss them all in detail, but for now let me attend to Roland Barthes, who most succinctly brings together the aesthetic, affective, and politically urgent character of the shimmer that pinpoints how it breaks with binary and dialectical thinking. My reading of Barthes is indebted to Gregory Seigworth and Melissa Gregg's methodological explication of how to outplay the paradigm of binary thinking in their introduction to *The Affect Theory Reader*, entitled "An Inventory of Shimmers," that enters here as a companion text.[21]

In his 1977–1978 course at the Collège de France, Barthes introduced figures, traits, or twinklings (*scintellements*) of the Neutral, selecting "that which outplays [*déjoue*] the paradigm," or better, "everything that baffles the paradigm."[22] Following Saussurean linguistics, the paradigm is formed of oppositional terms that produce discursive meaning when one term is actualized; hence, meaning is produced in conflict ("the choice of one term against another").[23] Barthes hits on the idea of a structural creation to break the implacable binarism: the Neutral being an amorphous third term that can parry meaning that suspends the conflictual basis of discourse. Though a nonexhaustive exercise to find examples of the neutral, I feel Barthes's commitment in the assertion that "'To outplay the paradigm' is an ardent, burning activity"; moreover, the methodological analysis of the Neutral is a manner in which to present the struggles of his time.[24] For my purposes, I locate the Neutral in the struggle to outplay the binary oppositions that structure the paradigm of sex-gender-sexuality, loosely distinguished by social and cultural movements concerned with trans* politics, intersex rights, and their complex and sometimes vexed relations to feminist and queer theory, what Judith Butler coins the "New Gender Politics."[25] Of particular interest—no surprise—is the trait of the Neutral that Barthes names "the shimmer," but also the figure of "the androgyne," which exposes the Neutral's gendered facet.[26] Combined, these twinklings bring out the sexual basis of the Neutral/Neuter while pointing to ways that Barthes's ultimate dream of having "an exemption from meaning" can be found in the cinema.[27]

The political will of the Neutral is found in aesthetics. In reflecting on a spilled ink bottle for the pigment color "neutral," Barthes considers the opposition between colorful and colorless.[28] In the subsection on "Shimmer," the monochromatic schema found in the paintings of gray shades, or *grisaille*, substitutes for the idea of a stark opposition paradigm—that of the overall slight difference, or the effort for difference, expressed in the term *nuance*.[29] The etymology of nuance is from *nuer* ("to shade") and from *nue* ("cloud") and shows how its meaning of slight difference or shade of color exists in the miniscule gradations and degrees of intensity. Barthes concludes, "this integrally and almost exhaustively nuanced space is the shimmer [. . .] whose aspect, perhaps whose meaning, is subtly modified according to the angle of the subject's gaze."[30] If trans is not identified as either/or, but depends on the "angle" of the subject's gaze emerging in different contexts, then the slight modifications of gender could be likened to the nuanced space of the shimmer. The Latin root of nuance, *nubes*, meaning "a cloud, mist, vapor," suggests the diffuse character of the shimmer's inchoate aesthetic. The subject in Barthes's quote above is a spectator gazing upon a visual text of some kind. (His examples for color contemplation are a self-portrait by Lao-tzu and Hieronymus Bosch's *The Garden of Earthly Delights*.) I would, however, like to leave open how the gaze adjusted to a trans angle might also open up a nuanced space that subtly modifies vision. The shimmer might not lie (solely) in the text, but (also) in the subject's angled gaze. Sara Ahmed tells us that "what we may feel depends on the angle of our arrival," an embodied point of view in the affective atmosphere.[31] How then might we become receptive to shimmers, or cultivate a practice of seeing its more-than-stereo optics?

Barthes describes the Neutral as having a state of *to pathos*, Greek for what one feels, that escapes the opposition of what one does or the passive state of *hè pathè*.[32] Thus, he suggests that to pathos (both active and affected, withdrawn from the will to act but not from passion) describes the "shimmering field of the body, insofar as it changes, goes through changes."[33] Dropping into one's own shimmering field induces what he calls the strongest minimal existence: "the passion of difference" after Blanchot.[34] The starting point to outplay the paradigm of oppositions and negations is attending to the shimmers of a process of change, not the positioning. Perhaps I sense some humor in his imagining of a future "science of shimmers," but he has also demonstrated a serious, long-standing practice to listen and watch for shimmering nuance.[35] This Barthes calls "the inventory of shimmers, of nuances, of states, of changes (*pathè*)"; he cheekily dubs it "path-ology" not to raise it to a metadiscourse but instead to nominate a Neutral power of being affected akin to Ahmed's "what we may feel."[36] Later he returns to how a path-ology might be practiced by situating the analysis within his own sense of calmness, a paradox of "emotive hyperconsciousness of the affective minimal."[37] The consciousness of the smallest shifts "implies an extreme changeability of affective moments, a rapid modification, into shimmer."[38] Shimmering affectivity confounds distinctions between from within or from without.

Barthes, writing on the shimmer, conveys a baseline ontology by proposing a primal form of affectivity that "oscillates between irreducible individuality and endless differentiation," as Laura Wahlfors describes it.[39] Available to anybody, trans modifications highlight this zero-degree ontology (as in a state of being) experienced as stable and fluid: stillness located in flux. Although the leading edge of transgender studies uses trans*, trans-, or transing to resolve the now outdated alignment of transgender with fluctuating gender identity and transsexual with a fixed gender identity, there has not been as yet a sustained investigation of this proposed trans ontology of change that might depart from an anthropocentric realm into aesthetics.[40] Combining Alfred North Whitehead's philosophy that the "adventures of ideas" reveal the history of the variety of human mental experience and Mieke Bal's interdisciplinary practice of "traveling concepts" that experiments with tracking the circulations of a concept, this book privileges the adventure of thinking the shimmer for the new understandings it offers of trans onto-epistemologies as emergent, affective, and processual.[41]

The neutral twinkling of the shimmer breaks with algebraic mathematical beginning and end points to consider "only intervals": the relation between moments, spaces, or objects, that which is in play.[42] Broadening Spinoza's definition of the body in terms of its *ability* to enter "relations of movement and rest," Brian Massumi writes that the "'relation between movement and rest' is another way of saying 'transition.'"[43] A body's ability as a power (or potential) to affect, or be affected, means that it is one with its transitions; and each transition is accompanied by a variation in capability that marks the degree to which a body tends to move toward a present futurity.[44] Such intervals of movement–rest form the basis of gender transitions, which are usually thought of only in terms of the takeoff and landing points of the crossing, as in male-to-female. The greater challenge of transgender studies would be to stay with the indefinite period or moment in suspension from the gridded paradigm, while fully acknowledging a tendency or intensity that suggests direction, location, context. With a gender transition comes a potential bodily change through self-multiplication across the shimmering passage of unresolvable disjunction in which we all live and breathe. For example, Eva Hayward writes from her trans-sexing perspective, but offers this advice to anyone: "Moving toward your self through your body is less about a horizon in which change stops than about how to embrace the endless process of change."[45]

Trans ontologies are process-oriented, rather than object-oriented. An appropriate trans method would centralize the pulses of affect guiding ontological movement and change. Seigworth and Gregg's "An Inventory of Shimmers," their introduction to *The Affect Theory Reader*, offers a highly useful guide to tracking the bombs, blips, and blooming of affect. The title clearly signals how they seek to harness Barthes's critical inventorying practice to an affect studies methodology in which research "becomes force then a matter of accounting for the progressive accentuation (plus/minus) of intensities, their incremental shimmer: the stretching of process underway, not position taken."[46] This practice of elucidating the glimmers of gradation is *trans*-oriented, not determination-oriented, in so far as it attends to the tendencies of transitions between movement and rest, "not position taken." Affect studies offers the richest set of vocabularies for describing "swarming, sliding differences," or "what so often passes beneath mention," as Seigworth and Gregg write.[47] Like the neutral seeking to outplay the paradigm, trans ontologies deflect the demand for definitive meaning of differences, showing this demand to be an offensive or misguided side effect of the "'fascism' of language."[48]

Guiding my chapters are the twin invocations of shimmering in relation to an incipient subjectivity and specific cinematic images that emphasize incremental shimmer within the frame or between frames. In terms of making an inventory, I conduct a formal analysis of shimmering affectivity in and between the bodies of viewer/analyst and film. It is an idiosyncratic method related to my cinephile practice of registering the continuous, shimmering gradations of intensities; or, I could say, of Shaviro's degrees of stillness and motion, of action and passion, of light and dark. As Elspeth Probyn writes, rapping her reader on the knuckles but kindly, "A general gesture to Affect won't do the trick. If we want to invigorate our concepts, we need to follow through on what different affects do, at different levels" to our bodies, our theory, our writing.[49] Eugenie Brinkema agrees, adding that Deleuzian fetishizing of affect's *potentiality* for its own sake often commits "the sin of generality"; in its place we need to get specific about how different affects become bound up in specific forms, in dense details, in order to access a vocabulary for articulating those many differences.[50] My writing oscillates between an empirical registering of the felt reality of relation that builds on (new) feminist materialisms and a formalist analysis of affects that brings me closest to aesthetics and its tradition of close reading. A theory of shimmering images uses concepts associated with formal, bodily aesthetics in place of less precise identity terms, such as male/female, masculine/ feminine, man/woman, which fall short of grasping movement and cause "grid lock," to borrow a pun from Massumi.[51]

This is not to say gender does not play a role—not at all—only that to get at its affective hold I necessarily need to set aside the fetishes of Man and Woman that cover over the gendering process that is underway. Barthes again proves prescient in that he turns to linguistic formations of the Neuter in which it essentially refers to the inanimate and/or nongendered.[52] It interests him how the Neuter has faded away in Indo-European languages and now, "faced with a ruling lack of the Neuter (of language), discourse [. . .] opens up an infinite, shimmering field of nuances, of myths, that could allow the Neuter, fading within language, to be alive elsewhere. Which way? I would say, using a vague word: the way of affect: discourse comes to the Neuter by means of the affect."[53] Might the Neuter's affective liveliness show up in the animated field of disjunction and conjunction? In this sense might cinema be an elsewhere for the Neuter, "not what cancels the genders, what combines them, keeps them both present in the subject [film], at the same time, after each other"?[54] The Neuter slips into the Neutral figure of the Androgyne that follows, a figure who for Barthes baffles the genital paradigm through presenting a complex degree of mixture.[55] Operating in an other-than-binary mode, the Androgyne's masculine and feminine fluctuation is taken by Barthes in a specific, limited way that I cannot follow further: "man in whom there is feminine."[56] In his concluding course lecture he apologizes for how poorly explored this final figure of Androgyne is, but at least his notes on the Androgyne do attempt to comprehend how a trans bodily effect, gender combination, or nonbinary gender gradient operates in a shimmering field of nuance. Although still a half-thought how to think the Neutral and Neuter in the Androgyne figure, in the years since transgender theories have come to offer a much more satisfying enfleshment of this figure modelled in posttranssexual embodiment, transgender politics, and the practice of transing.

At the heart of Sandy Stone's ground-clearing essay from the late 1980s, "The *Empire* Strikes Back: A Posttranssexual Manifesto," lies a theory of posttranssexual embodiment as that which refutes the binary imposition of a defined gender by activating a nonbinary, or combinatory, gradient of lived gender.[57] Stone's manifesto calls for making use of one's trans-embodied agency to bring forth all the territories between two unambiguous personae in a transsexual's history: the assigned gender that after transition typically becomes erased by the self-determined gender wrought through medical, legal, and/or social transition. Stone proposes that gender consists in visible signs that people read; therefore transsexuals are a genre, "a set of embodied texts whose potential for *productive* disruption of structured sexualities and spectra of desire" has not yet been explored.[58] A strict binary gender identity and the corollary mandate of an *un*disruptive transsexual expression become rewritten by those bodies that refuse to, or simply cannot, fit into the order of signs that conceal transsexual meaning. Thus announcing a self as posttranssexual means becoming a walking, talking sign of gender excess, showing off an overfull, fluctuating gender embodiment. Stone is emphatic that transsexuals "must take responsibility for all of their history" in order to reappropriate difference and to reclaim the power of the refigured and reinscribed body as a space of authentic nuance.[59]

Although the complexities and ambiguities of lived trans experience may to some seem to be false or unintelligible, I wager that cinematic aesthetics of the shimmer pattern the affective space of posttranssexual embodiment. My inventory of trans shimmerings seizes on filmic materials that productively disrupt structured sexualities and spectra of desire through cinematographic delinking and relinking. An inventory will always remain incomplete. Instead of working exhaustively, each chapter tracks the scintillations of trans-embodied "texts" within key episodes of experimentation in cinematic history: early trick films, docu-porn, and multigenre avant-garde flicks. Thus, next to and alongside the inventory of trans shimmerings runs a counter-history of cinema as a machinic linking and delinking of embodiment, morphology, and sexuality. In the next section I sketch the ways that a trans approach to film studies can open up the field to a radical revisioning of cinema's power to fascinate, radiate, and enliven.

Animating Trans-Inter-Queer

Shimmering Images follows the axiom that film is a subset of animation broadly construed. But *how* cinemas bring depicted and viewing bodies into animate and lively being is under investigative pressure. The writings of Alan Cholodenko argue that film "as such" is a form of animation, not only graphic art or digital film, but even live action, for "animation is the endowing with life and the endowing with motion" to the stillness of individual frames through the (artificial) movement of the projector or other animatic apparatus.[60] In other words, an animated image has a life cycle of movement and rest, stirrings and diminutions. To be clear, Cholodenko states, "Animation is the first, last and enduring attraction of cinema, of film."[61] Our attachment to the (non)human life of a film—neither dead nor alive, both dead and alive, confounding all either/or -isms—ruptures the proper hierarchies of intimacy. Film's shimmering pulses, flickering from dark to image to dark, death to life to death, bring us to the affective core of ontological enquiry.[62] If film operates as an apparatus for the animation of the body, cinema itself seems inversely to be animated by the morphing qualities of bodies. For trans subjectivities, film's challenge to bodily autonomy and affective sovereignty has special valence. The ability to animate and become reanimated lies at the heart of transition narratives that follow a trajectory of dying and being reborn, mapping onto the affective states of suffering body dysphoria and becoming happy through surgical and hormonal intervention, forming what some have called the dominant transsexual narrative.[63]

Stone's appraisal of the published autobiographies and personal files from trans women reminds us to consider not by whom, but *for* whom "the transsexual" was constructed: a fictitious character who goes from unambiguous albeit unhappy man, to unambiguous (presumably happy) woman.[64] Of course it is possible that the felt reality of one's self may relate to a singular binary identity: that of an unambiguous man or woman who orientates heterosexually before and after transition. However, for those who do not, their dramas of redemption nevertheless must comply with medical/psychological texts that determine the permissible range of expressions of physical sexuality and correct gender role presentation. Anything less than ideal femininity or masculinity would be grounds for disqualification from treatment. Early trans memoirs such as Jan Morris's *Conundrum* (1974) display this revitalization trope by drawing gender conversion scenes starring a God-like surgeon-creator/rescuer, who is inevitably a heterosexual male that validates straight female identity. Setting the standard in film narratives, Doris Wishman's "transxploitation" documentary *Let Me Die a Woman* (1978) stages an elaborate surgical scene glorifying medical expertise, curiously undercut by the sequences with trans women interviewees who explain that to access surgery one must dress the part of an appealing, young heterosexual woman. But we can also cycle back further into the Western cultural imaginary to find trans figures addressing godly parental figures that bring them to life.

The example is, then, in *Frankenstein*, James Whale's 1931 film adaptation of Mary Shelley's novel, where I find godly parental figures. The scene of the doctor bringing his patchwork creature to life most prominently sets the pattern for trans narratives that co-opt the surgeon's maniacal creative powers.[65] Although most Frankenstein scholarship focuses on how this unborn monster is an Other projected from the human psyche, the tale is also clearly one about the dangerous powers of animation. Dr. Frankenstein brings his creature to life on the operating table using a projector that he claims shoots out a "ray [that] endows the body with life." In a reverse anatomical theatre dissection, this re-vivisection galvanizes life as it shoots through the body. Is this not an apt metaphor for cinema's animating power and, equally, a vision of trans-sexing practices? The figures of scientist, surgeon, and filmmaker enfold in an orchestration of animating the light bodies—each can claim, in the voice of Dr. Frankenstein, "I made it with my own hands," but also the anxious declaration of "it's alive!"

Trans cinematic space offers a material means of achieving embodiment through cut and sutured images that are shot through with projections of desire. The critical move, I want to assert, is to understand that the animated trans body calls into question the naturalistic effects of biomedical technologies by comparing them to cinematic special effects.[66] A founding text of transgender studies, Stryker's "My Words to Victor Frankenstein Above the Village of Chamounix: Performing Transgender Rage," asserts, "As we rise up from the operating tables of our rebirth, we transsexuals are something more, and something other, than the creatures our makers intended us to be."[67] This claim to animating agency (heard in "rise up") returns in her more recent scholarly and artistic work on the first globally mediatized transsexual icon, Christine Jorgensen. Stryker describes her filmmaking practice for this experimental documentary as exploring the *cinematic logic of transsexual embodiment*.[68] Before transition Jorgensen had professional experience in the cutting room of a film production unit that Stryker conjectures helped Jorgensen to imagine how a surgical (cutting) room would similarly operate for her personally. In both cases, Stryker explains, the cutting of the physical medium of the image, the splicing together of images in new ways, the projection of the medium so that it becomes a public way to tell a story through those constructed images altogether form her practice of reassembly. This "cinematic logic" follows from the ways in which trans bodily practices are situated on what Stryker calls "the shimmering boundary between the real and virtual, the fantasized and the actualized."[69] I want to underline that the shifting scintillations of the shimmering boundary refuse to settle embodied or cinematic images into the diction of true or false, fantasy or actuality. The radical antistatic status of shimmering suggests a suspension of being either really there or not there, of being fully graspable. To become situated, or to situate oneself, in the shimmering of these boundaries opens up another way of knowing that does not rely on visual certainty. Shimmering suspends epistemological disbelief.

Navigating the fluctuations of the visual field as transgender, intersex, or queer comes with great risks, but also potential gain. For instance, consider the tremendous number of video blogs (vlogs) on YouTube that document and discuss physical, social, and emotional dimensions of gender transition. The start of one's transition on a trans vlog initiates being born as a media-body, which leads scholar Tobias Raun to dub them "screen-births."[70] Vlogging engenders the ongoing process of gender materialization by providing tools to dismantle and reassign certain gendered signifiers. Raun explains its appeal in that it promises (like transition itself) to make visible the identity that often begins as imperceptible.[71] This mediatization practice enables the vlogger to experience the image as an embodied subject, to locate their voice within the discourses of transitioning, and to connect with a greater community. Becoming seen or read makes it harder to be ignored, so the practice of visibility can be productive as a politics of interrupting dominant ways of categorizing corporeal selves. This rests, though, on the promise that increased visibility equals increased power in some direct way.[72] The result could equally be in shoring up the assumption that all real identities are visibly marked, which Peggy Phelan calls "the ideology of the visible" that as well expunges the power of the unmarked, unspoken, and unseen.[73]

Identity politicking that adheres to this ideology ignores at its peril psychoanalytical and deconstructionist explanations of how visibility is a trap. Phelan warns that it "summons surveillance and the law; it provokes voyeurism, fetishism, the colonialist/imperial appetite for possession."[74] You don't have to go in for deconstruction or psychoanalysis to see how it could be smart to make being unmarked and opaque your modus operandi, as decolonial scholars equally champion.[75] The ideology of the visible undergirds the natural attitude about gender, with its narrow belief in genitalia determinism from birth. Whether one wills it or not, transgender, intersex, and queer subjects are sometimes caught up in the trap of visibility, marked or read with the difference that makes a difference. Attention to the oscillations in shimmering reveals how and when subjects come to be marked and unmarked, which forms of recognition produce being seen or what optics render viability. *Shimmering Images* thus places *visuality* itself in the position of being the primary object of study, a move suggested by Mieke Bal.[76] For Bal, "visual essentialism" plagues studies of visual culture, assuming it already knows what is visual and what is not, forgetting the profoundly impure act of looking: rife with interpretative framing, complexly mixed-media, soliciting synesthetic sense perceptions, and bursting with affect.[77] Investigating visuality thus demands an analysis of the material, the affective *and* the epistemological conditions of vision. I bring forward this awareness of multiple levels to visuality in my analytical approach to the domain of trans cinema.

In the determination of my filmic corpus comprising "trans cinema" I am guided by Helen Hok-Sze Leung's philosophical summary of its potential dimensions: Does trans film feature self-identified trans characters, or ones that a viewer might recognize as trans? Should it be made by or starring trans people regardless of content? Must it be meant for a trans audience, have a trans aesthetic, or be open to trans interpretations?[78] She notes that the denomination itself is revealing, for "when and why a film is talked about as a 'trans film' tells us a lot about the current state of representational politics and community reception as well as trends and directions in film criticism."[79] Hereto queer's dominance as *the* optic for seeing disorder in visual culture at large (and within the New Queer Cinema specifically) has masked the uneven status of various gender and sexual categories that describe gender nonconformity, particularly as they intersect with racial categories.[80]

More generally, transgender studies reclaims space from gay and lesbian studies that often co-opts representations of gender variance (e.g., tomboy and sissy) into discrete categories of sexual identity. Gender identity runs along another axis than sexual identity; but sometimes they transect when one's embodied masculinity and/or femininity enables one to become erotically visible. Eve Sedgwick calls this a pleasurable clicking into visibility, into the grid of a certain optic (lesbian, gay, bisexual, hetero, etc.).[81] Nevertheless, queer theory that mobilizes the analytic of sexual identity can reductively render "queer" code for lesbian or gay, and deprivilege other ways of differing from heteronormativity found in "atypical" forms of embodiment such as transgender and intersex.[82] What should be avoided is the flattening of these diverse experiences through "saming," which is just as dangerous as othering these categories of experience.[83] To describe these complex affiliations in and out of visual culture, I borrow the aggregation trans-inter-queer from the Berlin-based political action and cultural empowerment group Trans-InterQueer, or TrIQ.[84]

The chapters in this book pivot on the interstice of trans-inter-queer in order to address the political tensions and coalitions between these bodies, movements, and theories, specifically in terms of their visual politics. I do so foremost by electing in my analysis of selected filmic works to focus on the portrayal of the disjunctions and conjunctions between *embodiment* (highlighted by trans), *morphology* (at stake in inter), and *sexuality* (taken up by queer). The films carry out an operation of assembly that enables some bodies to appear animate and have a recognizable life of their own; the specific genres, styles, cinematography, and, moreover, gender conventions provide the support structures. Paisley Currah, Susan Stryker, and Lisa Jean Moore conceptualize such a "transing practice" as that which "assembles gender into contingent structures of association with other attributes of bodily being, and that allows for their reassembly."[85] I interrelate the various trans-inter-queer reassemblages through how they challenge the regulatory forces that abet and maintain what Mel Chen identifies as a hierarchy of "animacy."[86] In Chen's hands, the linguistic concept of animacy is drawn into the biopolitical realm to describe the affective forces and tendencies that map racialized live and dead zones, broadening the field of (non)human life.[87] But crucially, animacies, in plural, in action, also displace the false binary of life and nonlife at the heart of humanism with an affective politics of ascribed orders and proper intimacies. Transing practices within filmmaking seize on this displacement of the life and nonlife binary at work in all cinema to access a contingent, provisional modus for depicting trans animacies. Despite spanning eras from the 1890s to the 1990s, the various shimmerings upon which I meditate critique the gendered and sexual terms by which life is constrained. Structurally the book comprises three chapters that highlight different modes of shimmering that occur episodically in experimental cinema cultures by independent filmmakers and artists: the shimmering of *phantasmagoria*, where it is located in the trick technology of mechanical reproduction; of *sex*, where it occurs on the surface of performing bodies through the generic framings of pornography and documentary; and of *multiplicity* that references dada techniques and cyborg politics in avant-garde affective forms.

The Moves:
Three Conceptual Models

In this book's chapters I offer three models for thinking "trans" based on lived experiences of transitioning that conceptually interconnect with cinematic practices for disjunction and conjunction. Each conceptual model is accented and highlighted by a typographic sign, namely, the cut of the forward slash (/), the suture of the hyphen (-), and the multiplier of the asterisk (*). These punctuation symbols forge new conceptual armature that I proffer as cinematic modes for thinking about the capaciousness of gender and as transgender models for transdisciplinary film analysis. In the cascade of three chapters, which flow across time periods, genres, and styles, I invite the reader to experiment with the affective and transformative qualities engendered by the cine-typographic technologies in Trans/Cinema/Aesthetics (chapter 1), Trans-Sexualities (chapter 2), and Trans*Form (chapter 3). Grammatically the symbols are a divider, connector, and multiplier. In the annals of transgender-related activism the symbols all have specific genealogies: the forward slash echoes with queer deconstruction moves; the hyphen, with hybrid culture and sexed identities; and the more recent asterisk, with digital inclusion through profusion. The cutting motion in the backward or forward slash in chapter 1 indicates a leap in transition time made possible through technological reproduction, and the ostensibly foundational aesthetic of surgical sex change. The hyphen in chapter 2 sets off a tentative modifying difference while also indicating a binding that draws together seemingly disparate or wounded parts. It develops from the investigation in chapter 1 of how cuts have been made, and to what effect, which may require practices of suturing through cinematographic means, erotic identification, or forms of disidentification. Uptake of the paratactical stickiness of the asterisk in chapter 3 references the (im)possible holding together of multiplicity, foremost of embodied identities, but also of affective forms present in filmic structures. Each chapter also draws on varied inflections of the shimmer, shimmering, and shimmerings that contour how cinematic creations negotiate perceived divided embodiment, illegible sexualities, and indistinct morphology—all persistent, unavoidable, stigmatizing tropes that negatively affect trans-inter-queer lives.

I begin with a consideration of how various cut and suture technologies, which bring together the medicalization of trans and intersex forms of life, can be reframed in terms of filmic techniques. Chapter 1, "Shimmering Phantasmagoria: Trans/Cinema/Aesthetics in an Age of Technological Reproducibility," examines the ways that the cinema of attractions, like new surgical procedures for "changing sex," reorders the sensible in an age of technological reproducibility. The model of cinema–as–surgical theatre bears out surprisingly literally in the practice of early filmmaking, flipping Stryker's insight into the "cinematic logic of transsexual embodiment" into a confirmation of the *transsexual logic of cin-*

ematic embodiment at work since its inception. I use the method of media archaeology to recover what Deleuze calls the "first light" of an era that creates the aesthetic possibility for something to appear as a shimmer, flash, or sparkle. The chapter proceeds by locating the "first light" of the phantasmagoria in a cultural series that includes the popular trick films of Georges Méliès (1890–1920) that vanish, substitute, and generally explore the changeability of the human body and the cultural text of "Lili Elbe," whose confessions *Man into Woman* (1931) were collectively assembled by her doctor, friends, and wife, montaging not only before-and-after personal photographs but also points of view. In particular I discuss the book's use of the third person, which positions the reader/viewer in alignment with a "machinic eye" to take in the astonishing facts of Lili's transition narrative that she acknowledges casts her as a shimmering phantasmagoria in the sense of a divided presence/absence. At the close, I examine how a set of contemporary trans artists practice a reparative form of temporal drag with the outmoded cultural imaginary of transitioning as an instant sex change. Zackary Drucker and A. L. Steiner's photographic collaboration "BEFORE/AFTER" (2009–ongoing) reweaves the phantasmagoric affect of surprise into temporally disjunctive before-and-after shots in order to resequence trans histories. The 911 photographs of Yishay Garbasz's "Becoming" (2010), which comprise a two-year documentation of her nude body before and after her gender clarification surgery, were transformed into the proto-cinematic animation of a handheld flipbook and into a life-sized zoetrope that highlights the trope of a divided being with overwhelming evidence of differential becoming. With their throwback phantasmagoric aesthetics these artists foreground the presentation of an optical trick to the viewer, to effectively tickle their desire for optical mastery while withholding a full reveal.

The next chapter continues an investigation into how trans subjects have negotiated the sex reveal specifically in pornography, where genital optics is closely tied to the documentary authenticity of the sexual performance and the performer's gender identity. Both kinds of sex reveals greatly risk the illegibility of the trans person performing for the camera's eye, and in extension for the viewer of docu-porn. Chapter 2, "Shimmering Sex: Docu-Porn's Trans-Sexualities, Confession Culture, and Suturing Practices," wrestles with the scientism of observation that echoes in the filmic rhetoric of "to see is to know." The aura of visual transparency

aids in producing an effect of the real within pornography and documentary genres. I open with Joan Scott's reading of Samuel R. Delany's
autobiographic *The Motion of Light in Water* (1988) that describes "the
saturation that was not only kinesthetic but visible," suffusing his sexual
experiences in bathhouses. Scott, though rightly wary of the metaphor
of visibility as literal transparency in the historical domain, undervalues
the evidence and authority of experience as it is *felt* kinesthetically even
as it is processed visually as the shimmerings of light beings, rebounding
off watery surfaces. Likewise, the hyphenated trans-sexualities on screen
(bi-trans, or trans-dyke, trans-fag) tend to only be appreciated for how
they satisfy the terms of visual essentialism or mobilize the mimetic medium of film and genres with a history of scientism to represent identities of desire. The essentialism of the image seems to carry over into the
essentialism of the identity represented therein. This generic framing accomplishes much for the activism-bent trans porn searching for ways to
correct the record, for sexuality has been largely a no-go area within the
respectability politics of trans communities, but it miscalculates the pernicious effects of a "permissible range of touch" enforced by sexological
narratives of transsexualism as deviant desire. I thus analyze ways that
docu-porns present "a set of embodied texts whose potential for *productive* disruption of structured sexualities and spectra of desire," in Stone's
words. This approach brings new insights into how experimental erotic
videos from Mirha-Soleil Ross (1997–2003) and mainstream porn features from Buck Angel (2004–12) critically, and affectively, put the sex
back in transsexual. At stake in these works are not only a visible but
also a kinesthetic saturation of sexual acts that I argue produces what
Foucault calls the "shimmering mirage" of sex. Sexualities are also disrupted through porn innovations: the early hybrid docu-porn *Linda/Les,
and Annie: The First Female-to-Male Transsexual Love Story* (1989) with
Annie Sprinkle eroticizes the productive failures of hetero trans-sex coupling, while more recently the racial realism in *Trans Entities: The Nasty
Love of Papí and Wil* (2007) by Morty Diamond pries "nasty" from damaging affective economies of race, sexuality, and gender. Last, I consider
the various videos for how they underscore the importance of sexual experience in trans "bodily aesthetics," in which a felt sense of one's body
can become sutured into an imperfect, wavering w/hole, not reducible to
genital fragmentation.

Leaning on the previous chapters' assessment of film's animating power to reassemble on-screen bodies through recourse to genre and gender/race conventions, next in chapter 3, I consider how two films operate as cyborgian cinematic bodies with the potential to delink and relink or even explode perceptual circuits. In this final chapter, "Shimmering Multiplicity: Trans*Forms in *Dandy Dust* and *I.K.U.* from Dada to Data to D@D@," the philosophy of images proposed by Henri Bergson and extended by Kara Keeling, in which images are not purely visual but a complex of affectivity, informs my reading of two multigenre cult flicks: *Dandy Dust* (1998, dir. Hans Scheirl) and *I.K.U.* (2000, dir. Cheang Shu Lea). Both millennial films deal narratively with collecting memory data (of other genders, of sexual climaxes) while materially exploding with rage, lust, fluids, noise, and genre twists. The multiplicity within their presentation of trans bodies in chimeric switch-forms is based on the partiality, but also the mutability, of the cyborg. Hence, I argue that trans*forms in these films are explicitly invoked in the image of the feared and desired cyborg, who appears cinematographically in odd composite images, fragmented and reworked through orgasms, code, memory, and in the shadow of an evil state apparatus. In *Dandy Dust* the titular trans protagonist racially morphs depending on his/her age, but also appears as a time-traveling mummy and a talking flame on the run from a mother's genetic engineering program, threatening twin siblings, and an incestuous father. In *I.K.U.* shape-shifting occurs mainly through seven forms of the replicant Coder "Reiko," but the narrative is also anchored in the FTM Runner character "Dizzy"—played by the African American actor Zachary Nataf, the only non-Asian person of color in the film—who works for the Genom Corporation and directs Reiko's orgasm collection mission. Closely reading the ways that these dark techno-porno films operate through puzzling and dada-inspired audiovisual special effects, I argue for how the cinephilic analyst must adopt a scanning gaze to be able to track the shimmering nuances of the affects built into its film form. Steven Shaviro singles out one quality of the image most responsible for filmic fascination, that is, the image's appeal to touch with its simultaneous exclusion: "I cannot take hold of it in return, but always find it shimmering just beyond my grasp." The elicited endless groping toward these film bodies resituates curiosity as a critical affective mode for bodies in transition. I propose that through curiosity one accesses the ability to break through habituated perceptual circuits, in short, to think otherwise. At the same time, a resituated curiosity responds to the rage of being made a mute curio or, perhaps worse, made vulnerable to transphobia that excludes monstrous trans bodies from the perceptual schemata for the human. Against the backdrop of shimmering boundaries used against trans bodies to discount their legibility, distinctness, and wholeness, the embrace of shimmering images by these films seizes the stigma as a source of personal and political transformative power, a survival technique for inventing livable conditions.

Shimmering Images brings the aesthetics of change into the glimmering limelight by attending to the role of affect in outplaying the paradigm in order to understand anew how surprise, suspense, disgust, fascination, rage, love, and curiosity parry our transitions forward into the nonbinary fixated politics of the Neutral. To the reader, I bid you repose in the intervals between movement and rest. If my writing as a trans lover has any impact, I'd wish for it to be so that you too can feel for the gradations, blooming, and bursts in your qualitative transformation, and hence the potential for change that lies at the heart of both transgender embodiment and cinematic experience.

ONE

Shimmering Phantasmagoria

Trans/Cinema/Aesthetics in an Age

of Technological Reproducibility

Opening a phantasmagoria show in Paris in 1793, Philip Philidor proclaimed to the crowd, "I do not wish to deceive you;
but I will astonish you."[1] The Enlightenment's investment in
rational, clear thinking achieved by shining a light on the
natural world takes a perverse twist in this popular form of entertainment that projects phantoms during an aural and visual dialogue between the living and the dead. The double view of trans bodies as both
engineered by medical science and as fundamentally illusory holds the
same tension, and protracted appeal, as proto-cinematic phantasmagoria
shows. In our twenty-first-century cultural moment when trans characters and talent are inundating televisual series, reality shows, and films,
yet still with their transition forming a main attraction and plot device,
it seems pertinent to ask, Are trans people the heirs of phantasmagoric visual culture?[2] Taking a historical view, Rita Felski argues that the
perceived undecidability of gender leads the figure of the transsexual to
become a metaphor for cultural crisis. Citing the epigram *fin de siècle,
fin de sexe*, Felski notes how the anxieties of suspended sex from the late
nineteenth century return before the millennium during the postmodern
moment in which "gender emerges as a privileged symbolic field for the
articulation of diverse fashionings of history and time," be they apoca-
lyptic or redemptive.[3]

What is missing in trans origin myths and interpretations of their existence—a bellwether—is an appreciation for how trans subjects narrate and represent their lives and thereby mold the available conceptual models of gendered embodiment. This chapter submits that diverse conceptualizations for trans embodiments and identities emerge together with phantasmagorical visual practices that offer them a horizon of intelligibility by interlacing science with entertainment. I foremost explore the continuity of a stuttering, flickering type of transformation as a type of shimmering found in the early cinematographic "fantastic views" of filmmaker George Méliès (1896–1912) and in the (photo) montage of Danish artist Lili Elbe's life writing (1931) about how she became a real girl that was later reprinted (referring to her "sex change"). At the close I consider how shimmering phantasmagoria return in the contemporary trans artworks of Zackary Drucker and A. L. Steiner, who collaborate on a photography series entitled "BEFORE/AFTER" (2009–present), and the flipbook and life-size zoetrope project "Becoming" by Yishay Garbasz (2010), documenting the year before and after her gender clarification surgery. Forgoing the foundational terms of either *trans* or *film* is imperative to tracing the phantasmagoria's lingering hold on how a transformative embodiment is conceptualized within visual culture. Following Elizabeth Freeman's queer historical concept of "temporal drag" to register the pull of the deep past on the present, I focus on how some trans bodies carry forward "the genuine *past*-ness of the past—its opacity and illegibility," that seems intransient and anachronistic, that is, unless viewed from the perspective of the phantasmagoria.⁴ To grasp the parallel and overlapping tracks of trans and phantasmagoria's temporal drag, I map the genealogy of an expansive trans concept interacting with invert, hermaphrodite, and deviant sex theories relying on the dichotomy of illusion/real, and I conduct media archaeology to trace phantasmagoric aesthetics of deception/reproduction across divergent cultural series.

A veritable mountain of literature discusses phantasmagoria as the name for the ancient or modern exhibition of optical illusions, or the literary creation of a shifting series of imagined phantasms, or the key term of intellectual and aesthetic discussions during the nineteenth and twentieth centuries. Straddling the era of incipient and full-blown technological reproducibility, Tom Gunning explains, "Phantasmagoria takes on the weight of modern dialectics of truth and illusion, subjectivity and objectivity, deception and liberation, and even life and death."[5] Or, as Terry Castle has shown, in the history of the phantasmagoria we can find the latent irrationalism haunting the rationalist conception of the mind, what she calls the "spectralization" of the world of thought.[6] Its persistence today in the syntax of trans lives and representation points toward the strong undertow of these larger categorical anxieties deflected onto gender then as now, and thus complicates the notions of transsexual and transgender as formatively modern or postmodern.

My argumentation goes against the grain of scholars such as Bernice Hausman or R. Nick Gorton who attribute the emergence of trans identities foremost to the development of surgical technologies by modern science and to the taxonomy of mental and sexual pathologies in sexology.[7] The evolving system of medico-scientific discourses certainly determines the so-called truth about a subject's status vis-à-vis differentiating between pathological and healthy definitions of sexual and gender practices. Trans subjects who articulate the feeling of being in the "wrong body" become a sign of pathology, and therefore a subject to reform back to health. But this view of trans embodiment is limited to explaining discourses of clinical experiences that arose during the modern era, however much of a hold they retain today in spite of competition from juridical definitions of self-determination.[8] In addition, I also contest the conclusion of trans scholars such as Jack Halberstam who claim this modern formation of trans has been superseded by postmodern theories that question any form of universal truth and challenges the fixity of all meaning, including the designations sex and gender.[9] In general, theories of gender performativity in queer and transgender studies embrace the philosophies that gender is more a fiction than a fact, and that identity is a potentiality rather than an achievement. Related to this malleable identity, technology for gender transitioning has accompanied changes in the economic and aesthetic landscape in which neoliberal orders increasingly favor plasticity. Here the prevalence of trans discourses of change are seen to orbit around the economic order, thereby becoming suspect for capitulating to late capitalist choice economies.[10] The growing investment in what Zygmunt Bauman calls "liquid life" and gradually more mainstream calls for fluidity in identity from celebrities like Miley Cyrus and Ruby Rose might well lead to increased possibilities for *some* trans subjectivities to become intelligible, while others become opaque.[11]

However, the modern and the postmodern claims for conceptualizing trans are primarily about epistemological correction, or uncertainty. Running through both claims, and both eras, is the perpetuation of the trans stereotype of *being* illusory or unreal, which places a heavy stigma on those who assert a trans identity. That is, the trans "onto-epistemological" condition, in which being and knowing are always already entangled, appears symbolically as either an aberration or a deconstructive supplement to constructed normal, natural, or healthy binary gender identities that match the sex assigned at birth, often referred to as cisgender.[12] The visual legacies of inscribing gender truths onto the visual body-as-text can be heard in trans vocabularies, such as being read (for trans), passing (for cisgender), female impersonator, or masculine presenting. Trans subjectivity is pulled taut between gestures of concealing and revealing with its literal translation into the violence of the genital reveal I discussed in the introduction. First I address the perilous investment in an one/none visual truth of sex and gender before coming to see how trans subjects engage the phantasmagoria *dispositif* to effectively shift the visual and discursive order toward a model of sensorial reckoning best described as shimmering.

Cultural Series:
Machines for Perceiving "Self-Evidences"

The experience of transitioning is often conceptualized as a visual effect of a personal disclosure, a "coming out" of the hidden epistemological closet into the revealing light of truth. Jay Prosser, for example, considers the transsexual to exist only during a medically assisted physical transition to become the desired perceptible gender. "The immediate purpose of transsexuality," he writes, "is to make real the subject's true gender on the body," and in this pursuit he names "the visual media" as being highly valuable for the "promise (like transition itself) to make visible that which begins as imperceptible—there but underexposed."[13] People who "cross over (*trans-*) the boundaries constructed by their culture to define and contain gender" thereby lose access to conventional evidence for making truth claims for their gender identity.[14] This places a tremendous amount of onto-epistemological weight on the indexical, referential, and highly visual dimension of their truth statements. The visual media of photographic images especially "realize the image of the 'true' self that is originally only apparitional" to others and potentially to oneself.[15] The photographic portrait accompanying written testimony functions, for Prosser, as an incarnation of gendered realness, bringing to the apparitional yet truer version of self as described in language a sense of heft paradoxically through its paper or digital materiality. In Prosser's brilliant analysis of how written trans autobiographies often integrate personal and artistic photographs, he is aware of the dangers of awarding visual media with less (perceived) mediation between signifier and soma than writing's rhetorical strategies. Borrowing language from Roland Barthes, the photograph, he notes, appears "co-natural" or fully in alignment with the bodily referent and even confused with it as it begins to function as more referential to the anchored gendered self (I am there, I am that) than the actual body that remains stubbornly in flux. In fact, the photographic portrait that realizes a true gender by index risks over time not offering the indexed subject a sustained form of gendered realness, but rather its illusion. The "now you see it, now you don't" quality of visual trans self-representation can function like a phantasmagoric technique. Like Philidor's disclaimer for his phantasmagoria, the production of visual gendered realness oscillates between deception and astonishment.

The optical device and conceptual vehicle of the phantasmagoria stresses the spectacular and spectral quality of bodies. Not only did the phantasmagoria incorporate the necessary, underlying lens technologies, perspectival physics, and techniques for capturing light for photographic arts, it also readied an audience eager to be astonished by cinematographic views. For a methodological frame to study the continuities between previous popular trick technologies and early film, André Gaudreault suggests the inclusive term of a "cultural series" for moments of transition through "intermedial meshing" between media rather than looking to pinpoint a historical rupture.[16] The process of institutionalization through the normalization of codes later set the animated views of cinema apart from other cultural forms such as magic shows and vaudeville theatre, consolidating it into a relatively autonomous media institution during Hollywood's Golden Age (1917–1960s). Even from a twenty-first-century point of view though, the series element of spectacular and specular bodies continues to play across differing cultural and media forms, linking together phantasmagoric aesthetic impulses with new technical advances. The cultural series approach that tracks intermedial meshing might also be applied to the scientific series of sexual intermediacy in which earlier notions of trans concepts were strongly related to homosexuality and intersexuality as well. Dating from the late nineteenth century, this kaleidoscopic blending and turning of trans-inter-queer inflections has a distinctly visual and psychosexual lineage. Take for example Magnus Hirschfeld's "Yearbooks for Sexual Intermediaries" (1899–1923), which consist of 20,000 pages of images showing the variance of psychic and physical hermaphroditism, transvestism, and homosexuality between the poles of what he called the "full woman" and the "full man."[17] These meshings of sexual intermediacy shifted again when judicial rulings compared intersex and transsexual claims to change gender status (1950s) and when homosexuality was largely replaced by transsexuality in a key reference psychology book on diagnosing mental disorders (1973).[18] My framing of phantasmagoria as a cultural series has the benefit of bringing together, and thinking together, two historical transitional moments: when technological reproducibility first affected visual culture by heightening the volatility of an audiovisual image, and when surgical and sexological science also first acknowledged the mutability of gender.

Michel Foucault's historical method of archeology that accounts for the dimension and direction of power in normalization processes can be usefully combined with studying minute transitions within cultural series.[19] His analysis of different eras focuses on the relation of forces that produce and deploy truth; power produces epistemological formations specific to a period's configuration, enabling something to be said to be, and another thing to be seen as, true. A cultural moment thus consists in the visible and the sayable that enables knowledge to emerge as self-evident. In parsing Foucault's archaeological method, Gilles Deleuze explains that an era consists of a geological threshold that breaks with the previous one through the transformation of *statements* (sayable) and *visibilities* (visible)—"an audiovisual archive"—that form bands of discursive knowledge and fields of nondiscursive knowledge.[20]

In the case of the phantasmagoria, I see that it patterns the supposedly self-evident or knowable visibilities of both cinema images and trans bodies as astonishing illusions or more generally as a shimmer. Deleuze defines visibilities to be "forms of luminosity which are created by the light [of the era] itself and allow a thing or object to exist only as a flash, sparkle or *shimmer*."[21] The "first light" of an era acts as a virtual visibility producing all perceptible experiences; it "brings forth visibilities as flashes and shimmerings, which are the 'second light.'"[22] Thus, the pervasive lights of an era can be analyzed as a potentate form that is capable of creating other forms and movements.[23] Deleuze proposes that in the same way that statements depend on their system for sayability, visibilities are inseparable from the machines that produce their seeability. Such visibility machines do not have to be optical machines like film projectors per se; they are more generally conceived as an assembly of organs and functions that makes something inconspicuously visible: producing a thing as a shimmering. Crucial to entering the visible field as a second light, then, is the proper relation to the machine that acts as a first light. Only then can one (or something) become a shimmer, created as a "light-being" both absolute in one's givenness and yet historical, because a being of light "is inseparable from the way in which it falls into a formation or corpus."[24] The phantasmagoria serves a unifying function, acting as a production and distribution center of light and dark, the opaque and transparent, the seen and not-seen—a system of light infused with power relations, as Foucault skillfully analyzes in "Diego Velásquez's" painting *Las Meninas*.[25] As a type of this first light, the cultural series of phantasmagoria not only literally projects a shimmering image, but also is a form of luminosity that allows cinema and trans bodies to exist as self-evident shimmers.

I look methodologically at how the cultural series of the phantasmagoria developed in order to understand how the sense of trans right about now is oddly not that anachronistic with trans from back then. Although trans identification and means to attain a gender transition then and now are clearly not the same, the lingering phantasmagoric aesthetic achieves a continued problematic sense of a sex change as self-evidently illusory by wavering on the tip of deception/astonishment. My archaeological method involves "breaking open" the self-evidence of an audiovisual cultural form that is suspended in the "strata" of an age, leading to the question, How did the era of technological reproducibility become filled with this particular cultural series of phantasmagoric shimmerings?[26] Principally, according to a media archeology perspective, as the means of image reproduction became more sophisticated so did the concealment of its production, contributing further to the sense of self-evident realness and the ever-greater popular success of phantasmagoric devices. The original phantasmagoria that used rear projection from behind the screen to keep the audience unaware of the lanterns became improved with new optical technologies of film that further hid the source of production by projecting images from behind audiences' backs. Jonathan Crary's historical study of visual devices and techniques determines that of the many competing optical experiences of the 1830s most disappeared by the 1850s because they were insufficiently "phantasmorgoric" in the sense of creating an illusion of the image's standalone realness.[27] Richard Grusin and Jay David Bolter find that similarly new technologies are taken up only when they come closest to presenting an unmediated reality (i.e., an illusion of the realness of the image because it appears unsupported), concluding that successful "remediation" follows the logic of transparency.[28] The persistent popularity of phantasmagoria since the 1790s is also accounted for by Theodor Adorno's Marxist analysis: "[phantasmagoria indicates] the occultation of production by means of the outward appearance of the product [. . .] this outer appearance can lay claim to the status of being. Its perfection is at the same time the perfection of the illusion that the work of art is a reality *sui generis* that constitutes itself in the realm of the absolute without having to renounce its claim to image the world."[29] The occultation of production through its concealment makes a commodity a "very queer thing," Marx noted, because it seems to take on an animated life of its own.[30] Hiding the production of gender, sometimes in plain sight with gender-marked clothing, gesture, and so on, enables one's outer appearance to do the work of "claiming the status of being." The very queer shimmer of a thing in the era of technological reproducibility shows up under the aegis of competing phantasmagorical optical novelties that create a world of images so real that they threaten to replace the actual experiences they represent.

The genre of fantastical stories of transformation also trades in the troubling division of illusion from realness. One of the first self-authored memoirs of someone who was relentlessly investigated for their "true" sex and gender identity was written by Herculine (Adélaîde/Abel) Barbin (1838–68), who also referred to herself as Alexina or Camille and was living in France during the phantasmagoria craze. Foucault came across Barbin's story through an entry in a sexological encyclopedia published by Auguste Tardieu that details Barbin's youth spent in an all-girl's convent school and later a women's teaching college. Foucault extracts from the personal narrative and surrounding medical documents an emerging social perception of monstrous and foolish embodiments that deviate from the ideal form of a singular sex—a new shimmer in the audiovisual archive. Changes of sex or claims of multiple sexes increasingly became considered as "insulting to 'the truth,'" or "not adequate to reality," and "seen as belonging more or less to the realm of chimeras."[31] Even if not an outright crime, sexual irregularity is suspected to be fictitious, a mere disguise that should be stripped off through the declaration of one's true sex.

Barbin captured the attention of medical authorities precisely because of her disturbing phantasmagoric appeal to lovers. These lovers were understood to be deceived and perhaps even desired to be astonished by Barbin's shimmering sexes: true and apparent. In Foucault's words: "But if nature, through its fantasies or accidents, might 'deceive' the observer and hide the true sex for a time, individuals might also very well be suspected of dissembling their inmost knowledge of their true sex and of profiting from certain anatomical oddities in order to make use of their bodies as if they belonged to the other sex. In short, the *phantasmagorias of nature* might be of service to licentious behavior, hence the moral interest that inhered in the medical diagnosis of the true sex."[32] Barbin's story does not relish in deceiving the medical or intimate observer, but it certainly savors the delights she experienced in not having a definite, identifiable sex. The world her story relates to readers "was a world in which grins hung about without the cat" in that it imparts how the identity of Barbin and partners had little or no importance next to the feelings that were shared.[33] This apparently "happy limbo of a non-identity" with its resultant affective intensification became rudely interrupted when she was forced by law to live as a man, and Barbin eventually committed suicide, her memoirs left at her side.[34] Her death portends the many trans and intersex people to come who also cannot find a way to live when forced to have a definite true sex that they either cannot abide or cannot convincingly produce. The phantasmagoria at this time thus dangerously tilts toward the modernist "one true identity" logic of a concealed referent, defining everything else as an illusion. I wager though that the cultural series of phantasmagoria continues in its development to model other visibilities with more accommodating ways of living as a shimmering.

If, as Foucault claims, the specific phantom of the eighteenth century was the transvestite and that of the nineteenth century was the haunting hermaphrodite, it is small wonder that sexological narratives about sexual intermediacy find their outlet as well in the cinematic effects of double exposure, substitution, and transformation.[35] The fantastic view that gender is transformable, and sex changeable, acknowledges an interest in the waning sense of incommensurable difference between the sexes.[36] The cinematographic shimmer of trans, however flickering in and out of focus with hermaphrodites and sexual deviants, indicates that long before Christine Jorgenson attained her international celebrity for having a "sex change" in the early 1950s, the visual field was peppered with sex change–type narratives and morphing imagery. In the scientific series of trans sex transformation, a significant shift occurred when Western scientific traditions of surveillance, measurement, and physical transformation utilized cinema to perform a "fantastic construction of 'human life' as a dynamic entity to be tracked, studied, and transformed in the social 'theatre' of the laboratory."[37] The ontology of cinema, in its special relation to animating life and suspending death in a cinematic theatre, strongly resembles the ontology of the trans body that undergoes surgery, which takes place in an operating theatre. In the phantasmagoria cultural series, cinema, with its system of editing cuts and suturing images, parallels the incisions and sutures that take place in a surgical theatre. Attention to the construction of human life with respect to the ways in which surgical and cinematic cuts refigure bodies may offer insight into the cultural and technical conditions that enabled trans identity to emerge differentiated from an otherwise perplexing limbo identity.

Walter Benjamin's 1936 essay "The Work of Art in the Age of Its Technological Reproducibility" offers such a theory of cinema with respect to its ability to cut into reality in order to reassemble the aesthetic experience of life.[38] In Benjamin's theorization of the cinema–as–surgical theatre, incisions occur on a number of levels: (1) the selection of reality to be captured on celluloid, (2) editing the celluloid, and (3) the viewer's reception of the edited film. First, the cinematographer penetrates deeply into reality's tissue to extract piecemeal parts, slicing into it much like the surgeon "makes an intervention in the patient."[39] Then, during the film's production, the editor assembles the various cuts to create another, transformed perception of reality. Finally, when this artificially "equipment-free" view of reality is foisted on film viewers, the film becomes the surrogate surgeon. Cinema has, based on successive changes of scene and focus made possible through the procedure of cutting celluloid, a "percussive effect" on the spectator: assailing him or her through the tactile quality of the unstoppable and erratic flow of cuts.[40] Film as a whole—not just at either its production or its reception—operates on an ailing relation with reality, in part caused by the phantasmagoric quality of commodities. Benjamin brings the discourse of surgery to bear on cinema in order to underscore the uncertain cultural and political consequences of interacting with reproductive technologies that bring enlivening novelty as well as deadening alienation. In the age of a global movie-going world, cinematic pictures become part of, if not the core of, what Susan Buck-Morss calls the "new urban phantasmagoria" of the commodity-on-display in which purely representational value is paramount.[41] How reproductive technologies are used and to what ends are critical questions not only for representation politics but also for how gender becomes reproduced in the operating theatre of the social.

Trickality Aesthetics:
Georges Méliès and the Quick Change

The model of cinema–as–surgical theatre bears out surprisingly literally in the practice of early filmmaking, flipping Susan Stryker's insight into the "cinematic logic of transsexual embodiment" into a confirmation of the transsexual logic of cinema at work since its inception. In 1888 Georges Méliès bought the famous Théâtre Robert-Houdin in Paris and worked as a conjuring magician some eight years before he started experimenting with new cinematographic devices. Playing the impresario in most all of his films, Méliès swapped a magic wand for scissors. "Méliès was one of the first to think of the cinema in terms of cuts!" exclaims Gaudreault, who points to the often overlooked stigmata of the numerous cuts found through all of Méliès's films, hidden in the upper corner of the celluloid film strip where the glue sutures together two distinct successive moments that comprise the trick effect.[42] The presence of scissors and glue indicate the slice-and-splice creative thinking that surgeons also apply. Even closer to the surgical cutting edge though was how along with developing his achievements in editing Méliès developed a penchant for demonstrating an instant sex change on film. Both the match-on-action trick edit and gender transformation are birthed in the origin story of his discovery of the stop-camera technique. It occurred one day through a happy accident when he was filming at the Place de l'Opéra around October or November 1896, less than a half year after he began filmmaking. He claims that "[. . . .] the camera I used in the early days (a primitive thing in which the film tore or frequently caught and refused to advance) jammed and produced an unexpected result; a minute was needed to disengage the film and to make the camera work again. During this minute, the passers-by, a horse trolley and other vehicles had, of course, changed positions. In projecting the strip, rejoined [*ressoudée*: glued back together] at the point of the break, I suddenly saw a Madeleine-Bastille horse trolley change into a hearse and men become women."[43] Gaudreault analyzes this quote to show that Méliès rightly belongs to the history of editing, as he is clearly aware from this moment of the possibility to glue together mismatching frames (that link different content by shared action) to achieve an astonishing effect.[44] This is the animated effect of the before-and-after photograph, speeding up the minute during which the scene became rearranged to an instant.

However, the quick change of men becoming women was perhaps more than just a lucky metamorphosis; it precipitated in cinematic aesthetics the avant-garde of the surgical and hormonal science of sex transformation by at least a decade.[45] Charles Darwin wrote in 1868, "in many, probably in all cases, the secondary characters of each sex lie dormant or latent in the opposite sex ready to be evolved under peculiar circumstances."[46] Méliès's filmic trick effect discovered a quarter of a century later seems to offer up this "peculiar circumstance" of sexual morphing as imaginable in the blink of an eye. This first substitution or stop-camera trick, Méliès says, sent him into a frenzy of experimentation: "Two days later, I produced the first metamorphoses of men into women and the first sudden disappearances [. . .]. One trick led to another."[47] Although Méliès used narrative, all his films are "trick-motivated" in that the story is accessory and theatricality is a pretext to the centering of what Gaudrealt coins cinema's inherent capacity for "trickality."[48] In the cinema's trickality one can grasp the transformative possibility of reproductive technology for human identity.

Méliès controlled the creation of his films in every aspect, which makes it all the more impressive that he was able to produce more than five hundred films in the years 1896–1913. Wanda Strauven assesses that of his intact oeuvre consisting of 170 films, at least a dozen focus on the transformation of a man into a woman, or a woman into a man, and sometimes with multiple changes.[49] For example, in *L'Illusionniste fin de siècle* (A Turn of the Century Illusionist, 1899), Méliès jumps from a table and in one fluid motion becomes his corsetted assistant, who gets on the table and in turn transforms back into Méliès as she jumps to the

1.1 Woman Before, Assistant leaping from the table (Georges Méliès, *L'Illusionniste fin de siècle* [A Turn of the Century Illusionist], 1899, Star-Film).

floor, and on again. The film's title, no less, claims this repeated quick sex-change trick to be the height of illusionary powers in an era anxious about gender roles (figures 1.1 and 1.2). Many more films, though, use examples of cross-gender dressing that flirt with the taboos instituted by then-recent dress reform laws such as punished Barbin once she was assigned to live as male.[50] Audiences of *Tentation de saint Antoine* (The Temptation of Saint Anthony, 1898) could safely witness the scandal of a crucified Christ transform into a scantily clad woman, or in *Nouvelles Luttes extravagantes* (The Fat and the Lean Wrestling Match, 1900) watch two women in fine dress suddenly become two burly boxers. Strauven contends that these *chirurgie filmique* (filmic surgery) scenes follow the logic of smoke-and-mirror transformation magic, but also science fiction.[51] Indeed, Méliès appears often as the stock character of the mad scientist, most famously in *Le Voyage dans la Lune* (A Trip to the Moon, 1902), signifying the excitement and dis-ease many felt with scientific progress. Many other films deal more directly with induced, surreal dream states that could reflect on the mid-century development of anesthesia (such as nitrous oxide, called laughing gas), which allowed for longer, more complicated surgeries because the patient would be pain-free and compliant. Hence, besides the technological improvements, a

1.2 Man After, Transforms into the director (Georges Méliès, *L'Illusionniste fin de siècle* [A Turn of the Century Illusionist], 1899, Star-Film).

new way of thinking, and perceiving, gendered corporeality, morphology, and sexuality takes hold in the filmic experimentation with highly gender-coded bodies.

Darragh O'Donoghue sees that the films stage the incredible manufacture of the cinematic image itself, writing that "It was as if Méliès intuited, a quarter of a century before Walter Benjamin, that the cinema was a reproducing machine."[52] The ability to reproduce not only had profound implications for the status of the art object, in that multiple prints could be made of films seen all over the world; human identity itself could be manipulated through its reproduction. Films such as *Nouvelles Luttes extravagantes* (The Fat and the Lean Wrestling Match, 1901) and *L'homme à la tête de caoutchouc* (The Man with the Rubber Head, 1901) demonstrate the sheer pliability of the human body as it transforms into something else, breaks apart by decapitation, or is manipulated in size; the assertion of identity and essence is continually fragmented or proliferated. Méliès created antirealist films that delight in the invented and artificially arranged tableaux; therefore it seems crucial to understand the actual surgical cinematographic process that occurred to produce these phantasmagoric filmic bodies.

Principally, the stop-motion effect is technically simple in that the camera operator is required to stop the motion of filming and then resume it, but in the laboratory the montage was also always recut on the negative to ensure that the desired continuity of action between frames match perfectly, which hides the splice in an unbroken rhythm. The splice proves that the perceived filmic instant is not just the instant of stopping, like that captured by a photography camera, but also a jump forward in real time. The on-match cut must be practically invisible to ensure the viewer experiences the continuity of time when introduced to any factors of discontinuity (man into woman, trolley into hearse). Different from the continuity system of editing that ensures smoothness in the narrative by suturing together cause and effect or diegetic relationships, Méliès used match-on-action cutting for magical ends rather than dramatic purposes.[53] Frank Kessler clarifies how trick films go against the presumption of a "cinematic specificity" that lies in the camera's capability for "reproducing visible reality"; instead the trick intervenes to manipulate "the exact rendition of the visual impression that an actual scene would provide to an eye-witness."[54] The illusion lies in the presumption of the perceived instant, that is, in the illusion of temporal continuity. This false sense of temporal continuity is "enhanced by the unchanging spatial arrangement" of the frontal shot with its fixed framing.[55] Although performed on the same stage, a gulf of difference lies between Méliès's real-time theatrical magic and the collapsed temporal instant of his filmic tricks: the location is not changed, the body is. The stop-camera edit provides a view of gender that is based on montage and assembly, departing from the naturalization of a body's gender that exists without a noticeable, conspicuous cut.

Early film scholars sought to correct film history's overemphasis on the sophisticated appeal of continuity editing in narrative films, glorified by the later development of the Hollywood system. Gaudreault insists on the equal complexity found within "early cinema's *alien* quality" owing to the "open field of enquiry and experimentation," and I must add that this experimentation largely pertained to film's form, which I submit correlates to opening discussions about the mutability of sex and gender forms.[56] Audiences preferring attractional aesthetics could indulge in the spectacle of bodies doing weird and wonderful things, such as going to the moon or having a sex change, scenes made possible through experimentation with cinematographic illusions, with (in-camera) editing tricks. The off-kilter alien quality of the world on-screen also generates more sinister gender-related visual tricks. For instance, Karen Beckman's study of the vanishing women of film and spiritualist photography claims that anxieties about the insubstantial and reproducible body were projected onto women.[57] Emblematic is the pioneering in 1886 of "The Vanishing Lady" magic trick on stage shows, which Méliès saw in London and redid a decade later in filmic form as *Escamotage d'une Dameau Theatre Robert Houdin* (The Vanishing Lady at the House of Robert Houdin, 1896). The shifting ground of the sexual politics of the new era is keyed into this visual trick; not just the process of literally vanishing women, but also the fading clarity of who is a woman, and what is her place, is put on display.

The instantaneous montage techniques used in early film seem attuned to the age's growing preoccupation with instant technologies found in an increasingly mechanical metropolis occupied by the telephone (1876), phonograph (1877), and automobile (1880s). Referring to the one-motion technology of the match, photography camera, and traffic signals, Benjamin looks critically at the haptic experiences that retrain the human sensorium to move abruptly.[58] For Benjamin, film plays a special—both aesthetic and therapeutic—role in the context of industrialization at the turn of the century. In film, "perception in the form of shocks was established as a formal principle," and thus has a decisive role in the epochal reconfigurations of the sensorium.[59] Freeman sees that each era synchs temporal orders to a mode of "chronormativity"; instant trick effects in early film are but one "mode of implantation, a technique by which institutional forces come to seem like somatic facts."[60] Film and video installation are "time arts," Freeman reminds us, in that they create a historically specific shared temporality that one can dwell within, pause, or remake. Méliès conforms to the temporal conventions of the instant, but perhaps also his film's sudden flickers remind us of the instant's construction, allowing us to pause and "desocialize" or "unbind the gaze" attuned to the historical condition of overlooking the temporal cut.[61] In the moments of before and after, sexed difference seems uncertain, like the celluloid that displays movement with "the flicker of presence, absence."[62] Trick films then embody the perversion of the age of reason in their phantasmagoric flash of the "*now* you see it, *now* you don't" apparitional body.

However, at the same time as the attractional techniques of early cinema began meshing with and transitioning into longer narrative sequences, the quick change of transvestite cross-dressing practices began to circulate within the scientific and popular press alongside claims to longer-term cross-identifications with the other sex. Hirschfeld's interest in helping people with "psychic transvestism," who have a desire to fully and physically become the other sex, led him to assist in the surgical transformation of famed Danish painter and Bohemian French socialite Einar Wegener/Lili Ilse Elvenes (1882–1931). Better known today by her adopted media pseudonym "Lili Elbe," likely given by her journalist friend and publicist Louise "Loulou" Lassen, Lili lived openly as a woman for most of her married life, supported by her wife and friends. When in her mid-forties (circa 1928) Lili learned she could undergo a highly risky series of operations to physically change her sex, she determined to document, and thereby narrativize, her transition in photographs and writing. I examine in the next section the resulting multi-authored archival document *Man into Woman*, published posthumously, in which her desire for a physical adjustment of gonadal sex to bring it into conformity with her strong feelings of being a woman aligns with a particular transsexual desire to leave one's assigned sex behind and inhabit the opposite sex. Yet, I argue, the version of Lili Elbe presented in the narrative writing and the before-and-after photomontage holds together the chrononormativities of the instant change and of the enduring self, specifically in the binding cut of the "and" that sutures the body of the before with the after as being self-same, even if radically changed.

Lili Elbe's *Man into Woman* Narrative:
A Photomontage of Before and After

From her rise to fame in the European avant-garde circles of the 1910s to 1930s as the mysterious muse of her artistic wife Gerda Wegener, who shared her devotion to theatre, carnival, and masquerade, to the press's fascination in 1930 with her miraculous transformation from a man into a woman, the cultural text of "Lili Elbe" inscribes her as a phantasmagoric figure par excellence. Her story narrates the achievements of the technical arts, carries the marks of a great visual illusion, and continues to astonish contemporary audiences who have flocked to see the Hollywood biopic of her life, *The Danish Girl* (dir. Tom Hooper, 2015; Eddie Redmayne plays Lili), which is based on the best-selling dramatic novelization of Lili's life from her wife's perspective, written by David Ebershoff (2000).[63] All this to say, like the cinema of attractions that promises shock and surprise, the meshwork around Lili Elbe's various incarnations of alluring, transformative gender representations and sexual confessions taps into the thrill of revelation, even as it holds back details. For example, in Gerda's extraordinary depictions of Lili in the guise of the idealized, sexually desiring New Woman beauty with immaculate makeup and in various stages of undress, her back is often turned to avoid showing genitals or a bouquet is carefully placed over them.[64] Lili's authorial distance as model and muse for other creators have led some to consider reading her own painterly oeuvre for telling details of how she perceived and created trans* aesthetics.[65] Although the factual and personal circumstances are lost to history, one thing seems certain: like the many trans (and intersex) people since whose personal narratives are sold to the press, Lili was troubled by the public exposure of her surgical transformation in the Danish and German press and sought, perhaps unsuccessfully, to regain control over her story through a multimedia book project with pictures, letters, and a story.[66]

Drawing on the available conceptual models of gendered embodiment as one (or the other) true sex, the narration and representation of Lili Elbe montages male with female personae, which effectively stretches out the before-and-after temporality into a stuttering story of shifting back and forth. The *Man into Woman* story celebrates Lili's achievement of being a woman and also recognizes the medical limits to actually changing sex, the procedures for which can create further nonbinary bodies. Hence, I see that both Lili's transsexual desire to inhabit womanhood and her continued sense of a nonbinary embodiment are presented, which is central to her attractional qualities. I privilege my emphasis on the presence of Lili's unresolved relationship to Einar (named Andreas Sparre in the book), resulting in a sense of her nonbinary-ness because it has been neglected by the cinematic rendering of Lili as a prototypical transsexual in *The Danish Girl* and by most historians of transsexuality who gloss over her self-understanding as a sexual intermediate. My attempt to hold together seemingly contradictory identity positions in the figure of Lili Elbe is done in the hope of drawing a more complex picture of how transsexual institutionalization took place vis-à-vis scrambling for turf in interlocking trans-inter-queer discourses.

Lili is ripe now, as she was then, to be recast into various pluralized meanings of transsexual desire and intersex embodiment. Although an authorial Lili cannot now be accessed beyond her letters and edited interviews, I rely on her main tool for engaging the orders of visibility to become a shimmer: the partially autobiographical book published posthumously under her pseudonym in 1931 in Danish, *Fra Mand til Kvinde— Lili Elbes Bekendelser* (From Man into Woman—Lili Elbe's Confessions).[67] The English version *Man into Woman* (1933) claimed to recount *A True and Authentic Record of a Sex Change*, namely "the miraculous transformation of the Danish painter Einar Wegener (Andreas Sparre)," and was said to be edited by Niels Hoyer (Ernst Hathern); it included an introduction by Australian sexologist Norman Haire, who practiced in London and was a known colleague of Hirschfeld.[68] The hybridity of the book's generic modes of confessional, medical dossier, and theatrical play encourages an involved, sensational reading, much like other popular epistolary novels of the day. By not including minute details of the surgeries it fails to be a true case study, nor is it a proper autobiography, because the author and editor are both anonymized and the text integrates dictations taken by friends and letters from her intimates. It is not surprising then that the book eschews narration from a central, stable point of view; the different voices present likely reflect how technically the book is a result of collaborations between six people and a publishing house. In researching the manuscript Sabine Meyer discovers that Lili Elvenes, Gerda Wegener, and Poul Knudsen (a friend of theirs) supplied records from the time period covered; these were initially edited by the journalist Loulou Lassen who then incorporated her recent interviews with the couple and Lili's surgeon. The editing task was taken over by their German friend Ernst Hathern (pseudonym Niels Hoyer), who produced a German-language manuscript; this version was proofread by Lili's Dresden surgeon Kurt Warnekros (pseudonym Werner von Kreutz), and was eventually translated back into Danish and edited at Hage & Clausens Forlag.[69] Although the book has no clear primary author, Meyer concludes that the medical authority of Warnekros/Kreutz, whose approval in the preface underwrites the validity of the confessions, ultimately authorized the German and Danish versions and frames Lili's legacy as being "patientized" and pathologized.[70] The effect of an authorial structure with such diverse investments in who Lili is and what she stands for is a book that pulls in multiple directions. In consequence, I must attend to the stylization of Lili as one that is hyperconscious of making her lived experience visible, of wanting to be knowable to an audience, and that is also aware of possible shocking impacts on society's understanding of sex and gender.

The most widely read German, British, and American publications of *Man into Woman* pattern the narration on a mixed hermaphroditic psychic and physical experience, interspersed with personal photographs that evidence her successful transformation, but challenge a firm before-and-after temporality. Appearing in frontispiece illustrations and sprinkled throughout chapters, professional portraits of Einar from 1920 and 1929 are surrounded by portraits and casual snapshots of Lili that appear to have been taken in the years before and after her surgeries (1926, 1929–31) (figures 1.3 and 1.4). The written narrative addresses the conflicted psychic state as an internal inversion: "Andreas believed that in reality he was not a *man*, but a *woman*," a state that required the removal of "the dead (and formerly imperfect) male organs, and to restore the female organs with new and fresh material"—a transformation that would enable Lili to survive and effectively kill Andreas, the man.[71] Stone identifies this division as a strategy of "building barriers" within a single subject to maintain "polar personae."[72] Although the divided individual is the same person, he or she must ultimately deny the mixture existing in one body—the mixture of s/he—by enforcing a divisive cut of he/she.[73] Now a staple of the genre to dramatize the moment leading up to a divisive cut symbolically and literally registered by submitting to a genital surgery, the multimedia presentation of Elbe in this regard retroactively indicates *Man into Woman* is the *ur*-text of trans life writing.[74] Despite the tidy title that propositionally defines gender relations in terms of one into another in order to indicate a progressive leap forward, the extreme use of a third-person narrator offers an unspecified, ongoing, subjective point of view of the protagonist before "Andreas had vanished." At the close of the book, unknowingly on her deathbed, she writes that she must use the third person, "as in a novel," when narrating the story of Einar/Andreas, for she "could not relate the story of Andreas' life in the first person," although she often found it "repugnant to speak of myself as of a third person."[75] The third person provides a distancing effect, but also one that felt offensive, unacceptable, possibly coerced. For the Lili figured in *Man into Woman*, although Andreas is as good as dead at a certain point in her transition, the spatio-temporality of before and after dividing masculinity and femininity remains unresolved.

In a key penultimate scene, the third-person narrator explains Lili's thoughts going in to what would be her last surgery: "She wanted to be a bridge-builder [. . .]. She had perhaps built a slender bridge across

1.3 Professional Portrait of Einar Wegener (Andreas Sparre), 1929. (No living or known copyright holder.)

that abyss which separates man and woman."[76] Lili here seems to embrace a gendered embodiment that moves across the "abyss of man and woman," appearing textually in flickers on both sides of the chasm. In this light, the portrayal of the protagonist as a man *and* a woman in snapshots sprinkled throughout the text unsettles Prosser's conclusion about how personal snapshots function to evidence further the semiotic unity or breach of the portrayed trans subject.[77] At first glance the images narrate: in first person "I have always been here," or, in third person, "He is no longer there." Their inclusion in *Man into Woman*, written by Lili but likely selected and placed by other collaborators after her death, animates the images into a photomontage that conceptually builds a taut connection between the appearance of a feminine persona and a masculine one. Although I cannot know which of the images were originally destined to be included in the book, the fact she was intent on having photographs of herself as Lili indicates what Meyer calls Lili's "staging strategies," which make it possible to analyze her agency within dominant discourses.[78] It seems that the book uses the visual and textual language of "sexual indeterminacy" not to undermine the reality of Lili's femininity or her agency

1.4 Portrait captioned "Lili, Paris," 1926. Photograph, likely taken by Gerda Wegener (wife). (No living or known copyright holder.)

to become a woman, but to indicate the ongoing labor of birthing her into an unknown, indeterminate future.[79] In the paragraph before that announcing this role as a bridge-builder (also written in the third person), the reader learns that "One day her confessions— and she smiled at this thought—would burst upon mankind as the confession of the first person who was not born unconsciously through a mother's travail, but fully conscious through her own pangs."[80] The confessions with the personal photographs thus seem framed as conscious elements of her self-creation in which she takes pride and joy.

Parallel to the effect of the photomontage's flickering of before and after, the opening puts the reader onto another track of a novel or screenplay of a fictionalized life told in the present tense: "The scene is Paris in the Quartier Saint Germain. The time a February evening in 1930. In a quiet street which harbours a stately palace there is a small restaurant, whose regular customers are foreigners, and mostly artists."[81] This is the precipitous evening before "Andreas" meets the gynecologist "Kreutz," and his first line is a hearty "Skaal!," toasting wine with a group of friends. With the first-person introduction of Lili taking place soon thereafter, the tale then breaks the rules of biography and asserts that it is not a medical dossier disguised as literature either. In puzzling over the text's diverse narrative structures, Meyer suggests to call it a "fictionalized biographical collage."[82] I agree that the text "collages" various types of materials, but the way in which the book achieves a new composite whole from fragments of other forms suggests a montage instead. The cinematic concept of montage also successfully accounts for the ways in which temporality in the presented life of Lili Elbe shifts around in unexpected and jarring ways. The text therefore teaches that holding attention is the best way to control the narrative, effectively by turning the instant into an everextending present.

Meyer's study of the press at that time makes it clear that Lili (and her coauthors) had limited scope for appealing to a discourse that would allow her to be accepted as a (trans) woman.[83] The fantastical dimension of the story, I want to stress, grates against the discursive authority of medical and legal experts who were consulted for the many press articles about her case. Through the flickering series of (photo)montages, the composite text of *Man into Woman* establishes a sympathetic, witnessing position of authority outside of any one of the characters. This position can be likened to the static camera that establishes a third-person position in trick films. The machinic eye set into motion by the moves of cinematography grants the viewer a limited omniscient position from which to experience the actors and props. As Benjamin points out, the audience comes to stand in for the camera's position and therefore becomes the "operator" or the surgeon who uses technical means to get at the reality of the natural world. Benjamin acknowledges this desire for immediate access to reality to be unattainable, but it nevertheless drives filmmaking as much as film viewing: "The equipment-free aspect of reality has here become the height of artifice, and the vision of immediate reality the Blue Flower in the land of technology."[84] The artistic training of Lili (as Einar Wegener/Andreas Sparre) perhaps not coincidently leads to their mastery of the landscape genre, which also practices the artifice of an equipment-free view onto a natural scene that encourages feelings of ownership in the viewer. As an artist, Lili intimately knows the power of technically produced beauty and the skill as well as the desire involved in conjuring the "blue flower." Taking up the role of the landscape painter of her own life, the narrative voice of Lili withdrawn into third-person subjective seems to adapt her skills of drawing how the landscape feels to drawing how the inner world of Lili feels.

The (photo)montage technique to achieve trans *poesis* through combining the forms of case history, (auto)biography, confession, novel, and portraiture can also suggest a falseness of a narrative that does not quite add up, or at least an unwanted duplicity. Stone voices disbelief in, for example, the after-surgery narration of changed handwriting and voice apparently achieved through castration: "He gazed at the card and failed to recognize the writing. It was a woman's script."[85] Once presented with the handwriting, the astonished doctor agrees that no man could have written it, remarking, "One thing after another is pushing out."[86] The nurse reports that Lili's voice also seems to have changed into "a splendid soprano" and remarks, "Simply astounding!"[87] Stone critically remarks that clinicians may take this seriously only when reading with "jaundiced eyes."[88] To skeptics and disbelievers, Jack Halberstam reminds that, "When we read transgender lives, complex and contradictory as they may seem, it is necessary to read for the life and not for the lie. Dishonesty, after all, is just another word for narrative."[89] Reading the narrative in terms of being guided through alternating substitutions, similar to trick effects in which we are presented with different bodies appearing in the same location, is far-fetched, but not, I argue, unusual within the popular visual culture of Lili's day. The framing of the phantasmagoria on her life narrative allows us to see the way in which Lili Elbe drew upon phantoms, chimeras, and other mysterious changelings in order to present a "person of my own kind," like the "mixed beings" in Plato's *Symposium*.[90] But the book suggests that Lili feels that in her own "sickly body dwelt *two* beings, separate from each other, unrelated to each other, although they had compassion on each other, as they knew that this body had room only for one of them."[91] Prosser asserts that "transsexuality is always narrative work, a transformation of the body that requires the remolding of the life into a particular narrative shape."[92] The shape of Lili Elbe as presented in the text quite remarkably does not put her realness under strain; rather, the plot thickens around the temporal irruption of her being and how to coax her into a sustained position in front of Grete (Gerda) who paints her, the doctors who agree to give her new life, and the photo camera operators who take her portraits. If Stone is suspicious of its authenticity, and if modernist scholar Pamela Caughie finds it too conventional a tale, it is perhaps because the gesture of a sudden surprising appearance has become a standard invention in trans narratives.[93] Although readers might "know better" now, we also seem primed to know trans as a shimmer through the pretext of incredibly fantastic transformations.

In sum, the phantasmagoric "body narrative" established by *Man into Woman* is as follows: Lili remains apparitional until Andreas is finally "pushed out" from the frame in a subtractive process of editing.[94] Gaudreault explains that resumptive editing in the camera (the stop-camera technique) consists in a sleight-of-hand disappearing act in which "one image drives another one out, one image is made to disappear and another takes its place."[95] The factor of discontinuity is central; one image's content seems to drive out another image, forcing a break that appears seamless. This is the complete opposite of the editing that typically occurs in the paradigm of narration, in which the factor of continuity in cause and effect is founded on the logical suture between the sequencing of shots. Borrowing from the film-editing paradigm of discontinuity, Lili's presentation does not have to provide one clear cause, or logic, for being a sexual intermediate. Today mainstream sexology and transgender studies alike acknowledge as much: plenty of reasons—personal and cultural—exist for transitioning, but scientifically or psychologically there is no proven or agreed upon etiology for becoming transsexual.[96] But in 1931, *Man into Woman* locked the attention-grabbing affect of surprise on to the narrative, wrought through authorial discontinuity, in order to effectively circumvent having to pin down a rational cause for her condition.

The affect of surprise, and to a lesser extent suspense, within a narrative context depends on disparities in knowledge between spectators and characters. Although narrative is where the content of knowledge is developed, a film's formal properties are responsible for conveying this information through set techniques and patterns for making meaning in film.[97] Edward Branigan stresses that the film viewer affectively latches onto the narrative in these ways depending on what is presented and how.[98] Put strongly, he writes, "Narrative comes into being when knowledge is unevenly distributed—when there is disturbance or disruption in the field of knowledge."[99] Suspense is based on predicting what is to come, or a future-oriented anticipation, whereas surprise is experienced intensely as being startled or not seeing something coming. Silvan Tomkins theorizes that the affective response of surprise is a "general interrupter to ongoing activity," and in this sense is "ancillary to every other affect since it orients the individual to turn his [sic] attention away from one thing to another."[100] Surprise is relatively neutral then, but also easily confused with the quality of the subsequent affective response to the new thing brought to one's attention (interest, fear, joy, distress, and so on). Like a circuit breaker, Tomkins describes "surprise-startle" as the affective complex that disassembles the subject experiencing a rapid increase in information, forcing attention on this new knowledge.[101] The attraction in cinema is the captivating element of the show; a moment of pure "exhibitionism" that acknowledges the viewer and their interest in being introduced to interruptions within narrative in order for it to fold into new patterns of meaning. Attractions alternate between revealing and concealing, Viva Paci explains, "in a way that is not dependent on the objects or time that precede—or follow—it in a cause and effect relationship."[102] The cultural text of Lili Elbe holds in tension machinic and narratological features of attraction: according to Strauven, when the spectator is attracted *toward* the filmic, it suggests a machinic and a bodily interest, whereas when images seem to move *toward* the spectator in order to direct their look, it defines a narratological interest.[103] *Man into Woman* positions its anticipated viewer so that they learn to become attracted to the patterning of newness, perhaps the better to accept "creatures" like Lili in their follow-up affective responses. The book therefore primes trans cinephiles whose affective response to its trickality via surprise would become positive on the basis of their bodily interest, and even welcoming of the disassembly of their subjective foothold in the narration.

The versions of Lili Elbe that emerge through *Man into Woman*'s multimedia aesthetics discursively work the system of visibilities to gain traction within the phantasmagoria cultural series of attractional images; however, I also want to venture that by taking her two family names from the Elbe River and the possessive form of the Danish word for rivers, *Elvenes*, the text covertly suggests a further a kinship to the phantasmagoria. Niels Hoyer explains in the editor's note that Lili chose her name "out of gratitude to the German city in which she fulfilled her human destiny," specifically the river surrounding the Dresden Municipal Women's Clinic.[104] The depiction of the bridge over the cut of sexual difference, which Elbe is said to embody, is prefigured in the text as the bridge over the Elbe River into Dresden, where the final surgeries are carried out. The symbolic meaning for the protagonist, one may surmise, is that the Elbe River marks the wavering boundary between the banks of man and woman. Elbe describes her first crossing of the bridge into Dresden and the water's magical ability to reflect the city's architectural feats, which "emerge from the shimmering water's surface" like "phantasmagoria."[105] Does the protagonist imagine that she, too, emerges from the Elbe's shimmering surface like phantasmagoria, a scientific and personal feat?[106] Although the extent and meaning of Lili's symbolic embrace of the Elbe River as her namesake is unclear, her legally chosen surname of Elvenes ("rivers'" or Lili of the rivers in Danish) strongly expresses an affinity with the ways rivers flow and shimmer rather than with the solid banks of identity. The built environment reflecting on the river's surface appears to Lili as apparitional and magical, a narratively focalized image that is included perhaps to reflect the protagonist's own struggle to make real and concrete the territory between the two sexes that flows through her.[107] The animating power of the flickering and shimmering of the book's montage sequences seems to bring Lili Elbe into being: the flow of a character over the cuts of perceived sex difference. The alternations of attractional and narrational techniques in *Man into Woman* comprise a central trans aesthetic of change that I see as being developed in this age of reproducibility and gender mutability to resolve the problem of how to sequence a life narrative out of sets of instant changes.

Reparative Practices of Cut and Suture:
Resequencing Trans Hirstories

Aesthetically, this era of reproducibility and instant change is today still seeded by the chrononormativity of trans before-and-after photography, which derives from the same tricks Méliès used to "effectuate instantaneous transformations" in the flick from one image to another, approximating the editing done with a scalpel.[108] Of course the reality of any surgically wrought change is far less speedy, not to mention the long time lapse between various surgeries or stages of a surgical change, and as presented in *Man into Woman*, a transition can follow nonchronological sequencing. The phantasmagoria's "techno-necro" roots of bringing the dead to life— by way of confusing categories dead/alive, truth/falsity, past/present— throws up an opportunity for contemporary trans artists.[109] In returning to the novelty of phantasmagoric aesthetics they purchase a discourse bent on disorienting juxtapositions. Retro-phantasmagoric images offer a cover for the awkward, impossible split framing forced on to the transsexual body "in transition" to both pass and be revealed, that is, to have a true and a false identity, to be dead or relegated to the past but still alive in the present. With a phantasmagoric vision artists can foreground presenting the trick to the viewer, to tickle their desire for optical mastery while withholding a full reveal. Knowledge of the technological mechanism that presents the vision does not necessarily undermine the reality of that vision. As Gunning puts it, the phantasmagoric effect is "I know very well, and yet I see. . . ."[110] Trans artists who invoke early modern optical toys and tricks not only practice temporal drag via a return to a so-called outdated medium, but also show acute awareness of the hangover of the true sex conceptual apparatus, for it drags on in contemporary sociocultural and certainly psycho-sexological discourses. Their harkening of these "throwback" concepts, aesthetics, and technologies facilitates time travel to resequence trans histories as well as their own transition histories.

Deriving from beauty, fashion, and surgical advertisements, before-and-after photographs obey the imperative to portray the self, improved. Thus the pairing of images might not necessarily cite a gender transition but is always gendered. The photography project "BEFORE/AFTER" (2009–) of Zackary Drucker in collaboration with A. L. Steiner occurs in the context of Drucker's performance, photographic, and video work that draws on her trans experience, particularly during the period 2008–10, when she first started physically transitioning.[111] The images currently circulating use some of the same trick techniques that Méliès pioneered in his films, for example, double exposure and duplex photography, which achieve cinematic aesthetics through capturing the moment of transformation in a single image. Other images use an opaque sheet recalling the vanishing lady trick, and more include diptychs of switched bodies back-to-front as well as switched bodies side-by-side. The project's cheeky joke is before and after what exactly? What event or temporal jump has taken place, on which body? Two bodies are presented, rotund and thin, large-breasted and budding, straight blond hair and dark curls, older and younger. Each masquerades as the other transformed, if we follow the invited trans logic of before and after. This series performs a preposterous split temporality distributed across dual, dueling bodies. The series has been installed wrapped around both sides of a corner and is also available in a printed postcard bundle one might thumb through. The multiples of "BEFORE/AFTER" made available simultaneously to the viewer trouble the search for the time of past perfect in which one event is supposed to have happened *before* another one in the past. Without anchoring in a before/body, which is the moment of the after/body?

Ducking the portrait's investment in realist resemblance, these split images suggest the viewer recall the magic simplicity used in theatrical and then cinematic magic acts of disappearance/reappearance, for instance by citing a sheet over a body. The blanket functions as a screen for our projections of which body might be more desirable: Steiner's curves or Drucker's leanness? It is unclear in which direction or into which body we place the unsatisfactory before and the desired after. The wonky double exposure of their bodies, seated and smiling, overlaid imperfectly, also invokes the ghostly apparitions of the phantasmagoria; but who is channeling whom here (figures 1.5 and 1.6)? It's attention to layering implicates a generosity of sharing a body, an act of gifting in which body areas and parts could be gained/lost through an optical game of addition, subtraction, multiplication, and division. Engaging Roland Barthes's theory of the photographic referent, Prosser writes that visual media promise to "realize the image of the 'true' self that is originally only apparitional," thereby incarnating the trans subject.[112] And yet these before-and-after portraits depict bodies cloaked in the transitioning narrative without

1.5 *Untitled*, series "BEFORE/AFTER" (2009–ongoing), by Zackary Drucker and
A. L. Steiner, double-exposure photograph (© Zackary Drucker and A. L. Steiner).

1.6 *Untitled*, series "BEFORE/AFTER" (2009–), by Zackary Drucker and A. L. Steiner, duplex photograph (© Zackary Drucker and A. L. Steiner).

any clear resolution of which would be this true self, or even which body should be taken as realized after the transformative event. The pairing of Steiner and Drucker seem to contribute in different, even contradictory ways to the notion of incarnating the trans subject via a radical split. Instead of a real woman emerging, transfemininity here incarnates through mutual longing.

"BEFORE/AFTER" takes a formalist approach to trans portraiture by ignoring who might be in transition, which is usually signaled by a named person in transition, even one in backslash like Einar/Lili. Instead its continued interrogation is of the aesthetic named in all the titles that comprise the series. Yishay Garbasz's two-year project of weekly self-documentation of her transition marked by a vaginoplasty, which resulted in a flipbook and large-scale zoetrope both called "Becoming" (2010), also uses seriality to foreground the forms her body takes over an expanded before/after time. The title's gerund *becoming* with its ever-expanding present futurity echoes with how the series presents a transition as progressively accretive instants. The 911 photographs of her nude body against a white backdrop show her one year before and one year after her gender clarification surgery on November 18, 2008, detailing the slight changes under way in hairstyle, nail color, facial expression, posture, and so on. Through appearing as "a straightforward look" at a physical transformation, as she writes,[113] the basic animation technology of a flipbook allows the viewer to control the movement of her becoming. Holding the book's edge with your thumb, you can flip forward, back, or stop to play "spot the difference" on the full-frontal body lying small scale in your palm.[114]

1.7 Installation view of "Becoming" zoetrope at the in Busan, South Korea, Biennial (2010), by Yishay Garbasz (© Yishay Garbasz).

By contrast the zoetrope project installed at the 2010 Busan Biennale in South Korea insists on the unique physics of Garbasz's movement.[115] Here a select number of self-portraits were printed life-size, then were lit from within the enormous wheel and cast spinning along in a rhythmic movement that follows the transition's physical changes. Crucial to Garbasz's decision for this format of the early modern optical device is that it injects movement into the images without requiring projection or animation from elsewhere[116] (figure 1.7). Not only is the documentation self-made, but also the display retains authority over the pace of Garbasz's bodily transformation. The flipbook and zoetrope animations insert a stuttering movement into her transition; the breaks in uniformity create small jerks that recall the shimmers resulting from the minute, overall "effort for difference," as Barthes phrases it (see the introduction). Despite her full-frontal nudity, the optical devices point foremost to the things unseen, to the nuance of where difference arrives. Sobchack makes the point that the pages "visibly stutter a bit as we flick them, reminding us of the temporal gaps in between, pointing to things unseen—cut out but nonetheless re-membered (pun intended)."[117]

These works meditate on the expansions and disorientations possible in the format of before/after, calling for a formalist approach to their analysis, "an impulse to dilate the aesthetic encounter as such, to *prolong* it by means of analysis and reading," as Richmond describes it.[118] The overt references to the format of optical toys, visual illusions, and the thrill of seeing human movement conjured out of still images shake off the hold before/after has on defining trans embodiment. In the dilated aesthetic encounter—walking around the edge to see where the series goes, flipping through the changing bodies and watching them whirl by—a formalist approach "reveals instead something hidden, yet nevertheless also given, in our perception and our feeling" about trans shimmers.[119] The formalism applied to the trans experience by these artists refuses to disclose a hidden meaning of who they really are; the highly self-reflexive choice of formats shifts into view the operations of the hidden structure of feelings that coalesce around their phantasmagoric bodies.

In anticipating the imperative for a trans reveal, these artworks seek to link the surprise associated with glimpsing the difference of a trans body to other affective responses than negatively tinted ones. Writing on the queer paranoiac's tenet that the violence of gender reification must be anticipated, Sedgwick explains that surprise is the one thing that the paranoid tries to eliminate through mastery of knowledge.[120] The necessity of forestalling painful surprises produces an anticipatory response she describes as proposing, "*Anything you can do (to me) I can do worse,* and *Anything you can do (to me) I can do first*—to myself."[121] While aware of how a reveal usually results in violence, these artworks—by taking a phantasmagoric form for their reveals—challenge the paranoid's unshakable faith in demystifying exposure. Following from Melanie Klein, Sedgwick explains that to a reparatively positioned reader (or viewer) it can seem realistic and necessary to experience surprise: "Because there can be terrible surprises, however, there can also be good ones."[122] The artworks pivot on the goodwill of the artist revealing something of themselves, but also on the viewer's goodwill to demonstrate openness to the new in the anticipation of the "after" shot, or what emerges in the becoming. The reparative assemblage of a new object—transition—with associated positive affects takes place through an anachronistic identification with sexual intermediacy—not coincidentally, I might add. Entering the reparative mode via the temporal drag of the phantasmagoria enables a resequencing of trans histories; it gives pause to reflect that if the past could have been different than it actually was, maybe the future will be too.

Reaching through a tear in the skin of time, these works extract life-giving substance from a culture that avows not to sustain them. The age of reproducibility in which the phantasmagoria rose in popularity also gave rise to the technological ability for projecting one's self: the trans/cinema agency to cut and splice together audiovisual images into a new sequence. The phantoms recalled from the dead also herald a posttranssexual moment à la Stone in which the binary personae do not have to be forever split, but shown in a lengthy progression (Garbasz) or out of synch (Drucker/Steiner). Through the delinking and relinking of images the phantasmagoric gender transitions reshuffle the sensorium of the artist and viewer alike. In discussing intercultural cinema, Laura Marks makes an addendum to Foucault's categorical orders of the sayable and seeable, which Deleuze tracks in film's audio and visual levels, that an order of the *sensible* is "the sum of what is accessible to sense perception at a given historical and cultural moment."[123] The temporal drag of the phantasmagoria in trans artworks might thus be a means of accessing across a wrinkle in time another organization of the senses in order to open up our cultural moment to a new sensorium that is in fact re-newed.

"Aesthetics concerns the struggle for control over the human sensorium," insists Sean Cubitt in *The Practice of Light*, which is why control over light and its mediations in the age of reproducibility is so charged—for Benjamin writing on the brink of fascism but also for trans representation created in an era of great violence against gender nonconformity.[124] The incorporation of the phantasmagoria haunting trans bodies into art-making practices reflects how "the machine is always social before it is technical. There is always a social machine that selects or assigns the technical elements used," in Deleuze and Claire Parnet's words.[125] Rather than seeing the phantasmagoria exclusively as either an ideological machine sustaining illusions or a process of demystification, Gunning persuades that its great capacity for producing startling effects could provide "an aesthetic model for the manipulation of the senses."[126] The showmanship, audience pleasure, and scrambling of what is perceptible by the senses all lend the phantasmagoria an air of highly politicized aesthetics. Rather than fostering credulity or incredulity, then, the phantasmagoria becomes a training ground for a sensorial reckoning of those psychic and affective currents of being that fall away from rational belief. The sensorial experience of trans shimmers may not be easily grasped or cast as real, but in the framing of a phantasmagoria, in which misty forms float into view and men incrementally or suddenly change into women, the so-called illusion is experienced as a real entity.

Finally, the reparative work being carried out on trans visual hirstories indicates that some trans bodies, more than others, appear phantasmagoric from a contemporary perspective.[127] The inheritance of trans phantasmagoric imagery with the specter of a horrific or hilarious surprise seems to be passed down mainly, if not specifically, to trans women who seem to carry the burden of "the genuine *past*-ness of the past—its opacity and illegibility."[128] One piece of evidence I already mentioned is the reinsertion of Lili Elbe into popular consciousness through the filmic narration of her highly sexualized transition in *The Danish Girl* (2015). In counterpoint, recent trans cultural productions also participate in the historical revival with films that reimagine the Stonewall riots by foregrounding the role of trans women of color and street queens such as Marsha P. Johnson and Silvia Rivera, who are honored in *Happy Birthday, Marsha!* (dir. Reina Gossett and Sasha Wortzel, 2016).[129] As the Silent Generation and Baby Boomer trans godmothers taper off, younger artists have started to grapple with making sense of the ensuing generational shift by investigating the query, What is our inheritance? To the question of how their life stories will be told, one can already find substantiation of a highly willing temporal drag, or identification across generations, in recent feature-length documentaries about the influential lives of the prison abolition and trans woman of color activist Miss Major Griffin-Gracy and the theorist and theatre-maker Kate Bornstein, and in the archiving of Flawless Sabrina's organization of a national drag beauty pageant and performance career.[130] The reparative impulse within these younger trans-led projects seems linked to an intransient and anachronistic identification that mixes up the temporal order of progressive narratives. These deeply historical projects enter their subjects into the phantasmagoric pantheon of visual culture as trans women who refuse both to fade into the population and to acquiesce to the logic of a full reveal. The next chapter continues an investigation of how trans subjects have negotiated the reveal but in the pornographic register, where genital optics are closely tied to the documented authenticity of the sexual performance and the performer's gender identity.

TWO

Shimmering Sex

Docu-Porn's Trans-Sexualities, Confession Culture,

and Suturing Practices

O n April 8, 2011, the Postposttranssexual: Transgender Studies and Feminism Conference at Indiana University opened with a moderated conversation between Sandy Stone, who coined the term *posttranssexual* in her 1988 manifesto calling for resistance to the medical model of transsexuality, and Kate Bornstein, whose *Gender Outlaw: On Men, Women, and the Rest of Us* from 1994 signaled a wave of new identities for nonbinary genders.[1] The conference title's additional *post* added to *posttranssexual* signals the historicity of the moment in which transgender studies had grown beyond psycho-sexological discourse into a field of its own, but it also gives pause to reflect on the political project of the previous era. Prompted by Susan Stryker to consider what changed in their various personal and scholarly transitions, Bornstein remarked that she now believes trans folks should "own that one of the reasons that we go through this change is about sex, desire, to be having it."[2] For her, the heady package of sexuality (identity, acts, bodily possibilities, and so on) continues to be a frustrating outlier to conversations about changing sex. Nothing less than an inadequate account of trans ontology is at stake, Stryker pointed out; for a trans subject, changing gender facilitates "a greater freedom of movement," yes, but that freedom is also "to move towards desire."[3] Although Stone was quiet at this moment in the discussion, her "Posttranssexual Manifesto" vociferously claims that the demedicalization of trans lives must involve the revelation of the "most secret of secret traditions," the ritual of penile masturbation just before surgery, which the manifesto refers to three times as "wringing the turkey's neck."[4] Through invoking this coarse euphemism Stone upends the protocol that silences trans people's self-guided experiences of sex and sexuality.

The medical model for transsexual diagnosis and treatment became established during the postwar period when numerous gender clinics set up shop mainly associated to university medical schools, prompting a more streamlined approach from the newly self-appointed authorities on the topic. A common source for recognizing trans experience for doctors and would-be trans folks alike was *The Transsexual Phenomenon*, a standard reference published in 1966 consisting of a lifetime of case studies.[5] In it sexology pioneer Harry Benjamin describes the strictly nonerotic behavioral profile of a "true transsexual" who would be suitable for surgery.[6] True transsexuals were expected to signal a lack of sexual desire primarily by expressing revulsion toward their genitals, treating them as, in his words, "disgusting deformities that must be changed by the surgeon's knife."[7] From the perspective of the clinic, hatred of one's genitals was "the cornerstone of the diagnosis," summarizes J. R. Latham, with self-loathing, especially of the genitals, essentially precluding any experiences of sexual comfort.[8] As a response to the typical clinical intake question "Suppose that you could be a man [or woman] in every way except for your genitals; would you be content?" Stone writes, "there are several possible answers, but only one is clinically correct."[9] The diagnostic protocol thus understood transsexual desire as directed solely at the object of the transition (changing the form of the genitals), foreclosing desire for others and for oneself.[10] As a result, persons seeking treatment modeled themselves on the people in the case studies, who did not talk about any erotic sense of their own bodies before transition, lest they be diagnosed as homosexual or a transvestite who could not access body-contouring treatment.

Transsexuality developed vis-à-vis the exclusion of autoerotic and non–heterosexually oriented forms of sexuality, and also with the structural absence of a space to consider sexuality specific to trans people who may or may not physically transition. Further, it bars consideration for those for whom gender identity "is something different from and perhaps irrelevant to physical genitalia," criticizes Stone.[11] The medical model actively desexualizes trans subjects by narrowing the parameters to heterosexual activity, likely in order to separate perceived "good" medical interests in proper trans-sex occurring after transition from the "bad" pornographic interest in hypersexed trans bodies (this I come to later). The narrow selection occurred in the clinic through the use of a protocol that determined the success of a candidate for medical intervention on the basis of her attractiveness to male doctors, or his masculine prowess in comparison to that of male doctors.[12] Success after surgery was measured in terms of achieving heterosexual penetrative sex, illogically making the completion of one sexual act the marker of a gender transition. At the heart of treatment guidelines lay the sexist underpinnings of transmisogyny, an ideology in which transfemininity is manifested by sexual availability to men and guided by hatred toward female agency. As Gayle S. Rubin announced in 1984, "The time has come to think about sex," specifically to investigate the sexual value system that hierarchizes trans-sexualities through divisions of a charmed inner circle of sexual practice/identities and the banished outer limits.[13]

Those who own wanting to have sex and experience desire in a changed embodiment do announce their existence; although they dare not speak in the clinician's office and do so only in limited measure in their autobiographies, they do openly express sexual desire in the margins of trans cultural production, in the "gutter" of film genres: in pornography. Rubin famously organized into visual schemes the normative social value and judgment of sexual practices: her research places pornography; sex for money; and transsexuals, transvestites, fetishists, and so on all in the clearly "bad sex" camp. In a footnote she clarifies that although she treats transgender behavior and individuals in terms of the sex system rather than the gender system, it is only "because transgendered [sic] people are stigmatized, harassed, persecuted and generally treated like sex 'deviants' and perverts."[14] Trans porn, then, arrives as doubly bad sex, casting social liability onto the trans person who performs in, creates, circulates, owns, or uses pornographic materials depicting trans bodies. Nevertheless, because sexual confessions in the clinic that deviate from a heteronormative script are muted—if not omitted—because of the risk of not gaining access to supplementary hormones or surgical procedures, trans pornographies offer at least a means of participating in sexual cultures. Michel Foucault's *History of Sexuality* describes modern Western sexuality as unfolding in a highly imperative confession culture marked by a *scientia sexualis* epistemology that invests in bringing to light all secrets of sexual thoughts, sensations, behavior that become telling details, re-velatory of a person's true self.[15] Trans-sexualities fall under particular scrutiny of scientia sexualis-organized medicine as their confessions in the clinical space relay the revelations of their sexual secrets as telling of their true sex/gender.

Dean Spade's autoethnographic analysis of the medical establishment regulating services for transsexuals concludes that the medical defi-nition of *transsexuality* requires the performance of being invested in gender norms, placing transsexuals in a double bind: "it is pathologi-cal not to adhere to gender norms, just as it is to [want to] adhere to them."[16] In the face of such compulsory compliance, Spade argues, we must listen to the multiple non-norm-adhering narratives that trans peo-ple produce outside of medical contexts.[17] Discussions about sexuality in the clinic clearly are far from true, voluntary confessions, as post- and post-posttranssexuals continue to decry the coerced silence on trans-sexualities.[18] Yet, today's "striptease culture," as coined by Brian McNair, valorizes mechanisms of exposure in the idioms of gender and sexual-ity.[19] Integral to the expansion of the pornosphere is an individuated pre-occupation with self-revelation and self-exposure. From McNair's per-spective, trans porn performers appear to position themselves in terms of a self-produced striptease, seizing pornography as a means to expose one's sexuality and become culturally visible in that way.[20] But are por-nographic "confessions" of sexual desire truer in this sense? Do visual examples of trans porn correct the record by better fulfilling the scientia sexualis criteria of *to see is to know*? Yes and no: pornography, like docu-mentary film, offers a generic framing that counterbalances the authori-tative weight of the clinic. Trans porn thus mobilizes a mimetic medium and a genre with a history of scientism to represent identities of desire hereto elided by the medical gaze. Further, I contend that the filmic me-dium of pornography also extends a different view on "the body"—trans bodies in particular—a form of visuality that undermines the genital optics of the clinic by suturing together a fuller range of pleasure-giving body images.

In this chapter I argue that under the pressure of confession culture trans pornographies generate truth effects by reproducing what Foucault calls "the shimmering mirage of sex," and they do so to various ends. First, trans porn guided by sex-positive activism and allyship breaks with sexual taboos reinforced by clinical parameters for the permissible range of touch, which are also absorbed into trans respectability politics.[21] The controversial 1989 release of *Linda/Les and Annie: The First Female-to-Male Transsexual Love Story*, depicting an affair between trans man Les Nichols and porn queen Annie Sprinkle, introduces the sexual appeal of transmasculinity and graphic acts with a neophallus. It campily embraces visual essentialism through the pornographic, documentary, and scientific framing of the images in order to secure the truth of the trans identity (and desire for it) represented therein. Second, commercial porn by Buck Angel and alternative porn from Mirha-Soleil Ross alike aim to delink the "genital optics" that determine the truth of sex (what's between your legs) from trans-sexualities. I focus on how the shimmering mirage of sex is produced in their pornographies through cinematic aesthetics of extreme close-up, through double exposure, and by rerouting genital fetishism through commodity fetishism. In the final case, Foucault's casting of the mirage as "the dark shimmer of sex" carries with it racial undertones that I explore through Morty Diamond's docu-porn *Trans Entities: The Nasty Love of Papí and Wil* (2007). The film's frank depiction of race play and discussions of colorism productively disrupt the cathexis of affective economies around "nasty." It brings into relief how the spectrum of desire for trans bodies is also circumscribed by whiteness. In accordance with how shimmering baseline ontologies are process-oriented rather than object-oriented, I conclude my discussion of the ways that the videos refute the object of genitals as primary to sexual and gender identity, and instead reorient to ongoing transing practices. Referring to the surgical and psychoanalytical concept of suture, I argue that sex can be a site in which a felt sense of one's gendered, raced body can become sutured to an imperfect, wavering w/hole, not reducible to genitals or skin, and that this can be redoubled in pornographic spectatorship. Overall, the audiovisual materials present a re-visioning of trans-sexualities that cleaves from the medical imagination of a true sex, which is not to say that trans porn has a more secure claim to authenticity.

My approach to pornography avoids determining whether sexual representation is either distorted reality or a revelation of reality, thereby taking up an antiporn or pro-porn position. Trans pornographies show how the optics that one might click into can be pleasurable, but also constraining. Although the regime of truth and falsity circumscribes what is intelligible and legible, visualizations of sexuality also point to the ways in which bodies become marked and unmarked as lacunae, that is, they perform a historicizing function. Joan Scott's 1991 article "The Evidence of Experience" issued a challenge—one still relevant now—to critical field studies to remain wary of what it means to become visible in the historical domain. Visibility taken as literal transparency, she argues, covers over how difference is established, the operations of difference, and in what ways it constitutes subjects who see and act in the world. In their accounting of trans-sexualities these docu-pornographies show self-consciousness about the vagaries of perceptibility. The shimmering nuance of difference, the effort for difference, the affective torsions, and the angle of the gaze are put on display. Before moving on to the shimmers appearing in filmic material, I first explicate the natural and illusive qualities of shimmering that associate sex and (trans)gender with being miragelike.

Shimmering Mirages:
Natural Illusions, Desire, and the Transreal

Foucault asserts in *The History of Sexuality* (volume 1) that modern societies are characterized by the epistemological operation of secrecy, "exploiting" sex "as *the* secret."[22] He is of course referring to sexuality here, but the meaning of sex acts cannot be thought separately from sexed embodiment, though they remain distinct. In the chapter "*Scientia Sexualis*," Foucault suggests the metaphor of a natural illusion, namely a mirage, to describe the way in which the truth of sex is secured by the injunction to confession. Foucault criticizes the substantiality of this sexual truth, writing that it is sought in the detailing of acts and sensations, "in between the words, a truth which the very form of the confession holds out like a shimmering mirage."[23] The shimmering element of truth-as-mirage is enticing, desirous, but ultimately unfounded. Nevertheless, the transformation that the quest for the shimmering mirage produces in the confessant is experienced as real, as constitutive of subjecthood.

Scientifically speaking, a mirage is a naturally occurring optical phenomenon caused by high temperatures that cause light rays to bend, wherein the viewer sees within their field of vision the refracted image of something located elsewhere. Most often the appearance of a mirage looks like a sheet of water—a shimmering oasis—that would be quite desirous to people living in desert climates, thus potentially, and fatally, driving them toward a false destination. There is a warning tone in the usage of this shimmering metaphor that resounds with the volume's treatment of sexuality as a whole. Its message is to beware of becoming caught up in the immense apparatus for producing truth by confessing one's sex; in "speaking sex" one invests in a regime of truth that sensualizes power. Confession, with its twin shadow torture, is a part of persecuting "peripheral sexualities," entailing "an incorporation of perversions and a new specification of individuals," which Foucault sees culminating in the nineteenth century when the homosexual becomes birthed as a species.[24] It is a ruse to believe that our liberation can be found "over there" in the shimmering mirage of truth; heading in this political direction is our undoing.

Transgender bodies, I intimate, gain new potency of meaning when secrecy shifts from revealing one's desire for certain sex acts to the disclosure of sexed embodiment. Written immodestly on the homosexual's face, Foucault writes, is a certain way of inverting the masculine and the feminine in oneself, resulting in an "interior androgyny" with telltale exterior signs.[25] The homosexual, like the transsexual, seems to have a misalignment of gender that through sexological diagnosis results in a "natural order of [sexual] disorder."[26] The miragelike ideological fantasy of pathologists is that gender perceptibility determines sexual individuation and vice versa. In this vein, everyday gender attribution forces disclosure on to transgender bodies, a constant invocation of shimmering sex. Recalling her experiences during transitioning, micha cárdenas explains how the perception of one's gender is miragelike: "I am aware of the slipperiness and multiplicity of the moment of passing in which someone's perception of one's gender can shift back and forth rapidly, like a kind of shimmering mirage."[27] Foucault's use of the term *mirage*, then, also describes quite accurately how trans bodies experience gender written on their bodies as a dislocation of truth, a false confession seemingly ready to be extracted. The so-called truth of sex is potentially multiple and incongruous, as we can read in cárdenas's reflection. The rapid shifting back and forth of perception, like the bent light rays, suggest that a gender mirage is an optical phenomenon in which shimmering visuality distorts any distinction between seeing and knowing, reality and truth.

In response to those people whose perception of her ascertains that she isn't a real "queer femme transgender woman," but "a man," or who try to make her choose between a man or woman identity, cárdenas says that she desires to be a "shape-shifter" and a "light wave."[28] The absolution from binary gender categories for a subjectivity lived as a light wave requires a new language to grasp a perceptual, and perpetual, shimmering self. Reclaiming what she knows as a new media performance artist, cárdenas coins the concept of the "transreal" to describe multiple shifting realities experienced by a subject who has been occluded from binary orders of realness. The transreal involves "the usage of reality as a medium," including augmented reality technologies that facilitate "crossing boundaries of multiple realities," and brings a nuance to her experiences of social immersion in this "multiplicity of worlds."[29] The transreal arrives in Samuel R. Delany's memoir, *The Motion of Light in Water: Sex and Science Fiction Writing in the East Village 1960–1965*, as an aesthetic practice of writing in such a way as to capture the shimmering of the permeable boundaries he experiences as a Black man who mostly passes for white, a gay man who mostly passes for straight, a writer who publishes science fiction.[30] His writing in two columns split by "material life" and "desire" follows from the feeling that he lives on different planets depending on whether he is perceived as white/Black, gay/straight. He explains that he started writing by forming parallel columns in a notebook; a tenuous binary split existed between notes for projects in the front and, in the back, his masturbation fantasies, until they interpenetrated as reality/fantasy, material life/desire.[31]

Delany's writing surfs the transreal of his life, detailing the shifting moments in which multiple realities hang together. A key example is when he discovers that his butch cousin and former camp counselor was the famous master of ceremonies named Stormy (Mary) in the Jewel Box Revue, a trans and drag variety show. Delany relates the vertiginous feeling as a shift in perception from solids to light waves: "It was as if a gap between two absolute and unquestionably separated columns or encampments of the world had suddenly revealed itself as illusory; that what I had assumed two was really one; and that the glacial solidity of the boundary I'd been sure existed between them was as permeable as shimmering water; as shifting light."[32] The book's framing motif is how a shimmering perception grasps the motion of light in water, the shifting between being a Black man, a gay man, a writer. In these cases Delany's multiple devalued identities occlude him from realness and instigate a transreal space of writing. Another moment is as he recalls pausing to watch the sun rise at the end of a long night having sex with men between trucks parked under the Manhattan piers, recounting that, "The water

shook and shimmered with the cobalt reflection."[33] This moment and another in the midst of domestic life places Delany in the role of observer:
"I stood watching the motion of light in water."[34] The concluding line to
the memoir explains that, "I merely want to fix it before it vanishes like
water, like light, like the play between them we only suggest, but never
master, with the word motion"; before vanishing from memory, however uncertain and discontinuous, his writer persona seeks to capture the
shimmering of his sex, his gender, his racial experiences.[35] In contrast to
Foucault's shimmering mirage that locates the constitution of the subject
in the extraction of (a false) truth, Delany's shimmering boundaries place
subject constitution in "the flickering correlations between" the columns,
which he likens to the light in play with moving water.[36] The motion, or
what I have been calling change, makes all the correlations temporary
and tenuous, as "evanescent as light-shot water, as insubstantial as moon-
struck cloud."[37] In so writing his experiences of shimmering boundaries
Delany queries the historical field and what it contains, or should contain, particularly the experiences that mostly remain in dumb ignorance
because the shimmering is "what most of us do *not* remember, what most
of us *cannot* speak of."[38] If the shimmer is hard to grasp, it is because it
becomes dislocated from sociality, not because it doesn't exist.

Joan Scott's article "The Evidence of Experience" opens with a reading of Delany's observations about the institutions of gay sex in the 1950s
and 1960s of his boyhood, especially the recounting of his experience of
a massive orgy during his early twenties in Saint Marks Baths, "a fact,"
Delany asserts, "that flew in the face of that whole fifties image" of homosexuality being a solitary perversion.[39] Her essay challenges the evidence
of knowledge that becomes gained through a vision of unmediated objects hereto hidden from history (gay sexual collectivity), and the authority of that experience, that is, the notion that "What could be truer, after
all, than a subject's own account of what he or she has lived through."[40]
Taking Delany too literally at his own word—"You could *see* what was
going on throughout the dorm" he writes[41]—Scott misses the aesthetic
practice in his writing of conjuring the transreal, of capturing a shimmering in the field of vision. The examples from his experience of an astonishing exodus of hundreds of men from the trucks during a raid and
the orgy at the baths make graphically clear how sexuality was structured into a visual regime that produced the mirage "that gay men were
isolated," marginal to society, asexual. This self-same visuality was rein-

forced through the extant institutions of subway toilets and public parks that accommodated male-on-male sex: it visibly cut up sexual acts into tiny portions so that this sex was barely visible to the bourgeois world, but also impossible for those participating in it to see it in its totality. Collective experiences of desire fell into the chasm "without any glimmering articulation at all" because these flashpoints of desire were visually split off from material life.[42]

I spend so much time with Delany's project of writing shimmerings into the perceptual field in *The Motion of Light in Water* because it models a way in which sexual representation does not have to accede to a dangerous distortion (a mirage) or a revelation (a confession) of reality, but rather might index a transreal space-time in which multiple realities are crossed. Whereas Scott accuses Delany's project of simply aiming at making experience visible, I appreciate how his documents of shimmering engage with the politics of visuality to cross the chasm of an era's structuration of discourse, and bring forward pockets of inarticulateness and imperceptibility. At stake in Scott's reading of Delany is whether the evidence of experience takes meaning *as transparent*—for example, through the metaphor of visibility—thereby reproducing rather than contesting given ideological systems.[43] The conjuring of a shimmering mirage of trans-sexualities need not always reinforce the terms of sexual truth extracted from confession, even when they mobilize those self-same terms. Delany's writing indicates that those occluded from realness, particularly via the omission and structured silencing of their sex, might find accommodation in existing sexual institutions, such as pornography. To become a light wave among multiple shifting realities, trans-sexual subjects have a long history of experimenting with interpenetrating the genre of pornography with realist documentary elements. In the next sections I introduce trans docu-porns and their variations on shimmering between the columns of material life/desire, the real/fantasy.

Annie Sprinkle's First Docu-Porn:
The "Realness of Social Context" for Trans-Sex

The 1989 video *Linda/Les and Annie: The First Female-to-Male Transsexual Love Story* (dir. Annie Sprinkle, Albert Jaccoma, and John Armstrong, 31 min.; hereafter *L/LA*) presents itself as a pseudoscientific documentary of a romantic encounter between a transsexual man and a porn star famous for parodying pornographic aesthetics.[44] The screenplay was first published in the men's magazine *Hustler* as the shock confessional titled "I Love a Woman with a Cock: Busting a Sex-Change Cherry (Photos and Story by Annie Sprinkle)."[45] The video pivots on what the sexual dalliance brings to Sprinkle, emphatically the "constant mind-fuck" that, she explains, is brought about by the sexual ambiguity of her lover's "surgically made hermaphrodite" genitals.[46] For his part, her lover Les Nichols embraces the self-identity of being a "freek" because he is a Greek freak belonging to outsider cultures. Coming out of the sex industry, the film was Annie Sprinkle's first attempt to "really create a new genre of docuporn," and because at that time it was not at all common to mix genres, the film was, in Sprinkle's words, "a breakthrough film breaking out of porn."[47] Sprinkle's exuberant artistic vision comes through in the multiple framing of a sexual encounter in *L/LA*, itself only a short segment in the film, embedded within elaborate sequences detailing how they started dating, an interview with Les about his sexual history, a scientific explanation of Les's phalloplasty complete with campy graphs, and a feminist trans-sexual manifesto from Annie calling for a future full of men with cunts. Overall, the video aims at bringing into public what had heretofore been "ob/scene," as Linda Williams uses the concept, that which heretofore was designated ob—off—scene or must be kept off the public stage and out of polite conversation.[48] The various framings of the genre experiment hang uneasily together as a practice of trans-sexual suturing; ruptures of seeming contradiction arise between the different generic expectations of realness in the sequences, throwing into doubt the transparency of their combined reveal.

A fundamental collision between edited sequences occurs in the midst of the pornographic sequence. Les and Annie are trying various sexual positions that will accommodate his use of a plastic rod in the neophallus for turgidity, but the rod keeps sliding out. He even tries inserting his own thumb into the hole at the base, but Annie pumps too hard on it and causes him pain. The couple has to stop, and Annie, deadpan, says in voice-over, "in spite of all the modern technology that went into making Les's dick, we still had to work out a few basics." The video then makes a hard cut to a scene wherein Annie goes into the kitchen to trim the plastic rod, picking up a knife while chatting and laughing. Suddenly, while holding the rod and knife, Sprinkle begins to weep uncontrollably and Les comforts her. Drowning out the diegetic sound, in voice-over she explains that she was overcome with the trauma of Les's suffering, and by sex and gender outcasts everywhere who face systemic violence: "I just started crying thinking about how much physical and emotional pain he must have suffered to change his gender. I cried for all people who don't love their bodies just the way they are. For all transsexuals who have suffered, many of whom have resorted to suicide. For all sexual persuasions who are made outcasts in society. [. . .] Les told me not to cry. 'It's been a wonderful odyssey. After all, I might not have met you.'" The kitchen scene abruptly ends in silence, with a blackout; a dissolve with synchronized sexy music slowly returns the viewer to the pornographic framing of the event, opening with Les's smiling face. In voice-over Annie recounts, "Les seemed quite happy with his new sex toy. He told me that watching the pleasure on my face made the pain of all twelve surgeries worthwhile." At that moment, Les successfully inserts his neophallus into Annie from behind. As *L/LA* shifts from foregrounding desire and fantasy in the bedroom to material life in the kitchen, the genres of porn and documentary interpenetrate, criss-crossing realities, capturing the transreal of their encounter (figures 2.1, 2.2, and 2.3).

As the video seeks to reveal "everything" in its exposé mode, the frames of realism shift to accommodate the different dimensions of the story's affective arc from light-hearted laughter to choking sobs. In this sequence, rather than offering a clean break between pornography and documentary, between the bedroom and the kitchen, a tension remains between their respective realities. This remainder, however, offers another kind of reality. The conflicted image of a porn star wearing sex-ready lingerie while crying functions to portray Les as real to Annie, specifically as emotionally real. Along with the set change, the emotional change shifts the video from the technological drama occurring in the pornographic register to a dramatic breakthrough in the love story. Her tears suggest that she understands him and the reality of his embodiment, which affirmatively gives her a pleasurable mind-fuck. Given the lack of necessity to include this scene, which would be probably considered a blooper or outtake in a commercial edit of a porno, the fact that it *is* included attests to the video's emphasis on Annie's coming to terms with Les—it is a first-person narration and primarily her creative work—rather than being framed as being about Les coming into manhood through his first penetrative sexual experience. As a result, the resolution of Les as an epistemological "fuck" becomes more crucial to the plot than Les achieving

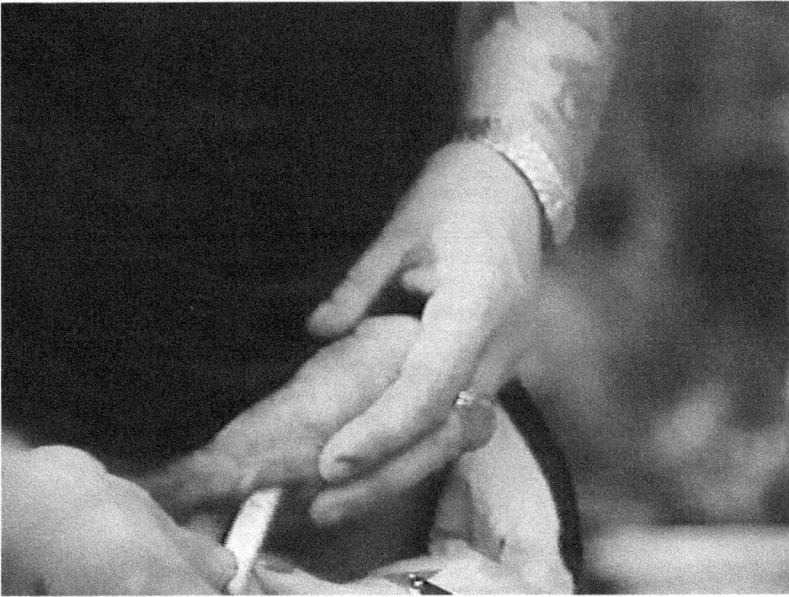

2.1 Annie Sprinkle assisting Les Nichols to insert a rod into his neo-phallus (screen capture, *Linda/Les and Annie: The First Female-to-Male Transsexual Love Story*, 1989, Annie Sprinkle, Albert Jaccoma, and John Armstrong, independent production).

the penetrative sexual act. Different from the description of the scene in Sprinkle's confessional essay in *Hustler*, the evidence crucial to her personal emotional coming out in the video benefits from another truth-effect, derived from its medium.

At the ontological level, film has a privileged relation to the real in that it seems to transmit to an audience impressions from the world "out there."[49] The apparently genuine tears appear in the profilmic world: I presuppose that someone is actually crying about someone else in a kitchen, which has been transferred to film.[50] Yet, next to witnessing this audio-visual synchronization of reality and overhearing their conversation, the video (typical of Sprinkle films) makes use of voice-over to relay her reflections on a hard political reality. The indexical tears thus become a sign of the film's social realism, which reveals a heretofore concealed political dimension of reality: people suffer because of what their body means in society and because of what they do with that body. Through the representation of the tears, *L/LA* becomes a form of (political) discourse. Although it registers a profilmic real, through its registration it

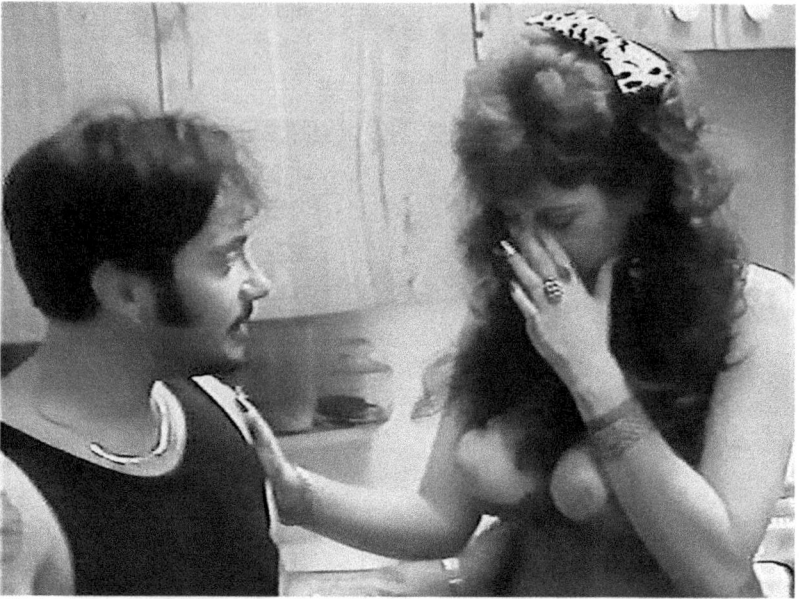

2.2 Annie Sprinkle crying in her kitchen while Les Nichols comforts her (screen capture, *Linda/Les and Annie: The First Female-to-Male Transsexual Love Story*, 1989, Annie Sprinkle, Albert Jaccoma, and John Armstrong, independent production).

also engages with the multiple codes that shape its effects, namely with realism as a mode underlying different genres. The genres of pornography and documentary both stage a reality through the "show" of events and the device of voice-over "telling" the image.

The show and tell of documentary, or evidence and argument, as film theorist Bill Nichols writes in "The Voice of Documentary," can be delivered through various strategies, for instance, from the direct address of characters telling their story in political films to the filmmakers' self-reflexive voice-over.[51] In each case, the dominant mode of "expository discourse" shifts according to the film's integration of visuals with spoken commentary or dialogue, which gives rise to its "voice." Hence, a film's particular style of showing and telling conveys what Nichols calls a "social point of view."[52] The voice of documentary-style film often calls upon the privileged relation of film to a profilmic real, but in equal measure so do video pornographies that simulate televisual "liveness" through low production values that grant a sense of immediate presence and spontaneity, thereby eschewing the spectacular mode of formulaic sex and stag-

2.3 Les Nichols smiling while successfully penetrating Annie Sprinkle (screen capture, *Linda/Les and Annie: The First Female-to-Male Transsexual Love Story*, 1989, Annie Sprinkle, Albert Jaccoma, and John Armstrong, independent production).

ing. Julie Levin Russo explains that this strategy for citing pornographic realness is shared by alternative porn cultures such as queer porn (and I'd add trans porn) and commercial porn.[53] Further, Russo usefully breaks down four ways that pornography is typically understood to have a privileged relation to the real, with alternative porn cultures alone demonstrating direct ties to real economic, political, and/or cultural processes, or a "realness of social context."[54] Most pornographies also seek realness of reception by acting on the viewer, realness of production by recording an unsimulated sexual act, and, most widely discussed in feminist porn studies, the realness of representation because images appear real as a result of their character and conventions.[55] The dominance of voice in docu-porns like *L/LA* inserts the social point of view to provide a broader, politicized sociocultural context to trans-sexual acts and to the potential effect of an audience's shared mind-fuck.

Remarkable to *L/LA* then is that the sexually explicit scenes are shown only with Annie's authoritative porn star commentary—never from Les's direct point of view. During the kitchen sequence, Les's voice speaking directly to Annie is nearly drowned out by her crying and enters into further competition with her voice-over. At the close of the scene, the sentences Les says are muffled by Anne's voice-over, but in her quoting of him ("Les told me") she also paraphrases his words, resulting in a kind of disconnected double speak. In general, Les is authoritatively spoken about by *L/LA*'s voice: especially via the character/director/creative testimony of Annie, the video seems to conflate its evidence—Les's body—with its *argument* that while transsexuals suffer for their perceived ambiguity, they are also desirous, not least because of their ambiguity. According to Nichols, the problem of conflation is common to the genre of documentary, which "displays a tension arising from the attempt to make statements about life which are quite general, while necessarily using sounds and images that bear the inescapable trace of their particular historical origins."[56] In Annie's voice-over during her crying, the gap between evidence and argument becomes stark. Annie stretches the moment of crisis in her personal experience with a particular trans man into a far-reaching political argument on gender oppression. Reflecting on the gap between image and statement, Nichols proposes that the extreme genre consisting only of visual evidence is pornography, whereas propaganda is a genre reliant only on expository argument.[57] Here Nichols slides into a radical feminist reading of pornography, such as that from Catharine MacKinnon, which discounts the mediation of pornography, problematically assuming porn to transparently register and reflect the real.[58] I submit that the video plugs the generic gap between documentary and pornography with the suturing staple of Annie's body, which mediates through her emotional display and her command of the video's voice during the apex of the story. The gulf between the show and tell, between a partly failed pornographic rendering of sexual experience and a propagandistic manifesto, nevertheless betrays a cracking in the video's generic "voice." The crack between the columns—the documentary's registering of material life and pornography's reflection of desire—shimmers between the formal dissolve transitions into and out of the kitchen scene marked by black screen pauses. The multiple shifting realities enliven *L/LA* as pornography that argues for a political future and as a political argument that offers pornography as its evidence.

While not based on the model of a proper confession, the seemingly out-of-control paroxysm of Annie's unfaked, unstaged tears and Les's big smile inflects the display of emotions and its interpretation with authenticity. The emphasis in the video on authentic emotions in combination with its staging of sexual acts indicates that its pornographic dimension of realness also relies on fantasy—not of the realness of sex, but of its emotional impact. Sprinkle's seducing voice-over and the video's reliance on emotional reaction shots solicit the viewer to *believe* instead of *observe* truth; *L/LA* entails much more than a straightforward use of representational realism. The emotional voice points a finger at its supposed real, imploring the audience to "Look!" However, as Judith Butler writes, "when we *point to something as real*, and in political discourse it is very often imperative to wield the ontological indicator in precisely that way, this is not the end but the beginning of the political problematic."[59] Similarly, the video's effect of pointing at phantasmatic "things" as real—the head-fuck, the pleasure, the pain, Nichols's masculinity—is to interrogate the variable boundary of the social phantasmatic from which the real is insistently contested. Pointing to the ontological becomes a way to point at the phantasmatic dimension and vice versa. In this way, the video's examination of the "mind-blowing head-fuck" might be understood as central to the performance of what Butler deems feminist thought can do: examine the circumspection of the (supposed) real.[60]

Sprinkle's fantasy of the transgender social context is elaborated in the closing montage, over which she speaks: "I imagined a new community forming of men with cunts, a new political force of women taking over the world as men." In a similar vein, Butler defends feminism's use of fantasy for political change in its task of (re)thinking futurity: "fantasy is not equated with what is not real, but rather what is not *yet* real, what is possible or futural, or what belongs to a different version of the real."[61] Sprinkle's strategic claim of Les's desirous masculinity suggests that the video participates in the protean dynamics of community and identity building, not merely offering up a pregiven real that appears transparently in the image. Its task is not to resolve the tension between real and phantasmatic, but to picture the crisis because the shimmering is "what most of us *cannot* speak of," to recall Delany. The simultaneous use of documentary and pornographic modes of seeing engages the discourse of positivism to seize on its fantastical dimension. Hence, rather than merely relaying a preexisting experience in evidence and argument, delivered by the generic conventions of pornography and documentary, the video's most crucial political work is in installing belief. As I view it, the video offers an exposé not only of transsexuality, but also of the epistemological gesture of exposing sex.

The film's debut and reception mark the development of trans sexual cultures that challenge the curtailing of trans-sexualities, in particular of the hereto invisible identities of transmasculinity, a curtailing achieved by sex-negative value judgments and coercively heterosexual assumptions about sexual pleasure. Rather than rewrite history though, it makes history: *L/LA* accomplishes the historical feat of bringing to the public scene knowledge of transsexual bodies in graphic, sexualized detail.[62] According to community leader Jamison Green, "Hiding ourselves may serve self-preservation, but it does not address the larger problem of social acceptance, acknowledgment that what we experience is valid. To be believed, we must be seen."[63] The voice-over places Sprinkle in the role of the trustworthy interpreter and diplomat between the world of FtM sexuality and the rest of society, then a potentially groundbreaking move for the nascent trans movement.[64]

However, Annie's love story with Les was met with controversy in the trans man community, which responded first in the December 1989 issue of the widely circulated *FtM Newsletter* by publishing an article called "*Hustler* uncovers an FtM." As Green recalls, "the *Hustler* article itself brought outrage and an outpouring of defensiveness from within the FTM community," whereas, "the general public hardly blinked."[65] The video version was screened during one of Louis Sullivan's group FtM meetings and some people stormed out, angry or embarrassed, or both, Green recounts.[66] Debates on the merits of the article and later the film raged in the newsletter for a year until Sullivan's death in March 1991 took precedence. Although some appreciated the "attempt to recognize the sexual desirability of transsexual bodies," most of the respondents felt that Les Nichols was not "an appropriate representative" for the general public.[67] For example, Green quotes a letter to the editor that claims Les was "*highly* eccentric, *extremely* exhibitionistic and *totally* irrepressible."[68] Implicit in this critique is that Nichols was not trans male enough, or heterosexually normative enough, perhaps because he seems to integrate the history and the physicality of the female-bodied "Linda" by enjoying (and showing) vaginal penetration. Although its docu-porn formula usefully mobilizes a "that's how it is" mode of visual transparency to resolve the mind-fuck of Les's trans body into pleasure, backlash against the video from the FtM community might be understood as discomfort with the extent of this strategy's success to sexualize and even potentially fetishize transmasculinized bodies. The policing of trans respectability along the lines of the proper clinical diagnosis reflects the transmasculine community's investment in remaining desexualized, to enforce the border of "bad" sex from "good" sex. One of the perhaps unforeseen effects of a negative community response to Sprinkle's earnest initiative was a dearth of commercially available explicit transmasculine sexual representation for more than a decade.

The Shine and the *Glans*:
Of Commodity and Genital Fetishism in Buck Angel

Until very recently visually sex-plicit material featuring transmasculine bodies was virtually nonexistent, leaving little to complain about except the lack of apparent interest or courage to create porn.[69] Raven Kaldera and Hanne Blank, the editors of the 2002 *Best Transgender Erotica*, offer the following explanation for the erotic invisibility of trans men: "Our sexual culture, by and large, runs on stereotyped femininity and fetishizations of the phallus."[70] In this context, the popularity of she-male porn, featuring cosmetically and even surgically feminized talent, but otherwise offering cock-focused imagery, seems obvious. Presumably missing in trans male porn is an erotically validating combination of sexual markers, so that neither attributes of stereotyped femininity nor the "schlongs that command recognition of sexual maleness" are dominant.[71] Defying this cultural logic, the commercial career of FtM porn star Buck Angel began with the website www.transsexual-man.com, launched in February 2003. Soon after, in 2005, www.BuckAngel.com seemed to carve out the niche commodification of "the man with a pussy," a tagline that is also his trademark, appearing at all times followed with the ™ symbol (figure 2.4).[72]

His webpage asserts that "Buck Angel *is* the man with a pussy," implying that the two terms are identical and exchangeable. Elsewhere it claims that he is "the original" man with the pussy, which suggests less worthy knock-offs of his product.[73] The commodification of Angel's particularly phrased transsexual embodiment transforms "Buck Angel," an actual person with a transsexual history, into a collectible item, a product on the website for sale in stills, in clips, or in DVD format.[74] Unlike Les Nich-

2.4 Examples of Buck Angel trademark on the splash page of his membership website (www.BuckAngel.com, May 2010).

ols, Angel has undergone no genital modification other than the effects of supplementary testosterone that typically encourages the growth of the clitoris. Further masculinization has been achieved through rigorous bodybuilding, and Angel's body is also liberally decorated with tattoos. As he discloses in the documentary *Secret Lives of Women: Porn Stars* (2008), while other porn talent require a gimmick, all he needed "was to be myself." The reality for most FtMs is that undergoing a phalloplasty to create a neophallus is too expensive and unappealing, as it bears a high risk of losing sexual sensation, so most FtM transsexuals are, in fact, men with intact vulvas.[75] The economic story of the evolution from the nameless "transsexual-man" to the registered trademark of "Buck Angel, the man with a pussy," speaks to the successful marketing of his transmasculine embodiment that exploits the sexualized charge of secrecy and exposure for financial profit, but also opens the door to new specifications beyond hetero-, homo-, and bisexuality. Foucault argues that the "concatenation" of local sexualities "has been ensured and relayed by the countless economic interests" that, "with the help of medicine, psychiatry, prostitution, and *pornography* have tapped into both this analytical multiplication of pleasure and this optimization of the power that controls it."[76] The sexual marketing of "the man with a pussy" makes use of pornography's role as an economic engine that implants new perversions and new local sexualities to grow potential fans and buyers.

Angel's pioneering enterprise as the first transsexual male porn star is set in the context of excessive visibility in an industry that makes ten thousand to eleven thousand films a year (Hollywood makes approximately four hundred), to the tune of $57 billion in annual revenue worldwide.[77] Angel's intervention lies not in entering or competing in this market in a different manner: like many stars between 2005 and 2012, he made a living by selling low-budget productions as photo sets, clips, and DVDs through a membership-based website.[78] Characteristic of his work, however, is the refusal to accept the traditional terms of fetishizing genitalia, encapsulated in his motto, "It's not what's between your legs that defines your gender," which decorated his website banner. Angel's motto, a transgender slogan of self-determination echoed in the works of Kate Bornstein, Riki Anne Wilchins, Dean Spade, and others, relocates the definition of gender away from genitals.[79] The repetitive format of Angel postings, in which his "man with a pussy" body is revealed over and again as not being a "man without a dick," stresses in its unavailability the fetishized element of gender—the penis—according to both Freudian and cultural norms. (For reference: in the "Fetishism" essay Freud writes, "we may say that the normal prototype of fetishes is a man's penis, just as the normal prototype of inferior organs is a woman's real small penis, the clitoris."[80]) Angel maintains that he did not want to create freak porn, or even trans porn, but rather porn that reflects a "community of men with pussies"; however, he continues, "in an industry where you can see clown porn and balloon porn, [ironically] a man with a pussy is horrific!"[81] Apparently, for Angel and his fans, the clitoris and vulva are not inferior on a man, but just what they were looking for. Angel's pornography, I propose, utilizes commodity fetishism as a wedge to assert an antifetishistic stance toward the genitals, offering a corrective to Freudian fetishism that underpins sexology's genital/phallic optics.

Without naming precisely what or who defines your gender, Angel's motto indicates that the thing, the "what's between your legs," is not *the* determinate sign, the referent that corresponds to the truth of gender. However, as Judith Shapiro explains, some transsexuals do acknowledge the social and clinical force[82] of "what's between your legs" as a determinate sign: "To those who might be inclined to diagnose the transsexual's focus on the genitals as obsessive or *fetishistic* [. . .] the response is that they are, in fact, simply conforming to their culture's criteria for gender assignment. Transsexuals' fixation on having the right genitals is clearly less pathological than if they were to insist that they were women with penises or men with vaginas."[83] In Shapiro's use, "fetishistic" refers to the focus on genitals as the principal sign of gender, a usage that derives from Freud's emphasis on the psychic consequences of recognizing—that is, misperceiving—anatomical difference.[84] In insisting on being a man with a vagina, Angel counters the social (and clinical) obsession with a singular marker that counts as the only criterion for gender assignment. The price for his negligence to be fetishistic in the proper way by demanding a penis, or at least a replacement, Shapiro informs the reader, is to become classified as pathological, or in the porn business as "horrific," as Angel phrased it. The transgression rendered by his transgender embodiment is the exposure of the social secret hidden in and by sexual fetishism: the fetishism of the correct anatomical criterion for gender identity, the absence or presence of a penis. This revelation, exposing the mysticism of gender as an unnatural and irrational association between referent and image, comes across as horrific. This horror affixes to Angel (and other transmasculine bodies) because his specific embodiment also fulfills the criteria of gendered "horror" attached to Freud's vision of the naked female/feminine body.

Freud describes sexual fetishism as a psychic action against the "horror of castration," which is experienced by the little boy in seeing his mother's genitals, imagining that something is missing, the penis.[85] "Probably," Freud muses, "no male human being is spared the fright of castration at the sight of a female genital."[86] Expressing sympathy with the fetishist, Freud normalizes, universalizes even, the nominal perversion. The psychic action, according to Freud, involves the fetishist's libidinal investment in nongenital objects that substitute for the woman's lost or stolen penis. Freud views the successful mental disavowal of the idea of threat as a helpful, if delusional, response to the threat of castration. He defines disavowal as a perceptual action, not a "blind spot in the retina" that a scotomization would produce, but an investment in a counterwish to cover over the "unwelcome perception."[87] The phantasmatic fetish appears more substantial than the negativity that defines woman: "something else [. . .] now absorbs all the interest."[88] The fetish object memorializes the threat as a foundation for sexual desire in as much as it erects a monument to another, more pleasing, idea.

Williams's analysis of the interaction of the two kinds of fetishisms suggests that the substitution object may itself be transferable: "The Marxian and Freudian fetishist locates illusory and compensatory pleasure and power in the gleam of gold *or* the lacy frill of an undergarment."[89] The phantasmatic yet material secret of commodity fetishism evidenced by its "gleam," I contend, might be substituted for the unresolved search for a pleasing frilly cover, or for the "money shot" that distracts from the so-called horror that Freud assumes all men see. However, rather than attribute this helpful fetish to the exemplary male fetishist, I want to suggest that "Buck Angel" the product and the person foremost profits from the gleam of the commodity fetish, not only monetarily, but also in securing an image in the visual field. In the trademark of being "*the* man with a pussy," Angel lays claim to becoming at least a "token of triumph," in Freud's words.[90] The term *token* in his analysis suggests a point of overlap between libidinal economy, the visual economy of commodities, and the monetary system. Hence, the image for sale—Buck Angel, the man with the pussy—can be understood to engage with the so-called unwelcome perception of the horror of castration in order to overcome it with the production of an appealing, triumphant token.[91] Stronger still, despite reneging literal surgical sutures on his genitals, Angel's pornographic body is a site for stitching together his transmasculine embodiment with a feminine part into what is for him a congruent, pleasing configuration. This suturing practice is rendered less through cinematic means of montage, however, than through the generic pornographic register that through image overload builds up deposits of desire into the shape of "sex," which can be molded into other, less conventional perceptible forms.

The relation of interchange between sexual and commodity fetish can be elaborated from Freud's development of fetishism, particularly the case in which his star fetishist collapses pleasure, the play of light, and a mode of affectively charged looking. Freud offers the following explanation for a young man's exaltation of a particular "shine on the nose" into a fetish: "The surprising explanation of this was that the patient had been brought up in an English nursery but had later come to Germany, where he forgot his mother-tongue almost completely. The fetish, which originated from his earliest childhood, had to be understood in English, not German. The 'shine on the nose' [in German, *Glanz auf der Nase*]—was in reality a '*glance* at the nose.' The nose was thus the fetish, which, incidentally, he endowed at will with the luminous shine which was not perceptible to others."[92] The glance becomes remembered as the *Glanz* (shine), although the word choice also seems overdetermined as a pun: *Glans* is German slang for cock.[93] Although Freud claims that the nose is the fetish, perhaps because of its phallic shape, it is hardly incidental that the fetishist converts the visual pleasure of self-directed looking (his glance) to the visuality of an external glow calling to him (Glanz). In other words, he retains his interest in looking, but now at a "luminous shine," an even better and more convenient pleasure that he re-creates "at will." Far from being a mere addition to the real object of the nose, the imperceptible shine seems closer to a fetish object: a semiprivate delusion that he wills into perception.

In its polysemic and fungible form, this exemplary shine (Glanz) structures fetishism's mobile, distorted, and pleasing perception of a dis-avowed secret. The pleasurable illusion of seeing sex, or of a phantasm of an immaterial phallus in the place of the vagina, might be likened to Foucault's suggestion of a mirage of sex. Foucault himself contends that sexuality might be described as a modeling of fetishism's core idea of irra-tional perception: "that there exists *something other* than bodies, organs, somatic localizations, functions, anatomo-physiological systems, sensa-tions, and pleasures."[94] This "something other" is a mirage, an irrational perception that appears real and true: again, in this passage, Foucault invokes the shimmering light of a mirage to provide a metaphor for the collective (mis)perception of sexuality. There, as much as in the fetishist's perception, the desire to see produces a pleasurable, if illusory perception of shimmering bodies. The invocation of the pleasurable shine on the sexed body of Buck Angel recasts horror into an enjoyable gleam. Angel's highly personal, privatized trademark has nonetheless paved the way for many more trans men to privately or publicly embrace their "secret" em-bodiments, thereby furthering the larger political project of delinking trans-sexual desire from its pathologized origins.

The Trembling Flesh of Mirha-Soleil Ross:
Obscuring Vision

The concept of sex, however, is a stand-in for something invisible, the in-substantial confession of desiring flesh. For Foucault, confession is pre-cisely about what *cannot* be seen or articulated: "stirrings—so difficult to perceive and formulate—of desire."[95] The transgression of sexual feelings becomes indexed by the reactions of one's material flesh, which constitute the basis of what is to be confessed. Beginning with its title, the experi-mental and sexually explicit video *Tremblement de Chair* ("Trembling

Flesh") invites a consideration of flesh and its animation.[96] The four-minute video stars Mirha-Soleil Ross unclothed and locked in a supine embrace with lover Mark Karbusicky, who was her longtime video editor and cocreator. The liner notes describe the experimental images as "A poetic meditation on the beauty, perils, and power of sexuality in a transsexual woman's body." Created in 2001 to install in a gallery exhibition, the video superimposes imagery of ominous skies, the eye of a tornado, and lightning flashes onto the lovers' bodies, which meld together to suggest natural powers colliding with sexual power. The cinematography of *Tremblement de Chair* also depends to a large degree on photographic effects such as double exposure and tinting to technically create visual shimmering. Apart from an effect of the desire circulating between Ross and Karbusicky, the notion of a fleshly or earthly tremor may refer to the fear caused by a tornado, or alternatively by the possible violence ensuing from an onlooker's disgust. *Tremblement de Chair* solicits its viewer to consider their flesh and its potential trembling: What might that affective response indicate about oneself? The tension between desire and fear circulating between the lovers and their viewers, I argue, arises from the notion that the affective response of trembling carries a weighted significance for sexual identity. That desire should function as a telling secret about oneself encases the aesthetic experience of *Tremblement de Chair* within the religious and modern-day framework of the "confession of the flesh." Through the notions of confession and truthful flesh, I examine the injunction to "speak sex" and explore in what ways *Tremblement de Chair* may be understood to "speak back to" the confessional mode in its imaging of transsexual desire.

A confession in common understanding is the pronouncement of a truthful statement about oneself, made by one person to another; however, not all statements are confessions. The statement must be shameful, difficult to express, and moreover revelatory of the "true" identity of the speaker, rendering the confession a feat of voluntary effort. According to Foucault's introductory study, confession operates beyond the religious context in that it is "a ritual that unfolds within a power relationship, for one does not confess without the presence (or virtual presence) of a partner who is not simply an interlocutor but the authority who requires the confession, prescribes and appreciates it, and intervenes in order to judge, punish, forgive, console, and reconcile."[97] Departing from the present concerns of the modern conception of sexuality, Foucault came to see the manifest technology of sexuality (apparatus or *dispositif*) as less important than the extent to which such technologies institute a social and true self.[98] Foucault himself submits to a confession in an admission of where his true interest laid at that time: "I must confess that I am much more interested in problems about techniques of the self and things like that rather than sex [. . .] sex is boring."[99]

The trembling transsexualized flesh of Ross bears the marks of a late nineteenth-century sea change in understanding physical sex and true identity, which is directly inherited by the paradigmatic clinical story of a true self overlaid with a discordant body. The confessions of the flesh in *Tremblement de Chair* concern the material flesh of sex as well as the flesh as sexual feeling, two kinds of flesh that can never be entirely disentangled, as Foucault himself demonstrated. The principal difference lies in the mode of confession of the stirrings and markings "so difficult to perceive and formulate": either the subject submits them in discourse or exposes the visual evidence that becomes inscribed in discourse through interpretation. The shifting movements of shimmering sex here translate formally to the trembling flesh, and tremors from nature's destructive power. The visual mode of the video largely relies on exhibiting material flesh as caught in the act of becoming stirred as well as marked, articulating a confession directed toward the viewer. In *Tremblement de Chair*, the virtual presence of the viewer stands in for the judging agent who wants to know the truth of their sexuality and the status of their sexed embodiment.[100] The authority of the viewer to assess a true sex, as Foucault traces, has a history in broadening the scientia sexualis from the experts to the public at large. Hence *Tremblement de Chair*'s visual intervention in depicting the obscuring effects of a so-called natural sex also contests the authority of outside interpretation: the lovers co-act and co-edit to superimpose their own truths.

Tremblement de Chair shows a sexually ambiguous body, no less a body in the midst of "licentious behavior," and hence a body in defiance of the morally minded medical edict of accomplishing a true and singular sex. The video begins innocently enough with an extreme close-up of Ross's right eye, pans to the left eye, and then slowly zooms out to her face addressing the camera, at which point she closes her eyes. An image of storm clouds washes over her face and buries her image, which then comes back into blurry focus. The next minute consists of a slow pan down and up her body, which follows the hand of her lover, his own body situated behind her, hidden from view. A bluish-white coloring outlines his muscular hand as it rests gently on her skin, seeming to hover over it as it makes its way over a tendril of hair. Appearing as though under, and yet a part of, his hand, the funnel of a tornado in a searing silver-white tint obscures whatever part of her body it glides across. The coloring of the overall image changes to a deep red as his hand, as well as the accompanying dynamic of the silver-white tornado, approaches a pert breast, moves down her belly, and in the same motion now caresses her nonerect penis. The image flashes to a bright white then fades to black before returning to a screen of branches covering the lovers (figures 2.5–2.9).

In the extreme close-ups, Ross's body becomes a series of revelations as the slow pan drifts downward. Her body is never given at once; one must anticipate and then integrate the different sections that are offered with varying degrees of perceptibility. The film's insistence on drawing out the revelation of her embodiment forces one to contemplate the diversity of physical markers that enable a reading of sex. From eye, to breast, then belly, and finally genitals, the viewer is asked to consider the relative importance of each segmented part to inform a sex judgment. The highlighting and obscuring of her genitalia, shown at the apex of the video's running time and as conclusion of the long panning shot, finally produces a quasi-confession of the transsexual secret. While, according to the ritual of confession, the film focuses on telling in detail, and through the examination of specific details, a sort of confession of the flesh, I use the qualifier *quasi* because the marking of a physical sex is never delivered as a singular and complete truth, disallowing conclusive judgment. In privileging a series of parts over a whole, *Tremblement de Chair*'s rebellious response to a hypothetical clinical intake is to refuse the synecdoche of sex in which one part—the penis—stands in for sexual identity entire. Instead the cinematographic effects in the montage sequence practice a filmic suture that draws together seemingly contradictory ways of being, perforce a trans manifestation of suturing a desired body from supposedly incongruous part images.

Furthermore, the intimacy of the imagery flouts what Stone describes as the medically enforced "permissible range of expressions of physical sexuality" by which good transsexuals should abide.[101] The obscuring effect of the double layering of images, a technical cinematographic effect of "double exposure," combined with added effects such as the changes in tint and focus all suggest a less than transparent access to Ross's sex-

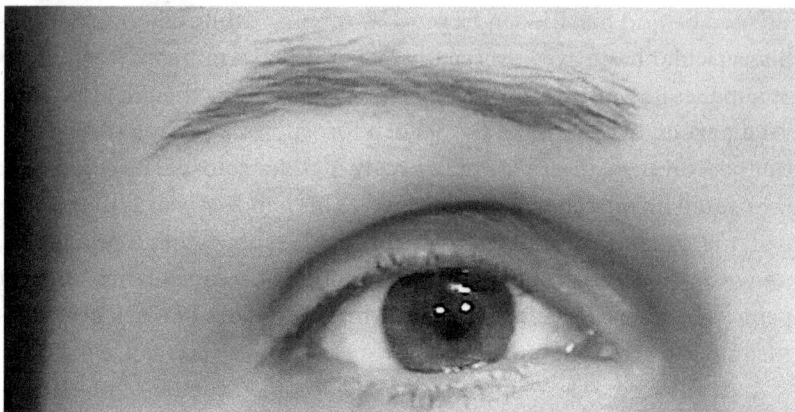

2.5 Close-up of Mirah-Soleil Ross's eye (screen capture, *Tremblement de Chair*, 2001, Mirha-Soleil Ross and Mark Karbusicky, V-Tape).

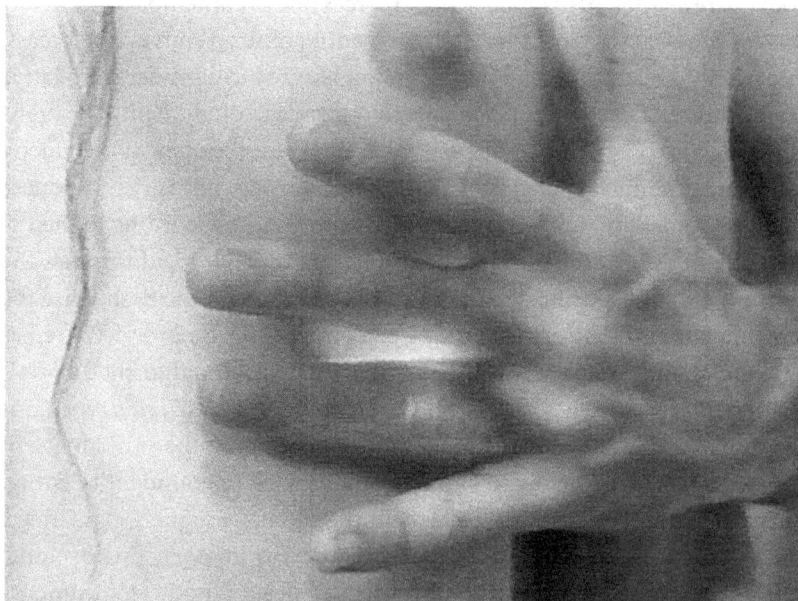

2.6 Close-up of Mirha-Soleil Ross's breast and the hand of Mark Karbusicky (screen capture, *Tremblement de Chair*, 2001, Mirha-Soleil Ross and Mark Karbusicky, V-Tape).

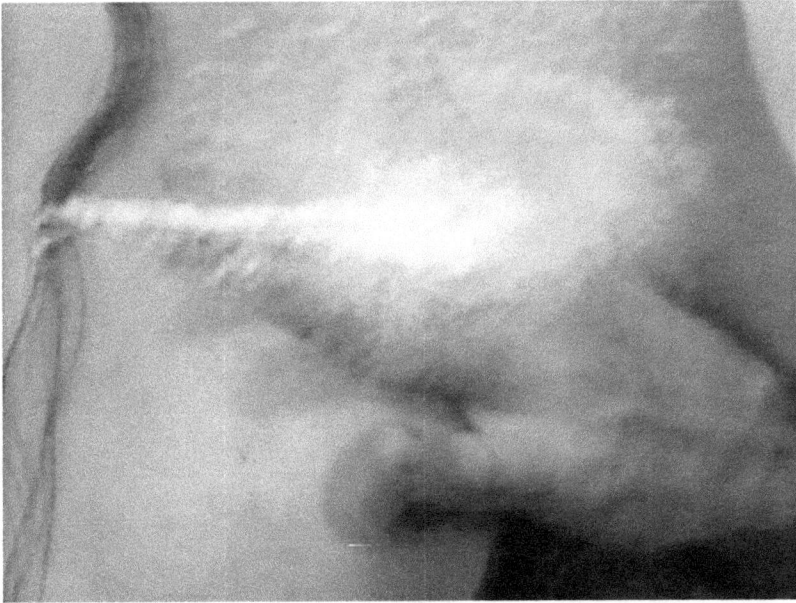

2.7 Close-up of Mirah-Soleil Ross's belly and the hand of Mark Karbusicky (screen capture, *Tremblement de Chair*, 2001, Mirha-Soleil Ross and Mark Karbusicky, V-Tape).

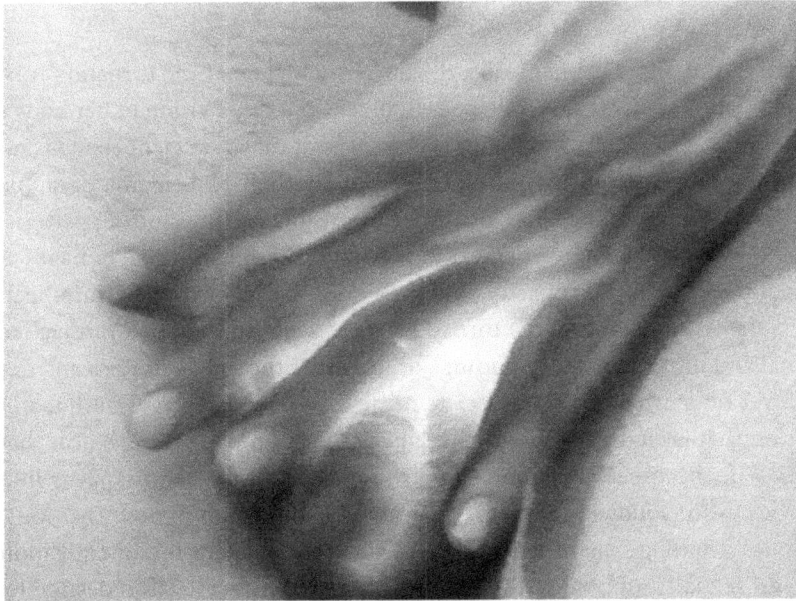

2.8 Close-up of Mirah-Soleil Ross's penis and the hand of Mark Karbusicky (screen capture, *Tremblement de Chair*, 2001, Mirha-Soleil Ross and Mark Karbusicky, V-Tape).

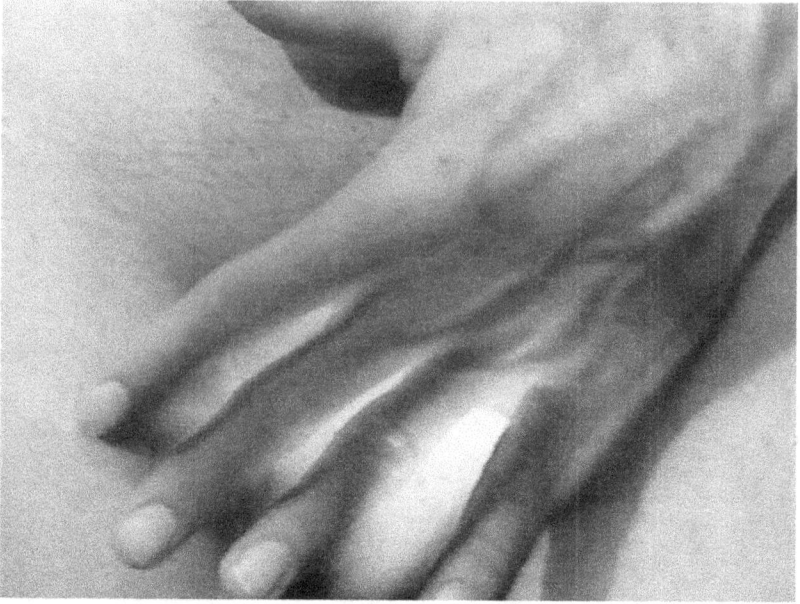

2.9 Close-up of Mirah-Soleil Ross's penis obscured by the hand of Mark Karbusicky (screen capture, *Tremblement de Chair*, 2001, Mirha-Soleil Ross and Mark Karbusicky, V-Tape).

ual desire. Most dramatically, the fiery white glow of the tornado's funnel, caught between the two bodies, blocks out one's vision of her body's tremors on one layer of the image, even as it may represent the tension of their desire erupting into trembles on another. The cinematographic effects of double exposure and other means of creating shifting patterns of light create changing degrees of perceptibility, but especially images of nature superimpose opacity onto their bodies. The forces of nature, such as the storm clouds and a tornado funnel, seem to suggest a miragelike natural illusion of sex "clouding" or haunting the image of Ross and her lover on another emergent epistemic level. The video stages an interaction that is characterized by the superimposition of a raging storm that literally becomes violent, insofar as the lovers ultimately disappear into the storm clouds (figure 2.10). Instead of a confession of flesh that indicates a wrong or sinful body, the reverse is depicted: the in-transition and sexually ambiguous body of Ross appears esteemed and desired by her lover. Only the intervening forces of nature threaten to obliterate it. The imagery of her (trans)sex and her desire struggle against the dark-

2.10 Image of the couple disappeared by a tornado formation (screen capture, *Tremblement de Chair*, 2001, Mirha-Soleil Ross and Mark Karbusicky, V-Tape).

ening forces of nature to become perceived and articulated. The slow dissolve image, though not a mirage, plays on the desire of the viewer to see through the inscrutable image of nature-as-such to possibly catch a glimpse of her truer self. But she and her lover never appear again. *Tremblement de Chair* thus inverts the terms of sex's political truth: the "natural" state of a singular sex appears as a destructive, shimmering illusion.

The Dark Shimmer:
Race and the Cathexis of Nasty in *Trans Entities*

In the final pages of *The Will to Knowledge*, Foucault returns to the metaphor of a true sex as a "shimmering mirage" to draw out the desire that influences the injunction to confession. Foucault writes that the mirage conjured up by the deployment of sexuality acts as a mirror, reflecting the subject in its own sex: "And it is this desirability of sex, that attaches each one of us to the injunction to know it, to reveal its law and its power; it is this desirability that makes us think we are affirming the rights of our sex against all power, when in fact we are fastened to the deployment of sexuality that has lifted up from deep within us a sort of mirage in which we think we see ourselves reflected—the dark shimmer of sex."[102] This false mirror shows only darkness, the shimmering shadow of sex rather than what Foucault presumes might be our truer, or differently true, selves. Foucault's method for correcting this vision involves reversing the supposed cause for its effect, suggesting instead that desire at the behest of sexuality causes a sense of political liberation. Foucault's metaphors of the "dark shimmer of sex" and the "shimmering mirage of sex" also operate on the basis of being taken as natural and self-evident because to the perceiver, sex appears as materially real. This insight can now be recast as a commentary on the pervasive ideology of "racial realism" that harbors the notion that genetic human races exist whose differentiation follows, or rather patterns, the same specification as sexual types. Like sexual essentialism that proposes the species of the homosexual, racial essentialism rejects the sociocultural context of racism for a natural taxonomy. The social value associated with skin color, Alice Walker tells us, in fact produces a hierarchy of racial categories cast according to the ranking order of "colorism."[103] Foucault posits that racial and sexual speciesism emerge through blood analytics that track the reproduction of populations; however, sex's humanizing cover for some bodies to enter the sexual field also, I want to argue, has a racial dimension. My attention to the shades of differentiation suggested in the "dark" of the shimmer run the risk of re-enforcing colorist sentiment, but might also aid in understanding how sexual representation can repurpose the values of skin color accrued through negative stereotyping.

My starting point for examining the dark shimmer of racialized sexuality is the film *Trans Entities: The Nasty Love of Papí and Wil* (dir. Morty Diamond, 2007), with the evocative term *entity* for the subjectivities of the docu-porn, and the descriptor *nasty* for the kind of love generated by these sexual entities. In modifying the concept of "love," *nasty* evokes contentious, layered stereotypes associated with Papí Coxxx and Wil Thrustwell (screen names). They both identify as trans, kinky, polyamorous, people of color (POC) and hence are aware that they are seen to embody cultural stereotypes for excessive, hypersexual, and thereby "nasty" ways of being.[104] Their embrace of being (and doing) nasty, however, critically exposes the whiteness and gender normativity saturating dominant, affective traditions of sexuality, including pornography. Moreover, the film's cogent vision of "nasty love" captures an affective intensity that seems formative of alternative sexual subjectivities: "trans entities." The film wrests the dark shimmer of sex from white supremacist optics underpinning clinical assumptions for the proper performance of transsexuality, including compulsory adherence to white gender norms, by asserting the sociocultural context of racism and colorism. The cathexis around nasty of concentrated investment into darkness and other devalued affective modes of being become a source of power and pleasure for these trans entities.

Featuring a real-life couple, *Trans Entities* consists of four parts interview-driven discussions on sex and gender expression, and three parts steamy, intimate, creative sex.[105] The inclusion of documentary-style footage of the personal lives of the performers trespasses an expected barrier in watching anonymous porn. Unlike the largely white and able-bodied queer porn, this video is forthright about race intersecting with disability by addressing the topics of nonwhite and explicitly African American and Puerto Rican trans identities as well as the kinky and d/Deaf communities.[106] It also contains a wide range of sexual scenes, beginning in the bedroom with an erotic game of Mercy, involving face and chest slapping, and, later, sex with a strap-on dildo. The next scene focusing on racial play includes a third partner, Chris, who is white, deaf, and a submissive. Chris joins Papí in being dominated by Wil. Finally, Papí and Wil role-play gangsters in an interrogation scene, the footage of which also shows the couple negotiating beforehand and giving aftercare. During the interviews, we are introduced to Papí and Wil's individual and collective thoughts on gender transitioning, polyamory, race politics, role-play, and spirituality. The testimonial nature of their interviews is established through the "talking head" device, their direct address to the camera captured in a medium shot. Whereas this documentary convention can stage distance or reflexivity when the interviewer is integrated, here the interviewer is edited out both visually and aurally. Instead, the eye-line of the speaker is made to match that of the viewer, bringing the spectator into alignment with the place of the director/cameraperson and thereby sutured in as a peer. The camerawork in the porn scenes differs in that two-camera editing is used to privilege the most generous view for a scopophilic eye (figures 2.11 and 2.12).

The first line of the film comes from Wil, who, fully clothed and sitting comfortably with his partner, Papí, states, "I identify as a trans entity.

2.11 Papí and Wil sit with their submissive Chris during an interview (screen capture, *Trans Entities: The Nasty Love of Papí and Wil*, 2007, dir. Morty Diamond, independent production).

I feel very much in touch with both my male and female side[s]. I wish there was something very much in between . . . I just, you know, found a word for it." Papí attests to having "always" been perceived as masculine because of their developed musculature and also feeling so, though not exclusively. Wil's identification with becoming an "entity" suggests a situational identity in process and certainly in transition. Papí also describes themself as a "trans entity," though they came to do so later, after identifying as femme, genderqueer, and on the masculine spectrum. For Papí especially, becoming a trans "entity" means radical "shifting" back and forth and "playing with" gender expression. The film's composition arranges the sexual scenes adjacent to personal interviews with slow dissolves, voice-overs, and musical bridges helping the viewer to transition from one format to another as smoothly as possible. The viewer might then see continuities between how Papí and Wil experience their sexuality and reflect on it. "The Nasty Love of" in the subtitle unabashedly points to the film's preoccupation with "nasty" elements becoming contrasted with Papí and Wil's loving relationship. Besides a catchy title, much more is at stake in the ways in which the affective force of the "nasty" aspects of trans-sexuality—transness, brownness, kink, and polyamory—enhances their loving practice of becoming trans entities.

Trans Entities can be noted for its unconventional depiction of sexual

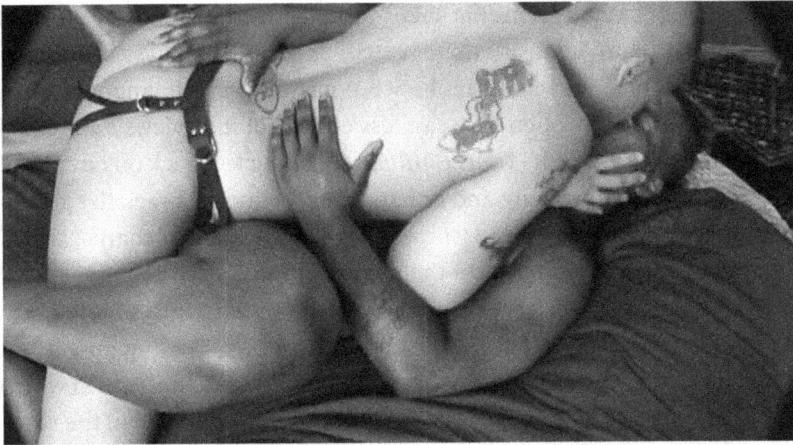

2.12 Papí and Wil kissing during sex in a bedroom scene (screen capture, *Trans Entities: The Nasty Love of Papí and Wil*, 2007, dir. Morty Diamond, independent production).

acts, including oral, genital, and anal intercourse, as well as kinky activities like spanking, bondage, and breath control. The inclusion of a range of more standard lovemaking to "nasty" sexual activities, however, is not the most unusual aspect of how this docu-porn presents sexuality. Tristan Taormino's review of "the new wave of trans porn" singles out an exciting counterlogic in its pornographic principle.[107] Whereas much mainstream pornography seems to reify the gendered norms of sexual behavior, the deeper we go with the protagonists into these sexually explicit scenes, for Taormino, the more "their genders become malleable and less significant than their connection to one another."[108] The transsexing of their shared transitions seems to be accomplished in part by their trans sex, by their generative enacting of nasty love. The possible conflict between nastiness and love seems to be resolved by the affective intensity—their connection—during the event of sex. The sex may be nasty, but it is so in a loving way. In contrast to most pornographic scenes, the sex is known, through interviews, to be consensual. The use of safe sex methods is highlighted with shots of reaching for condoms, gloves, and lube, most commonly depicted in queer and alternative pornographies that sexualize protective barriers. And each scene is embedded in a seemingly communicative and honest relationship. We come to associate their love with consent, communication, and care. Hence, the "nasty love" juxtaposition that takes place within the event of physical sex serves to only intensify their sexual, psychic, and physical connections. The shifting of intensities between nastiness and lovingness, visualized in parallel through the seamless editing of interviews and sexual scenes, seems to work in *Trans Entities* as looping feedback on circuits of desires. The commingling and enhanced resonances of racialized, gendered, polyamorous, and BDSM desires produce a heady charge, which might be examined in terms of their overlapping affective economies.

The mapping of "nasty" components onto declarations of love, such as Papí emphatically saying, "I love the fuck out of you," supports not only the flexibility of their gender expressions, but also the ways in which they perform racial difference. While the term *nasty* pops up in the video as a synonym for *sexy*, with highly positive connotations, it is also attached to their daring practices of on-camera racial role-play. In the culturally charged environment of pornography, film scholar Linda Williams points out that "the hypersexualization of the Black body (male and female) in some ways parallels the 'hysterization' of the white woman's body: both are represented as excessively saturated with sexuality."[109] In U.S. race politics, *nasty* became synonymous with obscene Black heterosexuality in the wake of 2 Live Crew's controversial 1989 album, *As Nasty as They Wanna Be*.[110] The taboos of Black power and hypermasculine sexuality are invoked in *Trans Entities* in the three-way scene, the second in the video's sequencing (figure 2.13). This scene stages a racially charged inverted relation of colorism power in which "Sir Wil" dominates "nothing" (Chris) with the help of "Pet" (Papí).[111] Although old South and plantation culture is not an explicit element of the scene, the use of collars and disciplining instruments to reinforce the dominant-submissive dynamic recalls the shackles and whips used for the enslavement of people. Props and power distributed according to racial difference, signaled primarily through skin tone from darkest to lightest, stimulates an erotic charge (figure 2.13).

In her discussion of interracial lust in films such as *Mandingo* (1975), Williams is careful to note that the intensity of the taboo relates to *knowing* it, and to being *aware of* the stereotyping, which is quite different from *believing* it.[112] The tension of the forbidden is explored in this three-way role-play organized by an inverted stereotype of racialized bodies: the person with the lightest skin is called "nothing" and is dominated by the person with the second-lightest skin, called "Pet," who follows or-

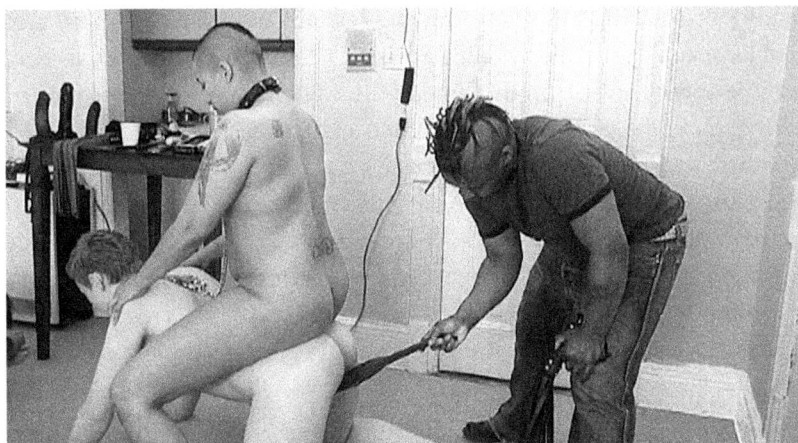

2.13 Wil dominates Papí and Chris in three-way race-play scene (screen capture, *Trans Entities: The Nasty Love of Papí and Wil*, 2007, dir. Morty Diamond, independent production).

ders from the person with the darkest skin, "Sir Wil." Wil explains that for him the charge in this scene comes from converting that which, as he says, is his "animalistic" desire into a controlled and clothed Master who tortures by giving orgasms. Together with his lovers, he develops through iteration a "refunctioned stereotype" of Black *and* white sexuality that will bring them all pleasure.[113] *Trans Entities* does not deny interracial lust, nor that "pornography acts as a racialized economy of desire," as Mireille Miller-Young writes, but mobilizes it "in historically new ways that are more erotic than phobic."[114] In paying attention to racial and cultural differences—discussing openly that they rejected white lovers before to avoid racial exotificiation, creating a sexual scene with a deaf person because Chris has, as they do, a separate culture from white ableism, affirming to each other that "I love your juicy lips"—*Trans Entities* works against the racist goal of "color blindness" operating in U.S. culture.[115]

The affective charge of "nasty" also suffuses the third scene between a backstabbing "criminal business partner" and a "crime boss," who gets even through interrogation techniques that involve knives and rough sex. This reanimation of the racial stereotype of Black people as a criminal underclass bucks what Miller-Young discusses as the "politics of respectability" in which Black women and men seek to gain racial respect by forming heteronormative, domestic, and bourgeois family relations.[116] In addition to acting out nonnormative sexualities of queer, contractual, public sexuality, this scene adds a "nasty" class component to the racial profile of their roles.[117] In this regard, throughout *Trans Entities* Papí and Wil explore the terrain of Sara Ahmed's "affect alien," who does not reproduce the line of what a community has determined is a "happy object," such as the family.[118] For Ahmed, affect "is what sticks, or what sustains or preserves the connection between ideas, values, and objects," and thus affect's economy can be mapped onto a moral, value-laden sexual economy.[119] During an encounter—for instance, the interrogation scene we watch— the affective atmosphere is always already angled insofar as "it is always felt from a specific point," an embodied point of view.[120] *Trans Entities* sutures together with the sticky thread of affect a rebellious configuration of trans-sex and of racialized embodiment. From the vantage point of their becoming trans entities, nastiness holds together a loving relation. Although love, like happiness, might be one of the most normatively moral affects, their means to seek it takes them far from bourgeois family relations and deeply into the realm of "bad" and morally suspect practices (genderfuck, BDSM, nonmonogamy), but still has the positive effect of generating trans entity ontologies.

In "Feeling Brown" José Esteban Muñoz analyzes the world-making of a theatre play that presents a reality structured by the affective overload of Latinx *latinidad*.[121] Like that play, *Trans Entities* eschews the cultural logic of heteronormative white respectability for the pleasures of its own affective performances of excess. As Muñoz stresses, the failure of Latinx (or other POC) to perform moral affective citizenship is *in relation to* the "hegemonic protocols of North American affective comportment."[122] From the point of view of the Latinx, "the affective performance of normative whiteness is minimalist to the point of emotional impoverishment"; it appears underdeveloped, if not a lack, in relation to latinidad fullness.[123] Given the "angle" of the U.S. racial atmosphere, Muñoz argues that seizing the stereotype of excess enables us to see the ways in which the presence of POC affective "excess" irritates and undermines the affective base of whiteness.[124] Hence, redirecting the stereotype vents fumes from a toxic characterization, creates an erotic charge, and resists feeling properly.

The contingent experience of excesses in *Trans Entities* runs along numerous community lines and against multiple cultural mandates. The doing of "nasty love" involves feeling "affective difference" that suggests affect might better account for the affiliations and identifications between radicalized, gendered, and ethnic groups that are in opposition or alien to other affective groups. It marks an affinity of resonance between racial and gendered outlaws. Their social experience can be described as "in process," yet nonetheless historically situated, contingent on the objects, values, and ideas that are circulating and stuck together with affect. The excesses of wanting, doing, and feeling more, a voracious desire to experience more pleasure, love, and life events, thus mark the affective overload of *Trans Entities*. In these many ways, the racialized sexuality and gendering of trans entities offered by the film materialize to be like the dense, full "black hole" space of Black women's sexuality that appears to be a void—but only to the nonracialized white observer outside of it, as Evelynn Hammonds brilliantly describes it.[125] The black hole trope portrays how these seemingly invisible sexualities emanate such incredible energy that they generate a distorting, perceptible effect on more visible white (queer) sexualities. Rather than appealing to the never innocent or uncomplicated register of the visual, the injunction of the dark shimmer of racial realism and the black hole of dense, excessive sexual affect produce distortions in the white structures of power and dominations, which determine what can and cannot be perceived or formulated in the clinical framing of trans-sexuality.

A Wavering W/Hole:
Trans Bodily Aesthetics and the Ontology of the Suture

Trans-sexualities in *Trans Entities, Tremblement de Chair, L/LA*, and Buck Angel films reside in a difficult to articulate spillage of affect that produces the nasty body, the trembling body, the crying sob, the alluring shine. Whereas sexuality typically is assigned transgressive meaning because its "stirrings" are difficult to articulate or because of the presumption that there is "something other than" cohering the various components of bodies, organs, pleasures, in these films the affective register of excess draws gender and sexuality into a new theoretical position. Trans sex and its affects, those forces that render the "mutability and specificity of human lives and loves," invite us to examine what falls outside or moves beyond the static framework of binary by-birth-assigned sex and gender identity.[126] The presumptions of a sexuality studies wholly preoccupied with sexual orientation (sex-coded object choice) at the expense of sexual practices feeds the ongoing lacunae of trans-sexualities on the same terms as clinical diagnoses.[127] Following from Bornstein, Stone, and others, a nonmedical conceptualization of trans-sexualities entails a departure from sexuality that is reliant on a stable identification with those whose sex or gender either mirrors or is considered oppositional to one's own.

Mutability first occurs through the body's affects and sensations, and to the ceaseless corporeal and incorporeal looping of the virtual and ac-tual. Second, in challenging the genital optics of species sexuality focused on heterosexual, homosexual, or bisexual couplings, trans sex opens to a different horizon of embodiment.[128] Underlying the process ontology of trans sex, engaged in by light wave–type bodies and shimmering shifts in perception, is the ongoing work of "bodily aesthetics" that Zowie Davy describes as the conjoining of the multiple body images of the social, sexual, and phenomenological body.[129] These divisions are heuristic de-vices to segment the spaces and times body images are consciously and unconsciously internalized and produced, which then affect further dis-cursive and material presentations of one's body. In the processing of trans bodily aesthetics, those normative judgments, but also reworkings of the aesthetic markers of beauty, ugliness, and desirability, help to stabi-lize body images, at least momentarily, into what Davy calls "(precarious) gestalts—unified wholes—which we identify or disidentify with."[130] The precarity of one's trans body images is partly to do with moving in to and out of particular times and spaces, but also because of what I see as the "suturing" required to conjoin these various and sometimes conflicting body images for different levels of identification.

The surgical term *suture*, like *cut* I explored in the first chapter, may re-call a sex-change network of metaphors, but I want to insist that regardless of actual surgical procedures and certainly alongside medical interven-tions, trans practices of suturing are integral to bodily aesthetics, partic-ularly of the sexual body. For example, trans theorist Jay Prosser conveys that "'sex change' entails a transformation of the body's surface" that hormone therapy begins and "surgery continues and radicalizes," which "consists in the surgical manipulation of the body's surface: the graft-ing, stretching, inverting, splitting, tucking, suturing of the tissues."[131] Prosser ends on *suturing*, suggesting that with surgical suture, finality is brought to bear on the transsexual subject. Although Prosser rightly de-mands we listen to the self-narration of trans embodiment, stories about sexuality in his selected examples fall to the wayside in his analysis. By contrast, Davy points out that "often the sexual body heightens awareness of particular intimate aspects of bodily aesthetics," with sexual experiences at times confirming or negating one's tenuous sense of wholeness.[132] *Trans Entities* draws attention to the necessity of others for one's bodily aesthetics to be accomplished with and through the sexual body, whereas *Tremblement de Chair* pivots on the destructive potential in the sexual body image imposed by others. In these trans sexual representations, pornographic conventions are clearly seized as an institution of sexual activity for narrating, materializing, and visualizing one's body. I suggest that in the uptake of pornographic self-representation, wherein an alternative counterweight to medically regulated forms of trans-sex and confession culture is offered, the posttranssexual or post-posttranssexual emerges agential in the process of changing their bodily configuration.

The Lacanian conceptualization of suture seems to afford a trans dimension in that the social, sexual, and phenomenological body images find precarious alignment through "pseudo-identification," a function he also terms "suture."[133] Although for Lacan this is an ongoing false recognition of correspondence between sentient self and seen self—for all subjects—the surgical synonym of suture highlights the way in which, through recognition, a body is pulled together in the mirrors of the visible world, mirrors existing at the level of the Imaginary and ratified at the level of the Symbolic. In capsule form, psychoanalytical suture is the joining of identification (that is *me*) and identity (*I am this, not that*). Hence suture names the click, or the zip, of the subject experiencing concurrence between the mirror's reflected sense of me-ness with the Symbolic's terms of identity (man or woman).[134] This conjunction, or the coincidence of ego and subject, might be understood as a pseudo-thing, but it nonetheless situates the subject in the social. Suture's function seems to break down in the transsexual "mirror stage," insofar as transsexuality is indicated by a failure of identification because of the noncorrespondence between felt self and reflected self. A trans divergent body is medically understood as the experience of noncorrespondence between the sexed body and gender. That state is then de-idealized to the point of mental distress, deemed a state of "gender dysphoria."

For Lacan, a coherent body is an ideal form, a form that Kaja Silverman in *The Threshold of the Visible World* contests as being available to all subjects at all times and at all levels.[135] Countering Lacan's presumption of the cultural norm that limits the fantasy of the Imaginary, and useful for countering pyscho-sexological assumptions of the dimorphic body underlying gender dysphoria, Silverman seeks ways of idealizing and enabling divergent bodies to practice suture. Silverman's rereading of the Lacanian ego clarifies the event of pseudo-identification; she indicates the ways in which cultural differences come into play in mirror scenes. She turns to Lacan's contemporary, Henri Wallon, who asserts that the visual imago, or "exteroceptive ego," is always initially *disjunctive* from the subject's felt sense of "ownness," or that which takes up space, which he calls the "proprioceptive ego."[136] Silverman suggests that the jubilant experience of suture during mirror scenes is not so much attributable to assuming the Gestalt but rather to the hard-won yet fleeting unison of exterior and interior egos. She writes that "a unified bodily ego comes into existence only as the result of a laborious stitching together of disparate parts," suggesting that the joint between these egos could come in many forms if culturally resonant terms were to exist for their shapes.[137] Furthermore, the process is unique to the body's history, to the way various cutaneous sensations have been registered and organized according to culturally distinct meanings. The sexual body is one such key, intimate place to perform the laborious stitching of seemingly disparate parts of the social and phenomenological bodies. For example, in the largely white dyke/trans BDSM communities that he studies, Robin Bauer notes that the "subcultural skills" of renaming and reassigning body parts enables participants to "stitch together imperfect gendered selves," even if this often comes at the price of overemphasizing social stereotypes around age, class, but especially race.[138] This ethnographic insight coupled with trans-erotic material invites an understanding of the sexualized body in terms of the ways in which sex and its affects may function as a gender technology.

C. Jacob Hale's groundbreaking essay on sexuality's transformative quality for transfolks, "Leatherdyke Boys and Their Daddies: How to Have Sex without Women or Men," offers more specifically sexual terms to Davy's model of bodily aesthetics transformed through inter- and intra-feedback mechanisms, that is, through relationality. Taking the exemplary experiences of leatherdykes who explore power dynamics in gendered roles, Hale's analysis ascribes transformative power to sexual experiences. He singles out Daddy-boy role-play that "sometimes functions as a means of gender exploration, solidification, resistance, destabilization, and reconfiguration."[139] Like Papí and Wil's use of sexual play to expand themselves into trans entities, Hale's interview subject Spencer Bergstedt describes SM as "a resource or means of learning more about myself and *growing*," and elsewhere states that sex is a "tool."[140] Used as a "gender technology," SM enables the phenomenon Hale calls the "retooling" and "recoding" of bodies, affecting a kind of transition, or departure, from the expected sexual mapping.[141] Through these reconfigurative sexual practices of "sexualized zones," Hale says that the body undergoes "deterritorialization and reterritorialization" in which genital sexuality becomes decoupled from bodily pleasures and the phenomenological experience of erogenous body parts can become transferred to other parts and even inanimate objects.[142] The usefulness of sex for transfolks is that regardless of surgical or hormonal transformations the body has undergone, sexual practices are an available means to resignify perhaps otherwise "off-limits" body parts.[143] "To change our embodiments without changing our bodies" is how Hale describes the potential in sexuality for growing multiple, context-specific, and purpose-specific sex/gender statuses, which is clearly how *Trans Entities* depicts the purpose of sexual scenes with changing personas.[144]

This alternative perspective on the functioning parts of the ego is helpful to understand the trans-sexual practice of psychically and corporeally rearranging and stitching together parts to match the exteroceptive ego to the proprioceptive ego in search of personal, sexual, and social legibility. Silverman alludes to how transsexualism has shaped her thinking when she writes that, "the 'gender-bending' of recent years has alerted us to the fact that the proprioceptive ego may not always be compatible with what the reflecting surface shows," leaving open the possibility that it can be made compatible.[145] However, she insists that a disjunction must *always* be overcome, which while stressing the general practice of suturing makes it difficult to articulate the trans-specific labor of stitching together a compatible bodily ego. Positively for my endeavor to account for the suturing practices of trans-sexualities, her use of Wallon points out that this disjunction does not give rise to embarrassment, nor a sense of incoherence, nor "seem[s] to produce pathological effects."[146] In this view, it is possible to have a maligned visual and sensational ego that requires continuous suturing without necessarily adhering to gender-normative, binary, or dominantly held values for bodily aesthetics.

"The goal [of Symbolic differentiation] is to confer ideality upon an image which cannot be even delusorily mapped onto one's sensational body," Silverman asserts.[147] Ideality is usually conferred on what is most culturally valorized. However, idealization as a practice, what she calls with Lacan "the active gift of love," can open up an identification, "which would otherwise be foreclosed by the imperatives of normative representation and the ego."[148] Silverman follows philosopher Max Scheler's terms of *heteropathic* and *idiopathic* identification: whereas idiopathic identification absorbs the other, through heteropathic identification the subject identifies at a distance from his or her proprioceptive self and corporeally surrenders its "specular parameters" for those of the other.[149] The more general term she uses for this ethical aspect of the field of vision is the "productive look," in the sense of being productive of a consciousness that idealizes the other as other. Mieke Bal notes in a review of *The Threshold of the Visual World* that Silverman makes the point, more clearly than Lacan, that "not every mirror image is framed by, clothed in a positive, validating response from the outer world, whereas the subject is dependent on such a 'ratification' for the formation of the ego."[150] If the outside world does not offer affirmation for the bodily ego, how does one find a loving ratification? How does one survive the cultural debasement that threatens to frame them? Cinema's ability to demonstrate the exchange of looks and thus extend the frame of the mirror seems useful for a trans subject with suture trouble.

Psychoanalytic discussions of suture have been explored in film theory since Jean-Pierre Oudart, in his 1969 article "La suture" in *Cahiers du cinema*, claimed that shot and reverse-shot sequences pit the viewer into a necessary *position of exchange*, a position that suture requires of the spectator to successfully (or not) enter into the operation of identification with the on-screen look.[151] The necessity of intersubjective eroticism to suture through conferring ideality has not been carefully explored by suture theorists, who tend to treat identification as an individual psychic experience of cinematic images and underplay, if not ignore the libidinal energy that Silverman suggests consecrates suture. This libidinal energy, itself not yet formatted into sexual identity, localizes the sexual body when it passes through the psychoanalytical "screen." Lacan nominates the screen, much like a film projection screen, to be a determining factor in the subject's ability to suture: it allows for bodily images to come together where the subject is locatable in the grid of culture. In contrast to the Gestalt mirror-image, the "opaque" and obscuring screen enforces an image that may or may not be pleasurable or comfortable for the subject: it is not necessarily ideal.[152] The understanding of the screen as ideological provides a productive distance between subject and self, a distance that Silverman stresses as indispensable to political contestation.[153] Relevant to trans-sexual practices is her suggestion that, at the individual level, one might substitute another screen-image for the conventional one, or even distort or resignify the normative image.[154]

In Silverman's view, the screen is managed as well as transformed collectively through the cultural imaginary, which is subject to historical change. Silverman insists that the cinematic screen, functioning as the repository of the Lacanian screen, can offer the "lighting up" of others as "an active gift of love": "'active' [. . .] might be said to qualify most profoundly that process of idealization which, rather than blindly and involuntarily conforming to what the cultural screen mandates as 'ideal,' light up with a glittering radiance bodies long accustomed to a forced alignment with debased images."[155] In clinical and cultural terms, debased body images include regarding one's genitalia as a disgusting deformity, or that a man with a vulva would be lacking, or that real gender identity is only achieved through heterosexual penetrative acts, making any other sexual script a double failure. Silverman's statement seems to be an endorsement for visual forms such as pornography and documentary that rework the shimmering mirage of sex in order to light up formerly debased images with a glittering radiance. The suffusion of light need not reinforce the ideology of clinical confession with its compulsion toward the revelatory and transparent exposure of sex secrets. Rather, the cinematic mode of catching the motion of light in water through docu-porn bathes the trans protagonists in the productive look of love, whether infused with nasty, futuristic, or even fetishistic sentiment.

In short, the minoritarian subjectivity that is de-idealized by the majoritarian Symbolic has recourse through the sexual body to negotiate and push back the erasure of their assemblage of "bodies, organs, somatic localizations, functions, anatomo-physiological systems, sensations, and pleasures" when it does not add up to the dominant materialization of sex. Muñoz describes this move of the "disidentificatory subject" as the employment of a third way, which does not assimilate (identify) nor reject (counteridentify) dominant ideology, but rather "tactically and simultaneously works on, with, and against, a cultural form."[156] By incarnating "bad sex" and by being the presumed bastion of white, male, heterosexist modes of looking focused on genitality, the cultural form of pornography has the benefit of centering all the obstacles trans-sex encounters for de-idealization. The corresponding strategies of disidentifying practices in the performance of pornographic trans-sex also cluster together the means to upend the mirage logics that debase some trans-sexual identities. The radical antistatic status of shimmering—even if, or especially if, visualized in the tropes of a mirage or a black hole—suggests a suspension of being either really there or not there, of being fully graspable. Disidentifying practices in trans-sex performance articulate means in which the visual essentialism of genital optics (that presumes to already know what is visual and what is not) can be placed under duress, particularly through bursts of affective intensity. The next chapter considers how experimental and avant-garde trans films at the brink of the third millennium posit the affects of interest amplified to curiosity through cybernetic film forms that transformatively commute the fear and rage of the chimeric subject.

THREE

Shimmering Multiplicity

Trans*Forms in *Dandy Dust* and *I.K.U.*

from Dada to Data to D@D@

onna Haraway's "A Cyborg Manifesto: Science, Technology, and Socialist-Feminism in the Late Twentieth Century" of 1985 captured the ironic zeitgeist of postmodern conceptions of sex, gender, and sexuality by advancing a theory of political economy consisting in fluid partiality.[1] The manifesto announces the cyborg as a mythic figure for our time, "a creature in a post-gender world" in which "we are all chimeras."[2] Haraway's detailing of the cyborg's origins and characteristics was empirically founded on the experiences of real cyborgs such as Sandy Stone, whom she interviewed and later supervised, lending a posttranssexual depth to the literary, end-of-millennium character.[3] The excitement over and fear of an increasingly complex information society that launched humans into space and cybernetics system theory into the Advanced Research Projects Agency Network (ARPANET) converges in the manifesto with opportunities to transgress gender in virtual realities, the desire to be free of gendered labor through artificial intelligence, and the rise of multifactor gender identity theories.[4] Not only cutting-edge military programs, but also the medical authorities involved with gender clinics conceived of bodies taking hyperplastic forms according to sex-design modeling.[5] Gender-chimeric cyborgs represent the actual and virtual manifestation of rapidly shifting multiplicities, coded switch-forms that embody the aesthetics of change.

The cyborg is typically located within the new information technology underpinning the virtual worlds of the internet and the World Wide Web rather than in the old technology of film worlds, following a perceived break between digital and analog due to new media digitization processes that integrate computing logic into all media cultures.[6] However, Kara Keeling's critical appraisal of twentieth- and twenty-first-century image culture identifies film viewing as the perfection of broader cinematic processes involving a cybernetic circuit of images in which a spectator plugs into a biotech interface.[7] "A film starts. A viewer creates various circuits between the present perception of the set of images that the film comprises and past memory-images available to make sense of the film," writes Keeling in her sensate-cognitive description of spectatorship.[8] Keeling follows Henri Bergson's view of perception from his 1896 *Matter and Memory* as a reduction of the present set of images shorn to fit past memory-images; effectively, perception is the selection of already recognizable images.[9] Bergson's model for affection posits one's skin as the regulatory boundary between the inside and outside of one's body, itself an image, which is different from other images insofar as it has the ability to group and organize all the other images that might affect it.[10] The body is thus a center of indeterminate action for a porous, affective perception process. Keeling uses the term "common sense" (borrowed from Gramsci) to refer to a commonly shared memory-image that anchors the schemata for sensory-motors in a collective set of "experiences, knowledges, traditions" that might link up during perception.[11] Common sense most often functions in the form of enduring clichés, but it might also enable an alternate perception if outlier or marginal recalled experiences pass through the subject's affective membrane into the copresent perception. In her analysis of popular and obscure film depictions of Black femmehood, Keeling banks on "cinema's ability to tear a 'real image from clichés'—an operation that breaks the sensory-motor link and extends a perception not into motor action, but into thought," which Deleuze tells us is the power of cinema's time-image.[12] Keeling directs her reader to consider how cinematic perceptual schemas and cinematic matter are crucial arenas for breaking with gender and race clichés, precisely because they work in tandem to assert broader cinematic processes that govern the selection of which images can appear and are likely to be perceptible, intelligible, and legible in their appearance.

In chapters 1 and 2 I demonstrated how assumptions about transsexual and transgender bodies can be plagued by the aesthetics of mutability and its failures, whether the enduring cliché of the sex change or of the suffering person whose body stubbornly refuses to change properly in the eyes of others. In relief, the specific aesthetics of change offered in cinematic images suggest alternative perspectives on understanding gender transitions. Like the trickality of the sex change from male/female and the pornographic trans-sexual, the experimental switch-form toys with deeply stigmatizing and encrusted commonsense understandings of trans people, namely as misguided monstrous cyborgs.[13] Nonetheless, two millennial films dedicated to avant-garde aesthetics and cyborgian ontology and politics stand out because of their activation of switch-forms for an alternate perception: (Ashley) Hans Scheirl's *Dandy Dust* (1998) and Cheang Shu Lea's *I.K.U.* (2000).[14] These films take on the crisis of seemingly unavoidable images that demarcate trans in terms of frighteningly chimeric body types, which persists twenty years on in invocations of trans predators and in fear-mongering "bathroom bills." The result is a distorted image of transgender medical care as biotech programs gone rogue, creating sexually deviant and cold-blooded transfeminine protagonists such as those at the center of psychodramatic films like *Dressed to Kill* (dir. Brian de Palma, 1981) and *The Silence of the Lambs* (dir. Jonathan Demme, 1991). To nullify this tendentious image, these trans-genre films remix sci-fi, neo-noir, pornographic, and splatter-styled images to create an alternative aesthetics of formal mutability based not only on hereto unthinkable transmasculine characters, but also on the level of film form. If form can be likened to the bodily elements of the films, then the volatility of these filmic bodies occurs in two dada-esque manners: the "male" and "female" protagonists continuously arrive in various physical forms, and the editing style decapitates the head from the body, separates the eyes from the head, and disconnects affects from bodies. The millennial avant-garde, I argue, dives into the wreckage of modernization's dark side, consisting of the ruins of the racially gendered (non)human, to forge an adequate vocabulary for trans* multiplicity in the cybernetic era.

The close connection between a transforming cyborgian ontology and hypertransformative film form in *Dandy Dust* and *I.K.U.* forces the question of how the phenomenon of morphing protagonists interrelates with shape-shifting genres and with narratives that refuse closure (both films have alternate endings and choose your own adventure–type plot moments). Many spectators walked out during both premieres, perhaps because their past memory-images could not be pleasurably or satisfactorily linked to their perception of the present set of images.[15] The multigenre quality of both films constantly shifts the horizon of expectation, leading to a highly deconstructed story/fabula frame. They require from the spectator a participatory meaning-making process that encourages self-reflexivity (What kind of film is this? What is going on? What am I expected to do?) that is more typical of avant-garde cinema; this results in a high potential for activating alternate perceptions of traditions, experiences, and knowledges in the cybernetic circuit of viewing. In this chapter I investigate how the transformative film form (the style in which the contents of the film are expressed, including the formal elements of shot, editing, narrative, sound) translates to the affective state of the film body, and further to the cinematic process of the plugged-in spectator. I wager that cybernetics systems theory and the related Deleuzian interpretations of "multiplicity" offer a better point of departure for this question of how affect modulates form and ontology than feminist psychoanalytic, phenomenological, or cognitive film theory, which tend to presuppose a fixed gender position or lack a gender-differentiated viewer.[16]

Cybernetics holds particular attention for queer affect theorists Eve Sedgwick and Adam Frank, who explain their turn to the work of psychologist Silvan Tomkins because he starts from another place than constructivism or essentialism when theorizing human behavior. Namely, Tomkins models the patterning of human affects on systems, whose psychic lives emerge in the cybernetic fold of their experiences not predetermined by any essential difference. Tomkins was working in the heady moment when systems theory forged a space between modernist and postmodernist brain-mind hypotheses that allowed for the "notion of the brain as a homogenous, differenti*able* but not originally differentiated system."[17] In other words, Tomkins is not asking "How are things different?" but "How do things differentiate?" This is a question about trans*life in the sense that Eva Hayward (writing with Jami Weinstein) describes it: "[Trans] is not a thing or being, it is rather the process through which thingness and beingness are constituted. In its prefixial state, trans* is prepositionally oriented—marking the *with*, *through*, *of*, *in*, and *across* that make life possible."[18] In her vision, trans specified with the asterisk refers foremost to a process of relating that situates and grows bodies, rather than to the identification of a particular kind or type of body. Delinked from an ontological condition of being, trans* is thus freer to refer to the process of life-generating relations that provide meaningful sets of bodies. The relation-making power of trans*life then is not unlike how Tomkins sees the affects generating and amplifying meaningful connections to the world. Both affects and trans relations exist insomuch as they make other existences possible and cogent.

Underlying these understandings of affect and trans* is a nondetermination model for differentiation processes in which things and beings become more extant than other things and beings, which also lines the philosophical notion of multiplicity. For Gilles Deleuze multiplicity is a main concept referenced throughout his writings on the philosophy of difference, developed from the ideas of continental philosopher Henri Bergson and mathematician Georg Riemann. Multiplicity opposes the dyad One/Many with the idea from Riemann that "any situation is composed of different multiplicities that form a kind of patchwork or ensemble without becoming a totality or whole"; this definition also shares the starting point of composing, fluid partialities within cybernetics-based understandings of conductors, nodes, devices, networks: systems.[19] In his book *Bergsonism*, Deleuze advances two kinds of multiplicities: extensive numerical multiplicities that characterize space (that can be divided up into parts) and continuous intensive multiplicities that characterize time (that cannot be divided up without changing in nature).[20] Further, in his theory of cinematic images, the *intensive multiplicities* closest to the amplification of affects are the most important for understanding the impact of the time-image in postwar films, with the irrational cut forming a paradigm case.[21] Divisive cuts without narrative purpose "come and interrupt the normal linkage of the two sequences; or in the enlarged form of the black screen, or the white screen and their derivatives," which Deleuze describes as "'anomalous' images" that form a mutilation breaching the time of eternity.[22] Deleuze also posits that multiplicity is the cornerstone of process philosophy's understanding of existence, for it names states of affairs called actual multiplicities (including ourselves), and particular intensive movements of change called virtual multiplicities (happening in parallel with changes to actual multiplicities).[23]

With the compact portmanteaux of *trans*form* I offer a word that captures the affective modulations that structure the differentiations of transgender transitions and transformations of form. The multiplicity of relations that congeal into cogent actualities cannot be known in advance; hence the asterisk designates the happening of a transformation en route to becoming an ensemble. The transforming differenti*able* body undergoes a quantitative process of transitioning (change in name, presentation, pronoun, hormonal balance, physicality) apart from, but also contingent on, achieving qualitative differences (change in energy, outlook, mental well-being). The asterisk in trans*form also marks the pure event-ness of the transformation; that is, we constantly miss the "happening" of the event: it never occurs in one instant whatsoever, but is "subdivided *ad infinitum* into something that has just happened or is going to happen, always flying in both directions at once," writes Deleuze.[24] Therefore the asterisk shape of six tentacular reaches (*) that Hayward theorizes nods to the desire for holding on to or grasping for connections among the swell of ongoing change bound up into an actual multiplicity.[25] The proliferation of trans* video blogging that documents personal transitions is one such example of the effort to capture the sticky solidity of actual multiplicities in the moment of virtual multiplicities giving shape to and amplifying trans*formations, and yet it always misses the happening of it.[26] Consequently, the asterisk in my term *trans*form* marks the space of gender multiplicity for a number of reasons: * represents a symbol for multiplication, * indicates an affect's intensive too-muchness as in "*#!?," * opens a jagged irrational cut into a film body's circuit, and * is the wildcard syntax for a digital command line that opens a search for all forms of gender variance (trans*vestite, -sexual, -gender, etc.). Asterisks are a notational technique to multiply the cliché and explode it, just like avant-garde cinema movements such as dada and Fluxus appropriate and amplify the common sense images that pass for perception to break through into new perceptual schemes. In these films, "the cinematic" assemblages of gender and race perceptual data flowing through cybernetic circuits of desire are intensified by dada nonsense to the point of orgasmic and spectacular death explosions that recede from any sense of finality, becoming instead another switch-mode in cinematic forms of life/death/life.

In the first section, before moving into a close reading of the films, I explicate how I translate to film analysis Barthes's affective method for reading shimmers by dropping into a Neutral state of pathos, a minimal state attuned to the fluctuations and flickers that modulate texts. Here I expand in new directions Eugenie Brinkema's neo-formalist film analysis for identifying the affects in formal details of shots and sequences, color and tone, namely by positing that these films first amplify the affect of interest to curiosity before other affects can be directed along the circuit of the film. Broadly conceived as the desire to know, curiosity is the affect of grasping, the tentacular equivalent for responding to irrational cuts and short-circuited film form. In the second and third sections I focus on different formal elements that compose the switch-form of the films in comparable manners. The films each proffer an indistinct sex/gendered bodyscape through the use of an interior animated "pussy-shot" and changes in scale, making spatial orientation akin to a "transgendered arsehole" that is emphasized by pixilation and granulation. Then I consider how wild compositions for going d@d@ results from the conjunction of adversary dada filmmaking techniques for representing sex and death with sinister plots about collecting memory data. In closing, I consider how curiosity as a survival technique draws on the affective form of rage to give birth to virtual possibilities and actualities of trans* life.

Although these films were conceived in the heyday of the New Queer Cinema movement, loosely defined by an attitude of "defiance" and open queer sexuality, they have been largely excluded from canonical considerations.[27] The formalist experimentation with the open-endedness of gender form and film form combined suggest that *Dandy Dust* and *I.K.U.* are more intelligible in the genealogy of feminist avant-garde aesthetics that interrogate the heteronormative categories of woman and man by deconstructing formal narrative conventions, such as coherent characters and plot resolution. Denise Riley writes that the "sometimes" temporality of gender need not undercut feminism, nor, I would add, does it undercut a trans*feminist film analysis, for *"Gendered self-consciousness has, mercifully, a flickering nature."*[28] This insistence on the at times temporality of gendered self-consciousness leaves room for an elliptical structure of gender in which one can sometimes align with an identity while also recognizing the impossibility to always be that at the behest of other identifications. The sometimes flickering temporality of these films, I argue, arrives in the switch-form of cyborgian partiality, shifting horizons of expectations, and pauses in the white noise of the shimmering void.

Drop in to Shimmering:
The Void, Minimal Existence, and Scanning

Dandy Dust opens with a low-whirring atmosphere underlying an extremely short shot of a glowing figure, a young Black child wearing a long white nightgown. Heavy break beats and horns kick up a notch into the film's signature sound, then the figure shifts suddenly up to the right before zooming left into deep space and into the dissolve. This image is repeated later with another version of Dandy Dust, arms outstretched (figures 3.1 and 3.2).

Dandy Dust was shot on low-resolution media like Super-8 and Hi-8 video between 1992 and 1998, then blown up on 16 mm celluloid film. With cinematographer Jana Cipriani, the director, editor, and starring titular protagonist Hans Scheirl invented "super-projection" processes of filming off of monitors, projections, and TV-proscenium rooms, resulting in constant up- and downgradings that rendered in the final low-budget film a granular, fuzzy-around-the-edges quality.[29] The video-film's budgetary restrictions became an aesthetic statement of a do-it-yourself "Fun-Punk" sensibility that exploits the sensuous quality of film through images peppered with cheap video special effects and mixed-medium formats, including animation and comix.[30] Scheirl wanted his extremely low-budget effects to produce an abstract sense of shape and saturated color that would become metonymic for a rich field of aesthetic experience more generally.[31] He was especially enamored of a "particular 'glow'"—produced by shooting on video, filming off a monitor, and then transferring the film image back to video—that made the film grain seem to come alive. This is because of the different speeds of the television scan and the film shutter that create an "evanescently flickering" image, created by the scanning fingers of the cathode-ray gun that draw and redraw the image thirty times as opposed to twenty-four frames per second.[32] He claimed, in fact, that the real protagonist of *Dandy Dust* "IS the film grain and the TV-noise [*Fernsehrauschen*, or static]," which aural-visually represents the interstitial space between technology and corporeality.[33] From the start, the viewer is dropped in to a white noise layered with cacophonic sound, unanchored in a void, and briefly shown a radiant, paper-thin character. How to closely read that which emits in a flash no stable form? Like tuning a television channel from noisy static, I proffer a reading method for the *pathetic* void, in the now dated etymological sense of

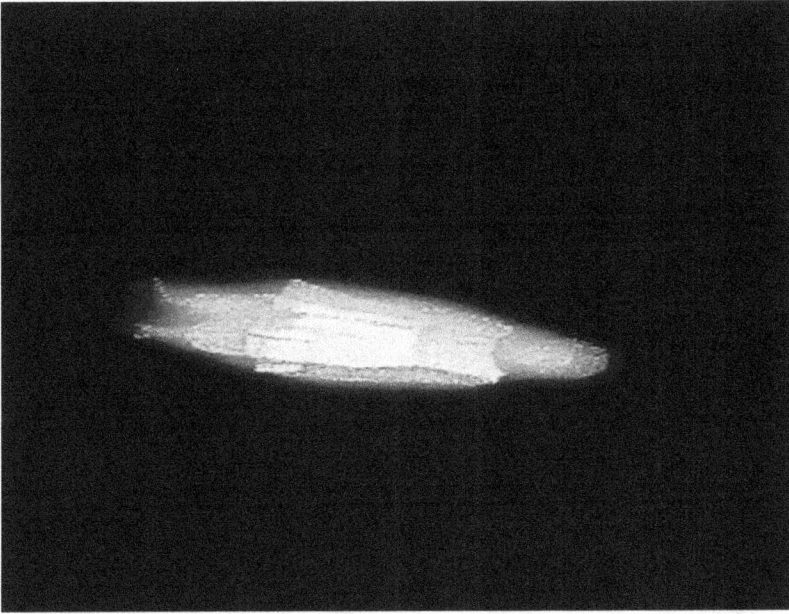

3.1 Young Dandy Dust flies through the void in the film's opening (screen capture, *Dandy Dust*, 1998, [Ashley] Hans Scheirl, Millivres Multimedia).

"that which is capable of exciting the passions," in which a state of pathos preconditions the image snapping into intelligibility. Resembling the *khôra* in Plato, the matrixial void of *Dandy Dust* is an overfull interval, not an empty space. This opening scene sets the affective stage, so to speak, by registering a low-level hum of affect. It drops the viewer into the shimmering void—to feel the minuscule gradient of change. *Dandy Dust* makes virtual filmic space the sievelike receptacle for pathos, for actual form: a kind of holding pen between being and nonbeing.

Film theorists must be cinephiles at heart, those who will risk surrendering to the cinematic processes that guide a plugged-in viewing. But how does this stance translate into film criticism and analysis? Brinkema's overview of the personal affective responses that embroider film analysis takes aim at how these theorists misconceive their own bodily responses for how the film's affective structures operate.[34] For her, a film does not concern itself with transmitting affects, but remains enigmatically, perhaps maddeningly closed. The affects, such as joy, disgust, embarrassment, grief, and anxiety, are embedded into formal elements un-

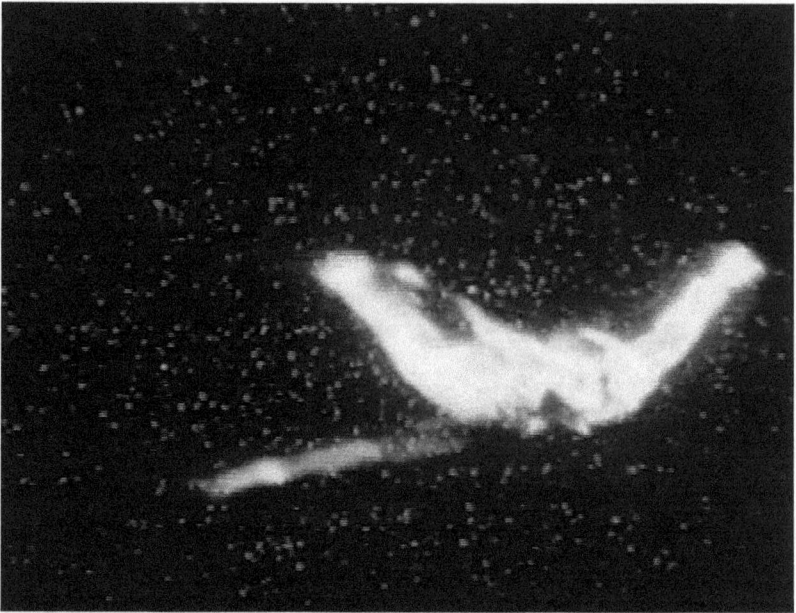

3.2 Older Dandy Dust returns to fly through the void (screen capture, *Dandy Dust*, 1998, [Ashley] Hans Scheirl, Millivres Multimedia).

concerned with actual human subjects. Media theorist Steven Shaviro's trenchant antipsychoanalysis film theory stance, which pushes him into elaborating an affective theory of film in *The Cinematic Body*, arrives to a similar conclusion as Brinkema. But in addition, Shaviro empathetically singles out one quality of the image most responsible for the analyst's/viewer's filmic fascination: the image's appeal to grasping contact in combination with its simultaneous exclusion from touch.[35] "I cannot take hold of it in return, but always find it shimmering just beyond my grasp," writes Shaviro, citing the shimmering quality of the image as what elicits his interest in the impalpable, teasing image.[36] Where Brinkema treats the film as a closed circuit one might detachedly observe from afar, Shaviro (and Keeling, implicitly) treats the film as a one-way circuit that imposingly loops the viewer in but also ruptures the ego at the point of fascination. It is interesting that both kinds of viewership expound an annihilated subjectivity.

In Brinkema's polemic to pay better interpretative attention to how the film's affective field is populated, she sidesteps explaining the ways close reading (her own, or that by any film analyst) requires affective training to withstand or cope with annihilation. Looking to the challenge of closely reading *Dandy Dust*, I think the interpretative mode of radical passivity or detached activity should not suggest a blank slate, but a minimal affective state, close to what Barthes names as a state of seemingly neutral calm brokered on the potential to intensify. Describing the "what" his calm is made of, Barthes notes briefly, "an immediate and precise consciousness of the smallest shifts of affect that attack my body (jealousies, urges to get rid of, fears, desires, etc.) → hyperconsciousness of the minimal, of the microscopic fragment of emotion = filings of affects → which implies an extreme changeability of affective moments, a rapid modification, into shimmer."[37] This neutral analyst is in turmoil, but they nevertheless have an observational power over the "emotive hyperconsciousness of the affective minimal" that is particularly useful for tracking how the affects operate in filmic processes.[38] Applying these observational powers to note and grasp conceptually the "shimmering field of the body, insofar as it changes, goes through changes," to *textual* nuances, Barthes calls for a science of shimmers.[39] He risks naming it *diaphorology*, for the Greek *diaphor* ("that which distinguishes one thing from another") combined with the suffix *-logy* (theory or discourse). An image's shimmering quality and the modifications of shimmers both refer to the nuances of hard-to-grasp splintering feelings, of hard-to-parse multifarious meanings. The shimmer thus describes the modulation in the text between the affects and the meaning; it is a differentiating force on the filmic body, the ripple effect of affect moving into the black dissolve, a sound signature that amplifies and disperses meaning. These are infrastructures of feeling, that is, aesthetic components given in the image, that elicit a grasping and grappling.

Like these scholars, I aim to describe and account for the nuances of cultural texts and the styling of difference that (we all agree) comes back to the particulars of a film's details; however, I want to refuse the kind of dogmatic close reading that would accord a final signifier on any element. In praising Christian Metz's practice of semiology for its attention to diaphora, the shimmer in filmic texts is for Barthes always "a shimmer in which different intentions may be read" according to the moment of intellectual discourse.[40] Here Barthes's notion of the historicity of shimmers indicates the importance of how differing "common sense" anchors influence a clichéd or alternate perception; it further implies that retrospective and intersectional reading techniques may influence the extent to which a film's affective structures work. The particular detail is never entirely open-ended, but nor is there only one meaning—for this would follow the One/Many dyad. The virtual multiplicity hovering around any actual detail might burst forth with competing meanings, not work, or perhaps work even better than expected. Filmic affects, what Scheirl calls "e/motions," are structures emergent in line, light, color, rhythm, which Scheirl claims is not so much represented as shown in its media-specific ways. "[*Dandy Dust's*] own self-irony makes it prone to humour or shock involuntarily," writes Scheirl about the textual polysemy of his chimeric film.[41] There is always more in a present image than commonly is registered in the perception of that same image; and even Brinkema's analysis of "passionate structures" within filmic images acknowledges how they exceed ideological address.[42] Affect is a matter of aesthetics, form, and structure; it is for us without being about us. The visual form and temporal structure enliven the body without being instrumentalist or functional in its expression. This is not to say that analysis is only relative or personal because of the "ambiguity" of a shimmer.[43] Rather than retreat from what falls out from our patterns of knowing, David Getsy calls for attention to their "particular, inassimilable, unorthodox, unprecedented, or recalcitrant" differences that exceed and undermine the supposed neutrality of taxonomies.[44] In turning to the passionate structures of these films, I'm accosted by the unorthodox patterning, enlivened by the excess of their address, and activated to track all the affective filings that fall out in their nuclear blips and bombs.

The importance of time, attention, and closeness in a formalist reading method can be seen in these films as converging on a method of scanning taken in a technical and poetic sense. The opening scene of *I.K.U.* is a stilted and pornographic reenactment of the love interest in *Blade Runner* (dir. Ridley Scott, 1982) between the replicant Rachael and Rick Deckard, a human detective specializing in tracking down humanoids and who is cast into suspicion as a possible fellow Nexus 7 series replicant.[45] Their proxies in *I.K.U.* are Reiko and Dizzy, who repeat the scene's lines, such as "Say, 'kiss me'" and "I want you," before Dizzy initiates Reiko's *I.K.U.* system through oral sex, then activates her triple-X wrist chip by scanning it. She has the programmed mode to transform into seven bodies (appearance types A–G) in accordance with her counterpart's sexual desires. This first Reiko version returns only in the final scene, to be re-

3.3 Reiko leaving to collect ecstasy data after Dizzy has activated her (screen capture, *I.K.U.*, 2000, dir. Cheang Shu-Lea, UPLINK Co.).

tired after she gives Dizzy oral pleasure, and he uses a dildo gun extractor to get her collected ecstasy data (figures 3.3 and 3.4).

Only just before this final scene is Dizzy given a title card introduction as an "I.K.U. Runner (FTM) type," a "SALARYMAN@GENOM." The abbreviation of female-to-male transsexual as "FTM type" rhymes with Reiko's XXX type, and calls for scanners with inside knowledge about what this "FTM" detail actually tells. Cast as Dizzy is Zachary Nataf, a high-profile African American trans man who founded the London Transgender Film Festival in 1998; Nataf stars opposite Ayumu Tokitô, a Japanese cult film and porn actress. Katrien Jacobs notes that "Reiko's acceptance of Dizzy's unusual penis is carefully registered" by a steady shot that observes her salaciously licking at his microphallus and eliciting deep moans.[46] The hard metal–enclosed space of both encounters is lit in stark blue and red chiaroscuro, with the shadow of fan blades languidly passing over their perspiring bodies. It introduces a formalist reading method attentive to light and shade, it centralizes the scanner technology for orgasm data in the narrative, and it uses slow camera pans and the rhythm of longer takes to insert visually and aurally contemplative shots. The film's style invites scanning of elements (what is here) rather than of plot (what is happening), which is reinforced by the familiarity with another film's plot transposed onto a futuristic 2030 Japan (what is different

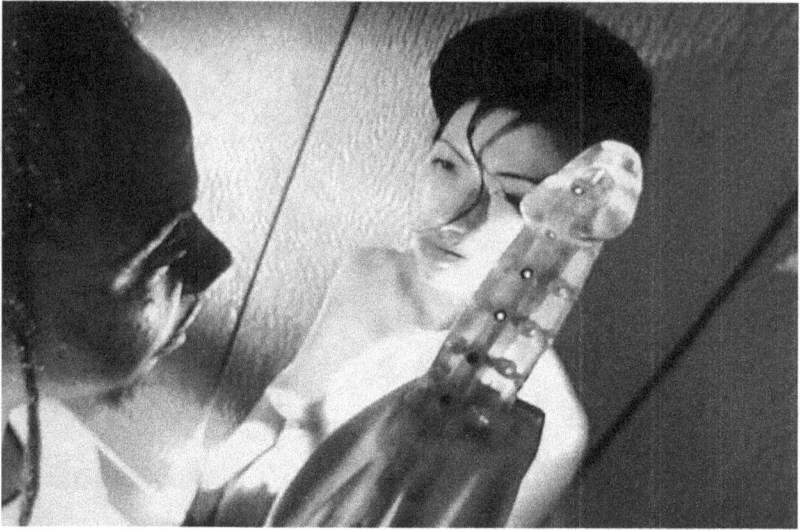

3.4 Dizzy preparing to extract ecstasy data from Reiko and retire her (screen capture, *I.K.U.*, 2000, dir. Cheang Shu-Lea, UPLINK Co.).

there). The viewer/analyst thus downloads the film like a webpage downloads the data that produce a visual field with clickable details we might "go into."[47] This scanning for detail is further embedded narratively in that each time Reiko goes out to collect data, the film restarts with a jump into a new avatar, signaled by a page with the player's info that appears to be "clicked" on and is emphasized with mouse click sound.[48] Rather than reveling in the new media convergence of computing culture with cultural logics of mass media, *I.K.U.*'s plot insists that the scanner reckon with the ways these bodily trans*formations are not seen as expressions of freedom (agency, desire, and diversity), for they are always under the control (command, programming, modulation) of the networked technologies of the GENOM Corporation.[49]

The scanner mentality also organizes how *Dandy Dust* repeatedly pauses to reshuffle or review events before starting again. "The film begins, again. Always again. Sometimes the film begins to begin again in the middle of the film, sometimes at the end. Sometimes it doesn't begin at all. Sometimes it just gestures to the beginning, as if to say, 'you lazy bastards out there in t.v. land, get off your butts and go start the film,'" collaborator Johnny de Philo writes in the catalog for *Dandy Dust*.[50] After the young Dandy Dust is shown in the opening shot before the ti-

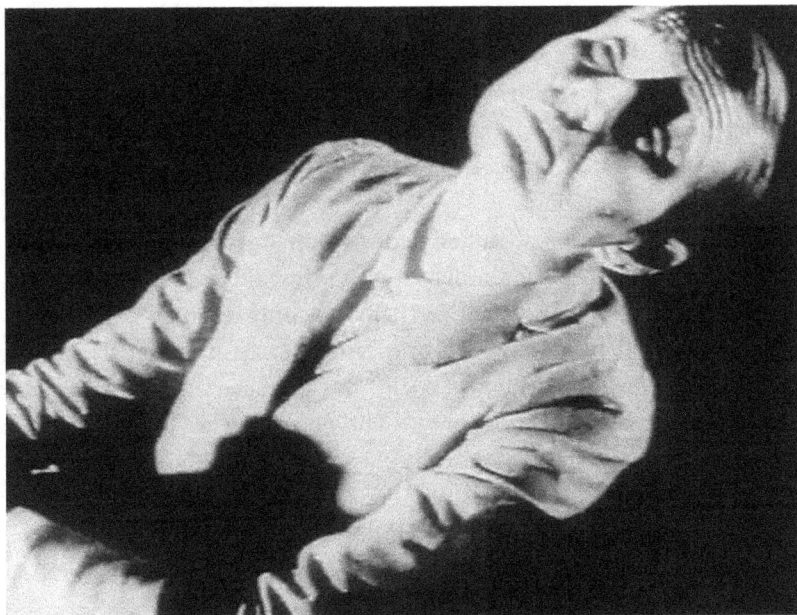

3.5 Older Dandy Dust rotating and contemplating within the void (screen capture, *Dandy Dust*, 1998, [Ashley] Hans Scheirl, Millivres Multimedia).

tle sequence, the next version—played by Scheirl in a tomboy/transboi aristocrat persona—appears for the first time in the film only in minute twelve. This character formation begins the journey the same way as the film instructs the viewer to "get off your butt." Rotating in a void, Dandy Dust seems to ponder the meaning of existence, while the narrator offers the advice: "Sometimes, when we know too much, we forget everything; Dust was bored from watching telly-vision" (figure 3.5).

Here to "know too much" means not knowing how to know new things, instituting a crisis of image perception. The protagonist suddenly notices a new planet flickering on the horizon and asks, "When did that grow? Let's go check it out!" Boredom cured in the instant of seeing a new planet and taking action, de Philo continues, sends Dust "flying into the projection screen of life, arms outstretched, whimsical and full of the kind of wonder only untamed horses and fashion models know is theirs for certain."[51] This is not a self-conscious wonderment, but a dispossessing curiosity that results from scanning the horizon until a tug of interest propels the film along and off on a quest to encounter that newness. Dandy thrice returns to a televisual monitor system to escape into a "trippy story" (read, disorienting and freeing) that consists of flashbacks of the present film told from other perspectives: an indication that curiosity "starts the film" over and again with an interest in scanning for newness like how one would zap channels looking for something good enough to cure boredom.[52]

From this scanning attitude I deduce a certain technical way of perceiving remixing televisual interest with filmic modes to decode which is more agential than imposed. In the film's companion text, "Manifesto for the Dada of the Cyborg-Embrio," Scheirl explains that the proper pronoun for *Dandy Dust* viewers and the characters is neither *she* nor *he*, but rather *cy*, short for cyborg.[53] The film's "ray" of attention has to be directed by the cyborg like "the electron ray, that builds up the TV-image in a few hundred stops per second," and the eye, "whose frantic micro movements paints [*sic*] the illusion of an image"; the ray of attention moves so fast from point to point across surfaces, layers, and dimension that it builds the "$n$dimensional space of experience."[54] Scanning is a participatory technology that constitutes the space and is not only about grasping the pre-formed elements of that space. The perspectival mode of scanning emphasizes how one's ray of attention not only connects with but also actively creates the image world through a cinematic process more akin to television channel zapping and internet webpage scrolling. Scheirl, along with many of his ensemble cast, was beginning to experiment with testosterone injections during filming, which resulted in female-bodied persons who often (yet not consistently) present as masculine, both on-screen and off.[55] The bold and obvious use of drag king dress for the father character Sir Sidore (Tre Temperilli), and for the gender-nonconforming characters of Super Mother Cyniborg XVII Duchess of Loft & Spire (Suzi Krueger) and twin siblings Mao and Lisa (Leonora Rogers-Wright), stresses the problem of reading for a true sex or gender attribution and activates instead a mode of scanning for details. The mixture of gender clues confounds a clear interpretative meaning, instead encouraging reflection on how a moustache or bare breasts, or bulging pants or short hair, function as affectively rich signs that might attach to father, mother, transboi, or dyke.

Scanning thus has a key role in close reading for nuance, traceable through the etymological root *nuer* ("to shade") from the old French *nue* ("cloud"), in the sense of scanning clouds for signs of imminent weather

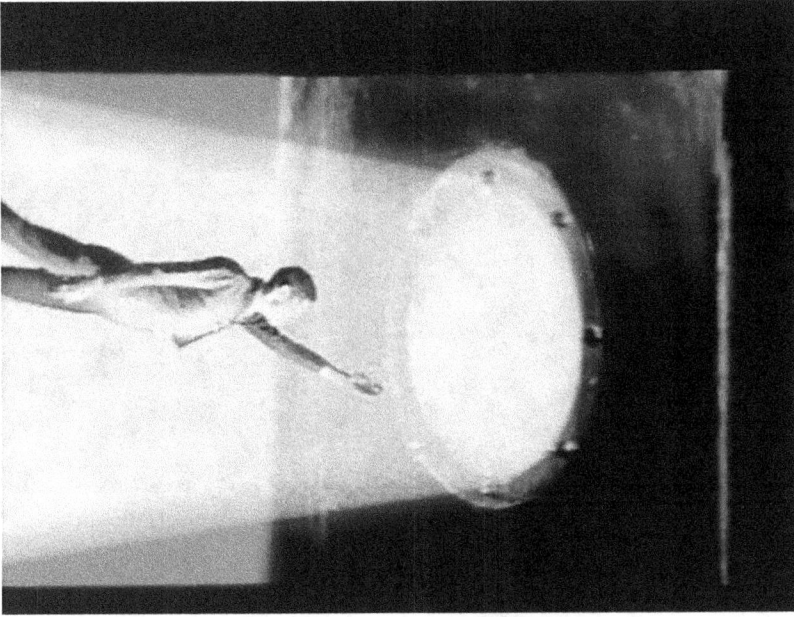

3.6 Dandy Dust flying into the movie (screen capture, *Dandy Dust*, 1998, [Ashley] Hans Scheirl, Millivres Multimedia).

or enjoying the play of light in the clouds. In Barthes's last writing exercise, *The Preparation of the Novel*, he returns to the life-long question of how style is the written practice of nuance, evincing a passion for difference that irradiates, diffuses, streaks (as a beautiful cloud streaks the sky).[56] The films float along a thin trail of plot, their contour realized by elaborate studio sets that stylize an exuberant mise-en-scène. Like the notion of a cloud that is visually alluring and yet shifts form, the atmosphere of the settings is saturated with a mobile, interpenetrating intensity of shade, color, depth, contrast (figures 3.6 and 3.7).

Filmic style can be compared to how Scheirl defines identity: the "cloud of the most probable whereabouts" for others and "the pattern written by the movements of the attention-ray" for oneself.[57] The cyborg character Dandy Dust appears as a dapper mid-1800s aristocrat, a dusty mummy, and a jaunty flame; the identity of the character is the interpenetration of these particles forming a dust cloud and with the dandy stylization of said cloud. The switch-mode between cy's appearances and between the seven versions of Reiko is unexplained; it is simply given as the

3.7 Tokyo Rose's Net Glass Show for businessmen (screen capture, *I.K.U.*, 2000, dir. Cheang Shu-Lea, UPLINK Co).

current or appropriate state-of-play for that part of the trip.[58] In restarting, scanning again, it is as though these films return to the "the scene of wild activities" in order to dip in to the void in the sense that Karen Barad gives: the void's raison d'être is for the "virtual exploration of all manner of possible trans*/formations" occurring like brain flashes.[59] The clouds moving, the lightning streaking, the charged atmosphere: these weather patterns write the films' affective stylization, calling for viewers/analysts to scan the sky for signs.

The ideal spectator for these films must look out and up to check for uncertain weather, but this interest is not returned. For humans, "the ability to be interested in the world" is so basic a function, says Sedgwick, that shame and disgust are the incomplete reduction or rejection of interest rather than an opposing polarity.[60] The interest-enjoyment scale is therefore a baseline kind of plug-in for other affects that might loop through a circuit into excitement, joy, humiliation, surprise-startle, or distress-anguish, forming a stretched line whose ends touch back to interest. Sedgwick and Frank point out that Tomkins finds a different place to begin than most psychologists of his day whose affect theories derive from fixed sexual and gender identities; instead he systematizes the drives and the affects that amplify them.[61] "The affect machine" Tomkins realizes, is a "separate but amplifying co-assembly" of the drives, effectively the directors of cognitive systems, because without the amplification of affects nothing matters, and with their amplification anything can matter.[62] Affective amplification is indifferent to the drive or object on which it works; it can recursively amplify itself without a referent, as in "it is enjoyable to enjoy," or "it is exciting to be excited" and so on. Not only does it not want for anything, or have a teleological output or outcome, it is also nonintentional. Formally, Tomkins's systems theory of affect introduces an absent center of human activity, behavior, and cognition, which lends itself to being mapped on to a formalist analysis of affects that amplify aesthetic elements and structures. In this regard I wish to expand on the methodologies of Shaviro and Brinkema by way of a systems theory for affect that will enliven my reading of the affective infrastructures of these films, without placing "me" at the center of their reading. As is my experience, the affective bodies of analyst and film may touch, but cinematic images run on a separate affect machine. It is to this machine that my attention is drawn, and it is by plugging into this machine that my sensorial-affective system becomes tinkered with in order to expand and exploit the virtual possibilities.

What then would entice the spectator to plug in to these cinematic perceptual schemata? The basic interest in the worlds of I.K.U. and Dandy Dust lies less in identification with wooden characters who form an absent center of emoting human subjects than in the puzzling abutment of oddly framed, angled, and scaled images, including of gender presentation, compounded by special effects and sound design. These are the hooks of the affect machine that might charge up levels of interest into a question of curiosity. These films invert the Enlightenment truism "to see is to know," establishing that the value of the passion for knowledge is to see whether "one can think differently than one thinks, and to perceive differently than one sees [. . .] instead of legitimating what is already known," as Michel Foucault describes the important intellectual risk of curiosity.[63] When cinephiles take this risk, as intimate, interested scanners of cinematic material, then they might stray afield from how they know their embodied selves.

Indistinct Cinematic Bodies:
Pixilated Pussy-Shots and a Transgendered Arsehole

The ungraspable quality of shimmering visual images is depicted in *I.K.U.* and *Dandy Dust* through a beguiling kaleidoscopic visuality that uses a mosaic of color, form, and scale. In each window on a sex scene in *I.K.U.* an actual digital pixilation and a composite audiovisual mosaic are used to depict the threshold from exterior to interior body cavities during sexual penetration, whether that be of a vagina or an anus. The space of the film worlds in *Dandy Dust* undulates along folds that collapse interior and exterior across the deathly Planet of White Dust, the incestuous Planet of Blood and Swelling, the bladder of Planet 3075, the time-traveling Mother-Ship in the shape of the uterus and fallopian tubes; a filmic trans*form that Scheirl calls "a transgendered arsehole!"[64] By critiquing the gendered notions of inside and outside, these films display a Pandora-type feminist curiosity to investigate what is hidden in the box.[65] Both cinematic bodies problematize the assumptions of a pure optical visuality that would judge a clear and distinct sex through vision's privileging of the externalized penis and a concomitant fear of the internal spaces into which one cannot or should not peer. The indistinct sex in these films is differentiated, just not into the form of male or nonmale; instead these cinematic bodies maintain a cyborgian switch-mode of forms comprising both/and that is displayed dazzlingly through the extensive use of in-camera and postproduction special effects. Through creating admittedly "unclear" sex pixels and gendered environments, the special effects that produce the streaking clouds of identity and the shifting scale of the body can be tracked. I argue that these films fail to appear properly in male or female sexed terms, and proffer in their indistinct and anally oriented trans*form a "transgender capacity" for perceiving differently, that is, not in accordance with dimorphic or binary assumptions and patterns.[66]

Sex is typically distinguished by referring to primary sexual characteristics of the genitals, and thus a critique of investing in a penile or vaginal heterosexual matrix might take the form of the indistinct anus. Guy Hocquenghem's analysis of the queer status of the anus salutes the gender-confusing and nonbinary possibilities of being "[s]een from behind," concluding, "the anus does not practice sexual discrimination."[67] The confusion of identity, which Hocquenghem elects to read in terms of neurosis and hysteria, might in today's intellectual environment be understood in nonpathologizing terms as a transgender capacity to trans*form. The switch-form possibilities activated by an anal perception, which I contend are at work in these films, engender confusion only if one tries to remain within the binary framework of either male or female. In *Abstract Bodies*, David J. Getsy suggests paying attention to previous unacknowledged instances of multiplicity and mutability in artistic forms that might cultivate these capacities, wherever they may be found, and not only at the site of proper trans bodies.[68] The emblem of a transgendered arsehole and the interior anus unlocks a virtual plane of multiplicity for gender and sexual identities; however, the trans* dimension of *I.K.U.* also relates explicitly to the hand-arm transformation into what might be called a "smart dildo" that is able to extract and memorize orgasm data. How does *I.K.U.*'s harnessing of an anal perception and phallic collecting tool demonstrate transgender capacity for switching modes that effects a trans*form moment?

The technological spectacle of Reiko's trans*formation and the data extraction appears in all of *I.K.U.*'s sex scenes and is the narrative motivation for those encounters with sex partners. The film takes on an explicitly machinic vision, shown from Reiko's perspective, signaled by typed instructional text about where to go and whom to target written out in computer command language. The *I.K.U.* coder's sexual partners of different genders and walks of life all appear entirely caught up in the heat of the moment when orgasm is approached, and they never acknowledge that Reiko's hand transforms from a fist into an extractive shaft—there is no reverse shot or close-up on their face that would suture a human connection to their experience. The graphic blur special effect at the site of penetration distorts the medium close-up of bodily interpenetration, then the sequence cuts to a digital morphing in anime style; a pinkish hand rotating and thrusting transforms in two stages into a live dildo-biotech tool. The animation technology simulates a nondescript interior bodily canal; Reiko's first encounter is with a middle-aged Japanese man in the sex/dance club *Harmony*; here on the main dance platform his rectum is entered during a three-way. Once his orgasm commences, the sequence cuts to a gridded data shot with a thumbnail picture of Reiko at the top left and in the middle a numerical uploading of the ecstasy data into the biodisc is graphically indicated.

I.K.U.'s hyperdigital game aesthetics recalls the special effects of its contemporary, the cyber-film *The Matrix* (dir. Lana and Lilly Wachowski, 1999), in which similar green-lit computer code appears to rain down in three dimensions and morphing is de rigueur.[69] Whereas the encoding of the maternal womb into the virtual is central to the narrative space of *The Matrix*, the sexualized digital environment of *I.K.U.* that the spectator plugs in to revises the cyberfeminist vns Matrix mantra from "the clitoris is the direct line to the matrix" to "the Pussy is the matrix."[70] The software-painted "pussy-shot" seems to achieve what Linda Williams claims is the ruse of pornography—visualizing female pleasure—leading to ever more spectacular substitutions of "the money shot" in which male ejaculate is captured in graceful slow motion, or leaping onto faces, spraying onto buttocks, and so on.[71] In fact Cheang's special effect pussy-shot is the same interior pleasure zone for any gendered character, human or android, the signal "inner" space the movie returns to regardless of "outer" appearance. Indeed, not just from behind are we all indiscriminately sexed, but inside our pleasure too lies a trans*formative capacity for suspending sexual polarity, so argues the film's formalist aesthetic. *I.K.U.*'s digital dick and pussy shots thus mobilize genital terms from pornography to critique its special effects for producing gender (such as cued or faked ejaculation). According to Jacobs, through the point-of-view pussy shot "we can observe the huge fantasy-object [digital dick]" entering a space that *I.K.U.* resolutely does not define as a female cavity or pleasure zone (figures 3.8 and 3.9).[72]

I see the pussy shot as offering a perceptual space of undifferentiated ecstasy data. The pause for the coder's memorization signals a study of sensation, "not as felt by moved bodies, but as wildly composed," to borrow Brinkema's phrase, in this specific cinematic special effect of mosaic pixilation.[73] The bodily transition each character undergoes with the assistance of Reiko's smart dildo has a distinctly composed form of sensation that is also numerically comparable, quantifiable, and reproducible. The special effect composition presents sensation differentiable in degrees of intensity and memorability, but tamable into a consumable, differentiated form of the *I.K.U.* brand of *iku* (行く), slang for "coming." Despite the hard-core aspects, Cheang has stated, "I did not make this film for masturbation. I made it for collective orgasm," airing a political ambition to break down individualizing of forms through sexuality and corporate capitalism. With a movie format that references multiuser game consoles, Cheang bets on the ability of technology to link multiple users

3.8 Reiko's female victim before her orgasm during the young lovers' scene (screen capture, *I.K.U.*, 2000, dir. Cheang Shu-Lea, UPLINK Co).

together in a quest for political collectivity signaled by the Japanese word *iku* that indicates an impending, arriving sexual climax. Semantically the refrain "I'm coming" in this film's orgiastic scenes of sex, always with multiple partners (mainly group sex, and Reiko is herself multiple forms), also reads as a welcome sign for "joining in" the sexual pleasure.[74] What exactly we'd be getting into is another thing altogether, for the visualization of ecstasy is determinedly undifferentiated by gender markers.

Digital pixilation or blurring is typically used to disguise someone because of privacy concerns, and yet *I.K.U.* brandishes this operational mode for the close-up shots of only some genitals, a nod to how a blur is typically used in Japanese pornography to censor pubic hair, vulvas, and penetration. That the film does not obey the legal code in its entirety, lingering clearly on bushy mounds and women receiving oral sex, implies the technical choice is to critique how the aesthetics of the blur operates in this cultural context. According to the *I.K.U.* website, "The *I.K.U.* data is made up of visual and voice data in mosaic" that are scrambled enough to produce the effect of indistinct sounds and images of a general and generic Japanese porn flick. Although the film's tagline is "This is not LOVE. This is SEX," one could also claim that "This is DATA BITS," or that sex is really just the mingling of bits. The pixilation itself becomes excit-

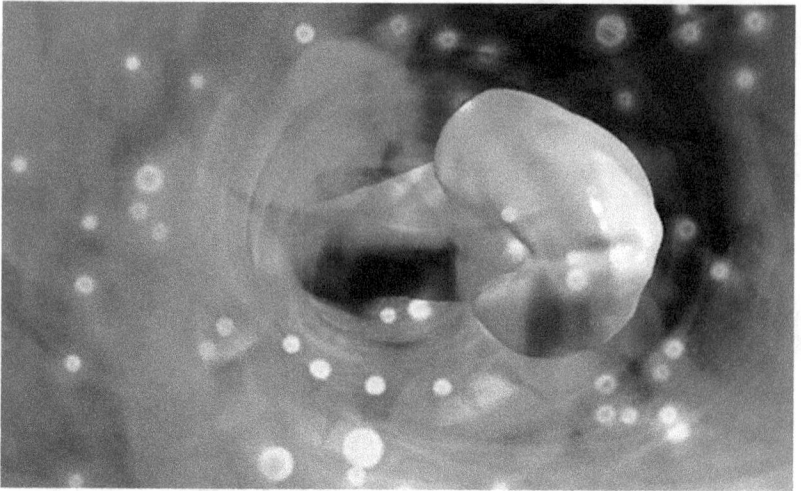

3.9 The "pussy-shot" during the young female lover's orgasm (screen capture, *I.K.U.*, 2000, dir. Cheang Shu-Lea, UPLINK Co).

ing, the moment of auto-affection when it is enjoyable to enjoy the rapid mixture of color and the rising cacophony of voices—intensification that one can drop in to. That *I.K.U.* sex conscripts the mutation of Japanese antipornography legislation of obscured sexual intercourse into the circuit of desire means that the mosaic convention has now become a trigger for sexual arousal. "That is to say that Japanese people have made themselves into an exceptional nation which is aroused by mosaic," in Cheang's words.[75] An experimental trip-hop soundtrack by Hoppy Kamiyama, whose most distinguishable English lyrics are "nice to meet you," further amplifies this fetish for psychedelic distortion. Like the whirling white noise in *Dandy Dust*'s clanging void, the high-pitched repetition of "nice to meet you" signals an endless set of virtual possibilities, namely for every meeting to lead to sexual exchange. The GENOM Corporation is the end recipient though, which makes each sexual encounter between human and humanoid rather more one-sided and akin to a data rape.[76] The implied violation of stealing someone's ecstasy data, commoditizing it, and selling it in vending machines for others to consume (in a bullet-shaped capsule no less) is the stark backdrop to enjoying techno-porno bodies who enjoy. The implication for just enjoying the enjoyment is that sex involves willing victims and customers. "Desire only exists when assembled or machined," writes Deleuze.[77] Cinephiles know this: cinesexuality is not about the actual sex on the screen, but in extending the circuit of desire through plug-in possibilities for the spectator, who can access the "nice to meet you" spaces for their own transing practices.

Where the fragmented cityscape of a futuristic Toyko in *I.K.U.* is actually transversed by the coder on the back of a motorbike, in chauffeured van, and by the metro, *Dandy Dust*'s planetary system scales up the spatial dimensions and uses time travel and spaceships to move along its organs, capillaries, and pockmarked surfaces. Stronger still, there is no naturalistic setting in *Dandy Dust*; the film was shot using low-tech means in a gutted building with built-to-scale sets. The wholly imaginary places conjured require imaginary means to get in to them. Dandy leads the way by taking drugs to alter consciousness, having dreams and nightmares to model cinematic ways to plug in.[78] The produced effect of rapidly shifting dimensions of scale is a result of a heady technical package of cinematographic effects. One reviewer in *Variety* compiles formats and tactics that include "frozen frames, fast-mo, tinting, B&W, 8mm, vid, clay/cut-outs/stop-motion animation, image distortion, multiple-image layering, doll-manipulation, miniature landscape models, plus plenty of simulated sex and yecchy, if patently fake, body-fluid 'gore.'"[79] This is only on the visual level; as in *I.K.U.* the soundscape is an equally challenging pastiche of found sounds, varied music such as punk and Strauss's "The Blue Danube," and "blatantly" postsynched dialogue that uses voice distortion that the reviewer says "further confounds the gender-unpinnable nature of characters."[80] Compared to the hi-tech value and feel of *I.K.U.*'s graphic, cool UPLINK production blown up to an impressive 35 mm aspect ratio, *Dandy Dust*'s kaleidoscopic vision is more like a riotous trip—it overloads and experiments with size to see whether it might get us to go somewhere.

The interest in multiplicity is not just philosophical, then; it is bound up with the aesthetics of rapid change that runs through the film at all levels: set and costume design, sound score, characters, and cinematography. The orientation to space therefore becomes ever more pressing in order to try to get a grip on the film. In *The Ecological Approach to Visual Perception*, James Gibson anchors the textural experience of images in their enveloping environs. Gibson suggests that vision in general entails far more than the anatomical structure of the eye, describing a kinesthetic vision that "registers movements of the body just as much as does the muscle-joint-skin system and the inner-ear system," and that this vision involves a relay with the felt environment, a process he terms "ecological" perception.[81] By attuning to the space, this sort of haptic visuality locates the perceiver *within* an environment, perceiving the significance of surfaces in relation to one's body. In Anne Rutherford's astute reading of Gibson for cinema experience, she suggests this perception is "more akin to a millipede than to a camera or camera obscura—a thousand tentacles feeling their way through a space rather than a single lens taking it in view."[82] Scheirl, who facetiously or not identifies as an insect and litters *Dandy Dust* with creepy crawly bugs, teases the spectator into becoming an insect like a millipede, fly, or earworm in order to trespass, slither, and fly through the filmscape's archly differentiated worlds.[83] In no particular order, the film world moves from the menacing parental lodgings on the Planet of Blood and Swelling, to the bloody laboratory of the flying Mother-Ship, and into Planet 3075's neon cybernetic bladder, in which naked, sucking hermaphroditic beings live connected by tubes diffusing nectar. The cinematic construction of such worlds in the aesthetics of a humid and lived corporeality maps *Dandy Dust*'s "filmscape" as a "bodyscape" consisting in outside cutaneous surfaces, inside body cavities, only to protrude out again. The oscillating dominant affects of boredom, curiosity, fear, and arousal associated with certain times and places only partly account for the constant fluctuations of the scale of space.

Scheirl likens the rapid movements across these spaces to a tight-ringed doughnut, infinitely folding "in/out/side insideout" to create "a transgendered arsehole!"[84] Embracing fleshy folds that seem gender-full rather than gender-less, Scheirl declares *Dandy Dust*'s corporeal scale to follow "the politics of bulge and cavity," in contradistinction to the dimorphic and binary pattern of the present penis or the absent vagina.[85] Grasping the film as a space of multiplicity emerging from the "arsehole" does not cancel out the other sexualized forms in the bodyscape. It revels in the sexually indistinct and refuses the imperative to maintain the self as singular. In the manifesto, and manifestly in *Dandy Dust*, embodied selves are reframed as a "complex system of inwards & outwards bulging hyrarchical [sic] identities with the potential to blow up to pieces."[86] This shimmering vision of transgender capacity to morph and undulate in peristaltic movements embraces the trans*form of bodily uncertainty. The raucously composed narrative that dances along this changing bodyscape flaunts a both/and calculus of identity parts.

Going D@d@:
Avant-Garde Decapitations

A dada interest in the body-in-pieces and the cybernetic collecting of data bits fuse in these audiovisual explorations of going "d@d@," an arty cyberpunk term made up by Scheirl in his manifesto. Death by fragmentation punctuates each film: death by decapitation is the spectacular fate of two raping men (a monk and Dandy's father) in *Dandy Dust* and *le petite mort* (orgasm deaths) befall all of Reiko's victims, who are left limply unconscious after being pixilated. The profuse use of simulated sex and death in *I.K.U.* and *Dandy Dust* draws on traditions from avant-garde filmmaking that announce a critical "adversariness" toward bourgeois society and a defiant attitude toward sexual mores.[87] Dada film experiments with developed vocabularies of revolt attuned to a cinematic audiovisuality that would capture sensation of physical movement, succession in time, and playfulness with cinematic codes for narration.[88] Next to poking the eye with shocking scenes of sex and death, these films exploit the impact of overproduced sound and the rearrangement of temporal conventions for self-hood, and defy narrative conventions for plot points in order to introduce decisive cuts into the usual circuits of perception and rewire the links between memory and clichéd images.

As one of the founding practitioners of Zurich-based dadaism, Marcel Janco stated that dada tendencies could be clocked "at two speeds": destructive and constructive, one militaristic and ballistic and the other overcoming static and mimetic conventions.[89] Dada at two speeds is an inherently cinematic arts movement in that new techniques such as the collage, cut-ups, assemblage, and photomontage all exercise cinematic methods for delinking and relinking perception. Thomas Elsaesser advances the notion that dada is reactive, in that it seeks means for "radically short-circuiting" how (art) objects acquire financial, social, and spiritual values, by embracing the "degraded nature" of the film spectacle.[90] The added degradation of the transcoding at work in transfers of electronic video to film exposes the impossibility of absolute fidelity; it can also, as in *Dandy Dust*, celebrate the distortion, breakdown, corruption as generative and productive of poignant moments forming around an erratically destabilized audiovisual image.[91] But the real aim of dada is the tyranny of the eye and total vision, Elsaesser explains. Resulting from inventions and apparatus for new means of representation and reproduction that came at the end of the nineteenth century, this tyrannical eye, dada artists gambled, could be gouged out by the "waste products" of its apotheosis in the moving picture—an anticontemplative cinematic perception engaged by slapstick and other popular genres.[92] In the face of the militaristic modernization that surged during World War I, avant-garde filmmakers reflected on how to live with death machines—a cyborg query at heart. It is small wonder that a classic dada film like *Entr'acte* (dir. René Clair, 1924) crosscut a runaway hearse with a roller coaster ride; the lifeless is converted into a frenzied composition of mechanical excitement.

If going gaga is about losing control and no longer being in possession of one's faculties, then going d@d@ adds a critical and technological cutting edge to loss of control. Created at the close of the twentieth century with reference to the new representational apparatus of TV, video games, net-porn, and genetic engineering, the model and metaphor of dada operative within *I.K.U.* and *Dandy Dust* places pressure on a totalizing psychic, erotic, and economic apparatus controlled by a dark state. The plots revolving around exploitative, nonconsensual practices of collecting human bits clearly stage anxieties about personal integrity. Dandy's overarching quest to learn about cy's "pedigree" is thwarted first by the twins, who forcibly remove cy's memory disc (from a brain hard drive), and second by mother Cyniborg's genetic engineering experiments to tamper with the family line. She recaptures Dandy, "my baby," from the pretentious pleasures of art school in an attempt to finish a genealogical experiment in her day care–cum–laboratory filled with body parts. Here the mutant family members rehabilitate their pasty white skin (badly slathered with cake makeup) with blood from fresh-killed babies (spurting from fountains at a dinner table), eyeballs attached to flies whiz by, human lips are stitched shut, and eventually Dandy is tortured with injections from oversized tools that suggest IVF needles. The genetic engineering of Reiko, who has no memories of her own, makes her a good foot soldier for the corporate theft of pleasure experience; she is a kind of compatriot of the seemingly blank, emptied Dandy. Both protagonists are decapitated by a loss of memory and personal agency—without any human rationalization they collect that which they do not have at the command of sinister, brutalizing forces. These twisted d@d@ plots revolving around stolen and traumatic memories recalls the use of the irrational by the dada art movement to critique the rationality of war, violence, and docility toward the state.

Reiko and Dandy's actual and metaphorical demise is shown to be far from a final termination. Although Reiko is retired with great fanfare by Dizzy's penetrating extraction gun, "Ending no. 1" shows her riding on the back of a scooter (driven by MASH, a retired girl orgasm coder who helps Reiko), and from one cut to the next they are out of the city and riding through the bucolic countryside to meet Dizzy, and perhaps to live happily ever after. ("Ending no. 2" reconstructs the same ending but to meet a beefy Asian gay male character, offering a sexual choice to the coupling.) The dead or alive plot twist in *Dandy Dust* features a theatrical "revelation" that all the other characters were played by Dandy (Scheirl in masked costume), which, while not the case, hilariously multiplies readings of how far-reaching the distribution of cy's cloud identity might be. Cy is also reanimated through the effect of a digital multiplication, shown in a video screen duplication of four, then eight, then sixteen, then twenty-four selves. Using the fantastical bent of dada that stretches back to the Méliès-type trickality (from chapter 1), the metaphoric decapitation and the reanimation of the protagonists indicate that death is merely a successive state to life. The switch-mode of life-death should not be considered binary, but a kind of on-off oscillation controlled by flickering frames. With screen deaths leading to screen births of the cy-embrio, death becomes another means for the multiplication of the self into different forms. "Only where there are multiple identities, fear of identity termination fades," writes Scheirl, citing virtual multiplicity in his reasoning for the aesthetic use of this technique.[93] The switch-mode between life-death is in step with millennial aesthetics of change that undermine the notion of one long-lasting gendered self. The temporality underpinning trans*form aesthetics is sequential and therefore multiple, comprising a set of "successive states of personhood" that Getsy conceptualizes for the ways that continuity persists in the same form or material despite reworkings.[94] In going d@d@, the self becomes a patchwork of successive states, with patch-ins and rebooting potential: so much for the finality of death.

Structurally the films both posit for autoeroticism a key role in rebooting after the loss of sensation/memory/agency, suggesting that sexuality is a reservoir for switch-form capacities and an antidote to death. In *I.K.U.* after Reiko C has smart dildo sex with Tokyo Rose (a peep show sex worker replicant), she becomes corrupted with a virus planted by a competing corporation. The film then cuts to Reiko naked in a white tub of water placed in an empty, sterile environment; she first presses on her navel switch and then masturbates to reset her system. Compactly, the film inserts an erotic switch-mode that patches over the problem of viral contamination, a sex-positive response to the haunting of sex by death in the age of the HIV virus. Autoeroticism in *Dandy Dust* also refers to a futuristic setting in order to rewrite the past, but results in accelerating cy's going d@d@. The historical setting is a European mansion circa 1780, in which the character "Spider-Cuntboy" (played by trans man Svar Simpson) visits Dandy in cy's bedroom late at night. Waking Dandy by stimulating cy's genitals, Spider-Cuntboy takes Dandy time-travelling to see a future self in order to speed up cy's sexual development. The masculine Dandy of the eighteenth century observes the Dandy of 3075: a breasted figure among other short-haired and breasted beings, naked on all fours, being filled by fluorescent tubes of fluid. Spider-Cuntboy remarks, "Dandy was so shaken by seeing his sexually-fluid self that he went nuts!" (figures 3.10 and 3.11).

Heavy, distorted techno music carries over from the future to the past, connecting temporal worlds through a sound bridge. The self-pleasuring scene, starring the future Dandy, initiates the uneducated Dandy's acting out of lasciviousness, including masturbatory rubbing on a tree, then rubbing food into cy's crotch at a fancy dinner party with dragged-up "ladies" and "gentleman." Eventually Dandy's bursting sexual feelings dangerously activate father Sir Sidore's lust, who finds Dandy copulating with a (sculptural) horse in the stable, puts on a screw-shaped codpiece, and "nails" Dandy in a gory rape homage to the Japanese horror-flick of *Tetsuo II—Body Hammer* (dir. Shinya Tsukamoto, 1992). The edited sequences following from *Dandy Dust*'s first autoerotic scene diverts the affective intensity of arousal from bodies into liquid flows. It locates it in the flashing red blood pumping the animated familial house, which seems to wash over from the flow of nectar and wets the stain on Dandy's white pants, then erupts in the spill of a party drink that later splatters even further in the burst of Sir Sidore's brains at the end of Dandy's pistol. Conceptually the dada dimension of the film's editing makes over desire into a spurting event. In both cases the self-touching transmutes the event of sexual activity into aggregate states of intensities through the acts of division, transposition, assemblage, and intermittencies of cinematic images.[95]

Affects also gel in the sounds of sex and death; like the head and the

3.10 Dandy Dust on Planet 3075, plugged into tubes of nectar (screen capture, *Dandy Dust*, 1998, [Ashley] Hans Scheirl, Millivres Multimedia).

eyes, the affects become disturbingly dislocated from the body. These filmmakers exploit the nonsynchronous possibility of a film's two tracks, especially bombarding the images of what passes for sex with an intensified sound layer. In *Dandy Dust* the physically halting and hokey rape scene is made difficult by the turned-up noise of a punk song, whose distortions clang and creepily repeat "Daddy! Daddy!" Although you can close your eyes, the assault to the ears is impossible to block. *I.K.U.* also uses overproduced sounds of moans, slurps, sucks, and smacks that effectively turn up the volume of the sex acts to a discomforting and disturbing level, so that the implied sexual activity teeters from arousing to gross to laughable. The intense self-reflexivity of these films registers as well in the heavy-handed use of lenses, like the fish-eye and tilting camera work in *I.K.U.* that visually distorts kissing and petting, and the flashes, dissolves, and time/date registration on *Dandy Dust*'s video images that announce "this is a movie." This highly self-referential and constant pointing to the filmic apparatus as illusion-producing machine shows an attachment to dada techniques for experimenting with cinematic codes.

3.11 Dandy Dust from circa 1780 reacting to seeing cy-self on Planet 3075 (screen capture, *Dandy Dust*, 1998, [Ashley] Hans Scheirl, Millivres Multimedia).

The ramped-up audio and visual tracks institute an ironic tone toward the use of clichéd images, which seem presented solely for the opportunity to "scrub" them in the manner Deleuze claims painter Francis Bacon attacks and peels back banalities of figure and form.[96] Stripped down to their core d@d@ nonsense, sex and death become the sweaty and messy business of fragmented bits crushing together and falling apart.

The perception under pressure is of sex and gender arrangements, though challenging racial alignments to these historical arrangements also plays a part. Dandy's changing appearance in terms of gender presentation, alive or dead, at different ages and with different racial characteristics, asserts a cloud mentality that de-essentializes identity traits, including race. Dizzy's status as the face of the corporation, the sole FTM, and the only non-Asian person of color in the film's world makes him remarkable, yet he is unremarked upon by any character or shot.[97] The seeming inclusivity of the racial economy of the *I.K.U.* product is further emphasized in a scene with a pill-popping white couple with British accents and a glamorously cross-dressed (gay?) Japanese couple, who equally yen for a sexual high as much as anyone else in the Japanese market. In the vein of avant-garde filmmaking that reacts against purity politics and rejects ontological suppositions, the use of mixed media, mixed race, indistinct gender, and the heterogeneity of their signifiers demands an acknowledgment of how bodies and perception can be rearranged.⁹⁸ An avant-garde approach to the sometimes of identity and to successive states of personhood introduces a chronopolitics dedicated to multiplicity. I believe that the disconnection of succession from progress introduces a sense of gender "transitional time" in which numerous movements become equally possible, as dance scholar Julian Carter posits from a choreography studies perspective.⁹⁹

The double ending of *I.K.U.* and *Dandy Dust*'s ending that begins to end at least five times (counting by the signal chord of the theme song) open out along the folds of the sticky asterisk in trans*form. The last image before the credit sequence is of Dandy Dust back in the shimmering void, that super projection screen of life that makes possible the contradictions of cy's multiple chimeric identities. Pants down around ankles, squatting with bottom in the air, a flower dart thrust into cy's anus, Dandy Dust blathers nonsense in between bursts of laughter. Cy gestures the viewer to join, "Come to me baby," only then to grab at the figurines of father and mother, of Sir Sidore and Cyniborg. The high irony of Haraway's manifesto ricochets back into the film's formal performance of ending: "Irony is about contradictions that do not resolve into larger wholes, even dialectically, about the tension of holding incompatible things together because both or all are necessary and true."¹⁰⁰ The films provide affective patches of arousal, fear, disgust, and an interest pumped up to curiosity in order to bear the tension of these "incompatible things" in their odd, if not ironic, d@d@ rearrangements of cinematic bodies.

Rage against the Machine:
Deforming the Schemata and Becoming Planes of Shimmerings

In the afterword to "Cinematic Bodies," Brinkema draws on the opening language of Ovid's *Metamorphoses* to expound on the multiplicities of bodies and the cinematic, of how they might be closely read, and of how they proliferate: "*As though the cinema were a machine ready to tell* *of bodies, changed to different bodies, changed to other forms.*"[101] These machined, engineered cinematic bodies, suspended between life/death switch-modes, are only uneasily postgender. They might accomplish the shock, thrill, or bafflement of gendered, racialized, species switch-forms. The plugged-in cinematic perception might rewire common sense into a somatechnical apparatus of alternative circuits of experiences, traditions, and knowledges. These cinematic changes to other forms do, as I have argued, place pressure on the symbolic stability of the human, with its underpinning racial grammars. But I want also to note the privilege of invoking the rhetorics of "turns," for the regimes of humanism, colonialism, and animalism are not over for some so-called postsubjects.[102] "Should we not should be suspicious of postmodern critiques of the 'subject' when they surface at a historical moment when many subjugated people feel themselves coming to voice for the first time?," queries bell hooks in reference to postmodern invocations of the end of blackness.[103] As Zakiyyah Iman Jackson notes, "calls to become 'post' or move 'beyond the human' too often presume that the originary locus of this call, its imprimatur, its appeal, requires no further examination or justification but mere execution of its rapidly routinizing imperative."[104] I want to resist the imperative to align exploding, limp, and severed bodies with a violent vision of postgender or posthuman consciousness. The expansion of common sense should not necessarily require the violent erasure of some bodies, even as it dissolves the stable forms of any body in particular. Hence, in closing, I address the multiple dimensions of violence inhering in the cinematic worlds and worlding of cinematic bodies—or, put simply, the rage against multiple violences faced by the trans*forming subject that become directed as rage against the machinations of gender and creatively dispersed throughout—shot through—the cinematic worlds of these films.

Let me return us once more to the void. In the voidlike spaces of these films, curiosity's driving force outward is limned with a rage against the ideological apparatus of transphobia that all too commonly plugs into racism and gender compliance mechanisms. Stryker has described transphobia as "a primordial fear of monstrosity, or loss of humanness" because it is difficult for some cisgender people to "recognize the humanity of another person if they cannot recognize that person's gender"; I would add that racial otherness compounds (if not instigates) this gut-level fear.[105] Cyborgian motifs in media representations often dovetail with the perceived threat of gender-changing persons, which justifies responses of hatred, outrage, panic, or disgust being channeled into discriminatory actions aimed at the perceived not-fully-human. The (implied) emotional and physical violence present in these avant-garde films therefore risk reinforcing the stigmatizing common sense about the inhumanity of chimeric monsters. The combination of affective forms that layer curiosity with rage and (self-)love, I argue, deforms the powerful hold of fear toward gender-changing cyborgs that remains present in contemporary cultures through trans exclusionary discourse and measures.

Through my close readings of films that tap into premillennial anxieties, this chapter faces the unavoidable confluence of the cyborgian technophobia with transphobic images of trans*life, particularly in the surgically and hormonally altered form. More than twenty years on, Haraway reflects on how the cyborg was "the despised place" of feminists circa 1980 because of its association with technocratic masculinist rationality and militarism.[106] The cyborg world of partial identification and contradiction therefore represented a terrifying, hopeless place to be feared for its system failures, dangerous viral contagion, and leaky boundaries. This fear continues to be expressed in transphobic tracts underwritten by technophobic approaches in (lesbian) feminist thinking about gender transitions, including early accounts by Mary Daly, Janice Raymond, and Bernice Hausman that are reprocessed and extended by Sheila Jeffries, Elizabeth Grosz, Germaine Greer, Julie Bindel, and more. In sum: they castigate any articulation of self beyond the sex assigned at birth as a scientifically duped fantasy, which paints trans figures into the mutant, scarred, necrophilic distortion of the cyborgian body. "Despising can rediscern its target," writes Jackie Orr in her reflection on Haraway's "A Cyborg Manifesto"; and for trans exclusionary radical feminists (TERFS) the monster may have changed name, but the affective apparatus for despising cyborgian types triggered by the fear of broken social bonds just as powerfully marshals hate toward trans persons.[107] Although Haraway declared that the despised place is no longer the cyborg, the reuniting of religious right and TERFS as bedfellows against trans rights to access toilets and other necessary services indicate that the anxiety that discerns trans*formations as "all bad" baldly persists.[108] To this fear of a "postgender" world, curiosity may be a survival tool for thinking "about a world without gender as we know it."[109] Curiosity thus must be turned away from stultifying relations that mark out a curious object, toward a trans*feminist curiosity about the mechanisms for differencing and how they might work otherwise.

Curiosity's life-making property, Sue Golding (a.k.a. Johnny de Philo) submits, comes from its power for trans*formative thinking: "It is amazing how people have survived some horrible things, and one of the things that have actually made them survive is curiosity, that is thinking the most famous radical question of all: Supposing that it could be otherwise?"[110] Golding's acknowledgment of the need to survive any range of "horrible things" suggests that curiosity is an affective technique borne of difficulty. Cinematic processes might play a special role in facilitating curiosity because of their ability to tear a real image from clichés, "an operation that breaks the sensory-motor link and extends a perception not into motor action, but into thought."[111] The violence suggested in the tearing is potentially a response to the ways that clichés recycle and thereby normalize into common sense images with horrible, stigmatizing (in short, violent) connotations. For example, Keeling's analysis of how anti-Black colonial mentalities become mapped on to cinematic reality draws insight into how rage can tear into clichés: in Frantz Fanon's words quoted by Keeling, "in order to shatter the hellish cycle, [the Black viewer] explodes."[112] It seems that in order to wield curiosity as a survival tool for thinking otherwise ("to extend a perception into thought"), a furious rage must identify the epistemological gridding of those conditions for arriving and appearing legible that need exploding. Trans fury fuels the deformation of perceptual schemata, namely the "highly gendered regulatory schemata that determine the viability of bodies" that Stryker identifies as what trans people are compelled to transgress in their transing practices. On the one hand, it is emotionally "imperative to take up, for the sake of one's own continued survival as a subject, a set of practices that precipitates one's exclusion from a naturalized order of existence," but on the other hand, transgender rage "furnishes a means for disidentification with compulsorily assigned subject positions."[113] Through the operation of rage, Stryker cites a trans*formational power to move through the field of deformation into which one has been outcast, and to seek to deform it in turn; she pronounces that "the stigma itself becomes the source of transformative power."[114]

In Stryker's "My Words to Victor Frankenstein above the Village of Chamounix: Performing Transgender Rage," these highly gendered regulatory schemata that organize antitrans logics are imaged poetically in the form of shimmering planes of watery light. To abandon the unbearable everyday images of herself—"self-mutilated deformity, a pervert, a mutant"—the essay turns from theory to the fantastic realm of a waking dream.[115] The sensation of being trapped in monstrous flesh, she suggests, feels like being trapped underwater. Desperate for air, she swims up toward the "shimmering light" dancing on the surface, only to break through and find more water pressing on her body, choking her: "Inside and out I am surrounded by it."[116] Describing the experience in first-person narration, Stryker becomes a swimmer caught in the ceaseless motion of gender's ubiquitous waters. She encounters infinite planes of this shimmering surface light that promises and denies release from the weighted water, caught up in an endless *mise-en-abyme* of life-sustaining possibilities that forever seem out of reach. The drama of the scene is derived from the swimmer's desire to survive elsewhere and then vowing to embrace the annihilating image that surrounds her: "*I will become the water* / [. . .] I am groundless and boundless movement. / I am a furious flow."[117] This "act of magical transformation" rendered by intensifying rage materializes the swimmer as a fluid form, identified with the flow across shimmering planes.[118] The act of identification with the shimmering surface provides the trans body with the material form of the wave. The final lines, "In birthing my rage, / my rage has rebirthed me," offer insight into how sensations and affects beget form even at the site of collapsed generic categories.[119] In this field of deformation and fury, becoming the shimmer is a means to outplay the paradigm.

"Performing Transgender Rage" in 1993 was one way to explode the essentialist and reductionist myths of gender that Gordene O. Mackenzie likens to the post-Newtonian paradigm shift that led to the discovery by the Hubble telescope of at least 50 billion galaxies. During the approach toward the third millennium, Mackenzie confidently cited an expanding gender universe in which "the transgender liberation movement is causing a 'wobbling orbit' where a smaller body (trans movement) is exerting a gravitational pull on a larger mass (society), causing the larger mass to change its orbit."[120] From the vantage point of an increasingly established field of transgender studies it might be hard to grasp what transgender rage has materialized, what kinds of thinking otherwise have been curiously pondered. My chapters here have each tried to demonstrate the rich, complex, contradictory fields of thinking trans-inter-queer linkages otherwise through the media associated to cinematic perception, from the phantasmagoric cultural series onward to digital video. Even the optical device of the Hubble telescope seems ripe for shifting trans* awareness and connections!

If trans*formative politics is to continue causing a wobbling orbit, then it requires a theoretically incisive understanding of the shimmer whose interpretation evolves with changing intellectual climates that find new nuances in the shapes and shades written in the clouds. Brinkema's conclusion that "[t]aking forms and affects as mutually consequent, reading for their shaping of each other, instructs us in a lesson about the possibility for the new, the not-yet vitality of both form and affectivity," ultimately calls for a lesson about the virtual.[121] As I have presented it, the virtualities of cinematic tracks to form disjunctions, glitches, degradations, and to extend cultural series into unforeseen directions, always harbor the ticking time bomb that might explode the past clichés in the present moment of recursively editing our collective memory.

Whereas Deleuzian understandings of multiplicity's virtual dimension press on the categorizations of kinds of multiplicities that take place in a generalized field, according to Barad quantum field theory helpfully clarifies how this space has the qualities of the void, in that it is *an endless exploration of all possible couplings of virtual particles, a 'scene of wild activities.'"*[122] What is cinema if not this scene of wild activities, the multiple and varying interactions among indifferently defined images and bodies, those activities generating, in Shaviro's words, "degrees of stillness and motion, of action and passion, of clutter and emptiness, of light and dark"? Returning to Stryker's poem about moving through shimmering planes, Barad replaces the swimmer metaphor caught within the gender schemata with her own intercutting of an electron in the void. The sense of dimension is toyed with in scaling down from the human swimmer in water to the electron in the void, both at the seeming mercy of waves. The effect is to sense the expansive and generative possibilities of "raging nothingness," as it "trans*figures fleshly possibilities": "*I am [a] wave [a raging amplitude, a desiring field surging, being born]*" she co-writes.[123] That light can be both a wave and a particle reminds us that its shimmering manifests as a both/and event: in its happening, shimmering is immaterial and material, surface and substance, a puzzling neutrality of this and that depending on the angle of one's gaze. On the cinematic projection screens of life, shimmering images beckon virtual aggregations wherein a "we" of a cinematic ensemble perchance comes together.

CONCLUSION

An Ensemble of Shimmers

n this adventure of following the shimmering light and its watery shimmers, I've attended to that which baffles the binary paradigm by seeming to confound its strictures, confuse its terms of engagement, or flummox the net that tries to capture meaning. In so doing, my attention landed within three arenas of great shimmering activity that outplay the dominant either/or paradigm for engendering meaning: the *aesthetic* with its gradations and intensities that register the nuance of difference, the swath of *gender* that binds and undoes subjects depending on the angle of the gaze or the angle of the room's atmosphere, and finally the *affects* that pulse within passionate structures and form circuitous loops through subjective perception. The chapters moved through inventorying the shimmering intelligibility of filmic and bodily surface, historically marked practices of light, and their engendering technological apparatus. In each I have tried to parse how shimmering images can conceptually accomplish a turn to the more-than-visuality, form an analytic lens, and become a critical practice for affirming transitional and nonbinary modes. That shimmering cinematic images are a norm in, rather than an exception to, perceiving these modes was harnessed to the project of transgender studies. Tackling the way transness has been privileged as a site of exceptional change, my parlay of shimmering images throughout the chapters was to show the steady or halting, but nonetheless ongoing bodily effects of delinking and relinking normative connections among sexed morphology, gendered embodiment, and sexual desire.

The figure of the appreciating cinephile was my tracking guide for keeping up with the interdisciplinary wayfaring of the shimmering concept. This trans-loving cinephiliac attracted to the shimmering images takes merriment in being astonished and joy in hearing the fascism of language thwarted. Barthes's Neutral is not a deconstructive or eroding maneuver, but one that requires the path-ologist (the scientist of *pathè*) to tune in to, or click in to, another mode, humming and thrumming, that might go unnoticed by dominant common sense. My effort here was to tune in to cinematic works that compel this mode, in one way or another, to accept their proposal, so that I might access another set of knowledges and experiences. In closing, I offer a last inventory of the ensemble of shimmers that have played together in an at times cacophonous concert, and that fashion this outfit of a book.

My final discussion herein of cinema aesthetics and trans embodiments and their intersections stages the transdisciplinary apparatus for trans cinema analysis that the book has enacted as well as demonstrates the potential for this apparatus to extend feelers into adjacent realms of inquiry and concern. The short two-and-a-half-minute digital video *103 Shots* (2016), created by visual artist Cassils and their crew in response to the mass shooting at the "Pulse" LGBT nightclub in Orlando, Florida, has formal and thematic qualities that speak to the five key dimensions of shimmering images addressed throughout the book and knits them together into a new ensemble.[1] *103 Shots* was created to memorialize the 103 lives forever lost or altered when twenty-nine-year-old Omar Mateen, a heavily armed U.S.-born security guard, entered Pulse around 2:00 am on Sunday, June 12, 2016, just before the club closed. He gunned down celebrants at this special Pride week "Latin Night," renowned for its cabaret and drag acts, killing forty-nine and critically wounding another fifty-four people.[2] This shooting, which occurred while Donald Trump was leading chants to "Build that wall!," can be seen as a culmination of hateful rhetoric against communities of (undocumented) migrants and gender- and sexual-variant people, which has only intensified since 9/11, in the "war on terrorism" era. Created in the aftermath of the largest murder of LGBT people in the United States, *103 Shots* addresses the grief of survivors and the fear of those in targeted communities, and affirms the ability to find joy in the midst of trauma. Made for and by the trans and queer communities over three days of Pride, it was filmed on location Saturday, June 25, 2016, at Dolores Park, San Francisco. *103 Shots* was released the following Monday on the online news site *The Huffington Post* together with an essay by Julia Steinmetz on the rebellion of queer nightlife, and it promptly circulated virally.[3] The video imagines through a proximate gesture the "reaction shot" of those who were shot down. In the space of a tight frame, pairs of two or three people press together, embracing, even kissing, until a balloon wedged between them bursts. Cassils chose this celebratory yet jolt-inducing action, along with the canned soundtrack of the Foley recording of balloons popping in a cement room, because one survivor said he thought the gunshot was balloons popping at the end of the party. The sound effect of the Foley recording of the balloon popping is used to enhance the sound of gunshots in films, making the "shot" in the video echo both the actual experience and the filmic. The effect is a disorientation of the indexical marker of sound and its related corporeal meaning for the identified bodies. The video therefore foregrounds the cinematic in an expanded digital network and also draws on the history of film's trickality aesthetics by experimenting with startling ways to intermesh bodies and images.

The shimmering passage of unresolvable disjunction in which we all live and breathe.

Technically, then, *103 Shots* is an example of "the disjunction between seeing and speaking" that Deleuze highlights as a cinematic practice, but that I have also investigated as being an important transing practice of reassembly.[4] This shimmering passage undulates over a lifetime, at times seeming to cohere into matching seen/spoken forms, only to break off again. Every body is subject to doing this suturing work of cohering a sense of self, of zipping a "me" up into the available brackets of one's surroundings. The film opens with the quote: "You're sitting there having a great time at the club and you hear what sounds like fireworks or balloons popping, / and you assume its part of the show, / and then you realize its not the celebration you thought it was," as the soundtrack of distorted exhalations plays over the typed white words on a black background. *103 Shots* takes a moment of extreme violent rupture, also of perception, in order to adjust the viewer's sensibility to the animate field of disjunction and conjunction that weaves and worlds subjectivity. After a beat, the first blasting shot is heard while in a tight close-up a muscular bare arm squeezes a mesh-covered back; in the split second you might perceive the

C.1 First embrace of bodies (screen capture, *103 Shots*, 2016, Cassils, independent production).

presence of two people but could only guess at their gender, relation, or what that gesture means. Flickers of black inserts pattern the next rush of close-up portrayals (figure C.1).

The bodies are shown on the beat of the shot going off, and the ricochet reverberations of the shot lingers as a sound bridge to fill the dark nothing space with a sense of dread. The headless bodies thump together, a grim embrace around the balloon that is barely visible in some close-ups. Their squeezed-tight torsos rhythmically press together, fall apart, then collapse together again. Then a woman's face of shock registers the violence of the ruptured balloon skin, stinging latex that snaps back (figure C.2). Cassils describes the performance of trans in their artistic practice as "a continual becoming, a process oriented way of being that works in a space of indeterminacy, spasm and slipperiness."[5] In *103 Shots*, however, Cassils is only momentarily one of the eighty-odd participants in the performance-action, and is not easily identifiable; the spasm is distributed over all the bodies whose shudder, twinge, and recoil mark this space of indeterminacy.

C.2 First reaction shot of a face (screen capture, *103 Shots*, 2016, Cassils, independent production).

A trans method centralizes the pulses of affect guiding ontological movement and change.

The inventory of shimmers method that I adopt from Barthes, following Seigworth and Gregg, is based on the principle that trans ontologies are process-oriented rather than object-oriented. Hence this method refutes treating the film as an autonomous object, formally distanced from the context-imbuing social affair in which it arises and from which it derives meaning. *103 Shots* is not just a labor of love created by over two hundred volunteers, it is also a manner in which Cassils sought to present the struggles of their time, a time that calls for collective feeling-action. These collective pulses of affect dilate the cinematic sound images of *103 Shots*. It is notable that the owner Barbara Poma named her queer club Pulse in dedication to her brother John, who died in 1991 of AIDS-related illness, so that his pulse would live on.[6] This pulse can be heard in the soundtrack's faint slowed heartbeat mixed into ambient music, which plays alongside the additional "shot track." The doubled, layered tracks effectively press together the sound and image, bodily form and lifely content, that aesthetically brings out the affects—of surprise, pain, discomfort, and bursts of laughter—blooming on the faces and intermingling with hard kisses and grips. Attention to this intersection of colliding affect, at speeds fast and slow signaled by the slow motion layered with fast editing and real time, gives space to experience the affects secondhand and to process disbelief at the tragedy. The video draws out the force of expression that forms and differs the body, that of a diverse group of people coming together, but also enjoined by the affective force field generated by the wider media coverage, and felt by viewers in the punch of the short-film format.

A collectivity of traumatic public affects, then, but zinging with what Ann Cvetkovitch calls "the messy legacies of history," cannot be conveniently managed into the LGBTQI2S acronym for a single diverse community.[7] In Elijah Adiv Edelman's recounting for why the Pulse murders of mainly Latinx trans and queer lives have been forgotten, he stresses (quoting Jasbir Puar) the pernicious effects of whitewashing brought on by homonationalism that depends on "the segregation and disqualification of racial-sexual others from the national imaginary," evident in mainstream gay and lesbian movements' disregard for immigration rights, sex worker rights, and the incarcerated.[8] *103 Shots*, I propose, recomposes those forces of disaggregation to cultivate negative affects as possible resources for political action. The corpus of trans cinema that I've assembled in these pages testifies to the resourceful reclamation of negative affects, which is not just about "transforming the base materials of social abjection into the gold of political agency," as Heather Love points out.[9] Negative affects are also valuable as a diagnostic tool for discovering what Raymond Williams calls "social experiences in solution."[10]

Alongside the inventory of trans shimmerings runs a counter-history of cinema as a machinic linking and delinking of embodiment, morphology, and sexuality.

Bringing forward Pulse's place in HIV art-activism, *103 Shots* borrows the exact font from the confrontational posters and stickers of graphics the direct-action group Queer Nation used in the early 1990s, a conscious design choice to pay forward their impactful work (figure C.3). The specificity of the video-making taking the form of a collective direct action is also a reference to Gran Fury's way of working, which was an ACT UP spin-off art group addressing the ongoing HIV crisis. Formally the reason for choosing an intimate action is to recall Gran Fury's 1989 public service announcement plastered on buses across major U.S. cities: its tagline

C.3 Front of Queer Nation graphic used for the title card at the end of the video (screen capture, *103 Shots*, 2016, Cassils, independent production).

"Kissing Doesn't Kill: Greed and Indifference Do" is written above photos of kissing couples of different ethnicities and genders and set against a white background, much like then-popular Benetton ads.[11] The black-and-white video aesthetic also "dates" it to a historical moment, or at least removes it from the legacy of color film and video that connotes a bright reality. Each chapter in *Shimmering Images* also seeks to excavate the historical strata that embed the seeable "visibilities" of trans-inter-queer as a flash, sparkle, or shimmer, while other relations become opaque. In this manner I broached Foucault's dark shimmer of sex and the shimmering mirage of sex as potentially contested by visual pornographies that draw out the racialization of nasty sex, the eroticization of gender malleability, and the commodification of fetishized genitals. I also found that trans-inter-queer intelligibilities do not require transparency, but rather rely on the screen of culture to block out some meaningful relations while pressing forward others.

The (dis)articulating joints of trans-inter-queer gave a focus to my tracking of these shimmering visibilities. My corpus selection did not capitulate to analyzing only widely circulated North American film materials, as I wanted to show the potential for transnational inventories of visibilities. Moreover, the materials collected also bear cross-comparisons that show the uneven hangover of modernity cast over different geopolitical sites, genres, and their assembly of trans-inter-queer cinematic embodiments. For example, European temporal drag of sexological imagery is evident in the invocation of the hermaphroditic body that is transposed on Lili Elbe's 1931 phantasmagoric depiction of intermediacy and onto *Dandy Dust*'s 1998 cyborgian chimera. Locating a semblance of trans in different strata demonstrates the accretion of sex-design onto ideals of bodily integrity and self-determination, which appears in different value systems ranging from sexual intermediacy to gender nonconformity, or even of diversity of sex, gender, and sexuality. That these various forms present as shimmerings to outplay the paradigm attest to why trans cannot—and should not—be pinned to one mode of film/bodily being (an ontology). The nonexhaustive effort to inventory shimmers can also be used more broadly as a film analysis method for describing the prepositional space of relation and connection that affords delinking and relinking processes, for instance, through formal experiments with perceptual flickering, or dissecting the institutional cinematic setup.

However, the question of history is also particularly charged for transsexuals, as Stone insists, in that posttranssexuals "must take responsibility for all of their history" in order to reclaim the power of the refigured and reinscribed body that shimmers with nuanced difference.[12] *Shimmering Images* offers a framework to circumvent reducing gender to the problems of recognition, and thereby it challenges the notions inherent therein of being either visible or invisible. By understanding that the lights of an era produce a machine for visual intelligibility, I have been able to learn in what ways trans becomes caught up in the shimmerings of cinematic processes, materials, and perceptions. Examining the cultural series of cinema, the genres and their frameworks that allow and disallow some readings of transness, my analysis shifts away from focusing on representation as a means for social and political recognition to instead consider the conditions under which trans appears. That is, I center the study of the affective, synesthetic, technological, and social ensemble that comes together to purchase trans being and becoming. The inscription of transsexual is what Stone was first concerned with: the technologies that mediate trans experience, and the overlord institutions that have tried to mediate trans with discrediting theories, meanings that would from the start disallow access to seeing trans bodies, much less hearing trans voices.[13] This critical approach to transmedia is what I'm trying to foster in the lineage of Stone via Stryker, and in the media creatives since them and before them. The historical "void" of authentic trans images therefore should not be seen as an empty void, but overfull and ready to become again a scene of wild activities. The tentative corpus of trans cinema aesthetics I've formed here already show that connections across intellectual, historical, and spatial divides can be built and sustained in ways that shift the paradigm to an other (re)arrangement of knowledge, sensation, pleasure.

> *Trans cinematic space offers a material means of achieving embodiment through cut and sutured images that are shot through with projections of desire.*

The sound of shots tears through *103 Shots*, the overproduced, enhanced versions of the diegetic sound of the balloon squished between bodies to the point of breaking. That many of the people embracing also elect to kiss each other on the mouth means that in the moment of rupture, their lips are also often torn apart (figure C.4). This sound-image generates a poignant tone around the desire to remember and to assemble together surrounding the Pulse tragedy, but also around the desire to become erotically visible.

Clicking in to the optics of being erotically viable, and having a body that enables that form of visibility, was and remains a key motivating factor for many of the trans scholars and media-makers I discuss. Stone's proposal that gender consists in visible signs that people read, therefore concluding transsexuals are a genre, "a set of embodied texts whose potential for *productive* disruption of structured sexualities and spectra of desire," is a leitmotif that I track in trans docu-porns and multigenre cult films.[14] In *103 Shots* sexual celebration during Pride hinges on harnessing queer erotics for resilience, to gift in a gripping embrace the rearrangements of knowledge, sensation, and pleasure. My stake in hobbling together cinematic aesthetics and trans embodiment was to enable analysis of the parallel, intersecting tracks of transitional and cinematic bodies that attracted cinephiliacs and lured them into the apparatus to become part of the ensemble.

The groping motion of embodied thinking that Shaviro describes in relation to an image always "shimmering just beyond my grasp," and that *Dandy Dust* invites, consists in the subject seeking a foothold in the image, or a handgrip to guide toward knowability. Knowledge becomes the most elusive outcome of the process initiated by the spectator's evaluated

C.4 A kiss torn apart by a ruptured balloon (screen capture, *103 Shots*, 2016, Cassils, independent production).

response to shimmering images. The spectator's dalliance with cinematic bodies performs what Shannon Bell terms "pornosophy," a philosophy that emerges from the carnal.[15] Philosophy here refers to the love of investigation and to the critical analysis of knowledge, which both might be pornified by the carnality of the subject. The practice of pornosophy, Susan Stryker elaborates, consists in a "refusal to discredit what our own carnality can teach us."[16] Pornographicity in the cinema takes advantage of the potential for a carnally dense vision that engenders shimmers by disrupting the bands of desire that structure sexuality's limited spectra.

If film operates as an apparatus for the animation of the body, inversely, cinema itself seems to be animated by the morphing qualities of bodies.

Film has the power to raise the dead, and in *103 Shots* bring to life the experiences of those whose lives were taken. The dangerous powers of animation in a less-than-human form are spread across the cyborg, the horrifying transsexual monster, and the ghosts of the magic lantern. Each example plays on the interrelated animating power of cinematic technologies and trans-sexing practices. A surgeon/film operator brings a transformed subject to life through cuts and sutures on a material strip, run through a projector that shoots out a ray of light to endow that body with life. The history of filmmaking, I venture, has been marked by the logics of cut, suture, and multiplication, each offering different sets of aesthetics for their kind of change. The intensely cut-up visual style of *103 Shots* demonstrates a frustration with visibility as a primary mode of politics. It seems eager to allay voyeurism and surveillance, but also to avoid generating a visual essentialism of the event. The fast-cut editing that offers snippets of reactions foregrounds in touching gestures the impossibility to touch the bodies, and in its tight close-up camera work paradoxically manages to widen the frame of the event in Orlando to include other trans and queer temporalities and spaces. By rerouting this crisis through other forgotten crises, other protests and public intimacies, *103 Shots* activates the virtual and heralds a potential new ripple in common sense.

Cassils has said of their image-making practice, "I want to try to hold together the struggle of both sides: the endless inversion of celebration into violence, and empowerment into harsh realities."[17] In a similar way Stryker's swimmer encounters the endless inversion of shimmering planes that flips the harsh reality of gender into empowerment. These watery boundaries of gender are met with a rage that enables her to transform fleshly form into the flow. The rage animating *103 Shots* and the viral sharing of the video seem to activate this cinematic apparatus in order to transform the bereaved and the targeted into a "we" in the face of divisionary and exclusionary affects. Every instance of cinematic projection is a singular event, fundamentally conditioned by the malleable dynamics of its specific time and place, but also, I have demonstrated, related to the shimmerings of the cultural series—phantasmagoria, trick films, documentary, pornography, cult flicks—that proposes a different kind of ideal spectator (thrown back on themselves) and generates transformative passionate structures. Hence I'm writing against the ahistorical understanding of a cinematic apparatus's totalizing vision of an ideology.[18]

As practices of light change, the introduction of ways and means to shimmer changes one's capacity for perceiving trans movement, that rustle, nuance, and effort for difference that generates life itself. Cinematic bodies are thus the "illusive flesh" that L. H. Stallings invokes through a stanza of poetry from Robert Hayden, titled "Monet's Waterlillies": "Here space and time exist in light / the eye like the eye of faith believes. / The seen, the known / dissolve in iridescence, become / illusive flesh of light / that was not, was, forever is."[19] The illusive flesh of light is a shimmering in its teasing scintillations, beckoning yet elusive. Stallings refers to illusive flesh to point to the form of metaphysical gender that is less than attached to a "unified body" and therefore only seems to be deceptive or illusory. The notion of this kind of nonattached flesh is a staunch counterphilosophy to embodiment that raises questions about the representation of Otherly human bodies, those forms of life and being that exceed the biological.[20] It comes close then to the transreal of cárdenas and Delany, whose intermingling realities generate trans world identities in order to displace the columns of a unified social body or racial, sexual, or gender identity.[21] This nonattached, elusive, and only seemingly illusive rippling flesh of light offers a means of locating "new genres of the human"—those subjects who live, imagine, and desire as Alexander Weheliye recovers from Black feminist philosophies, but which Stalling sees as "incapable of challenging the assumed materiality of sex and gender in the West" that renders their appearance as less than fully human.[22]

These subjects, and this incipient subjectivity of trans embodiment colored by the aesthetics of change, emerge in the repose, in the intervals between movement-rest. *Shimmering Images* only elusively here and there pins down the promiscuous shimmers of light, grasps the transition, but so does film analysis more generally. After all, perception, like qualitative transformation, and the aesthetics of change are moving targets.

NOTES

Introduction

1. Minnie Bruce Pratt, *S/He* (Ithaca, NY: Firebrand, 1995), 104.

2. Steven Shaviro, *The Cinematic Body* (Minneapolis: University of Minnesota Press, 1993), 255–56.

3. Gilles Deleuze, *Foucault*, trans. Seán Hand (Minneapolis: University of Minnesota Press, [1986] 2000), 64. For an extended discussion by Deleuze of the relation between speech and vision, soundtracks, and image-tracks, see "The Components of the Image," in his *Cinema 2: The Time-Image*, trans. Hugh Tomlinson and Barbara Habberjam (Minneapolis: University of Minnesota Press, 1986).

4. Going a step further, Patricia MacCormack's conceptualizing of spectatorship as cinesexuality ("the desire which flows through all who want cinema as a lover") relates a polymorphous sexuality to cinema (lacking gender, sexuality, form, or function), rather than the structures of cinema to binary gender/sex matrices, in *Cinesexuality* (Farnham, UK: Ashgate, 2008), 1. I use *cinephiles* as a broader term inclusive of spectators and filmmakers attracted to cinema's potential as escape from systematicity. I follow Rashna Wadia Richards's *Cinematic Flashes: Cinephilia and Classical Hollywood* (Bloomington: Indiana University Press, 2013), which argues that cinephiliacs seize on surplus signification within the image to locate audiovisual pleasures outside the advancing of narrative.

5. Susan Stryker, "The Transgender Issue: An Introduction," GLQ: *A Journal of Lesbian and Gay Studies* 4, no. 2 (1998): 149, my emphasis.

6. This is the charge leveled at Marjorie Garber's use of transvestism (rather than the identity of transvestites) by Vivian Namaste in *Invisible Lives: The Erasure of Transsexual and Transgendered People* (Chicago: University of Chicago Press, 2000), 14–15.

7. Laura Mulvey, "Afterthoughts on 'Visual Pleasure and Narrative Cinema' Inspired by King Vidor's *Duel in the Sun* (1946)" in *Visual and Other Pleasures* (London: Macmillan, [1981] 1989), 29–38.

8. Jacques Lacan, "Some Reflections on the Ego," *Psychoanalytic Quarterly* 23 (1954): 11–17.

9. Kaja Silverman, *The Threshold of the Visible World* (New York: Routledge, 1996).

10. Danielle M. Seid, "Reveal," *TSQ: Transgender Studies Quarterly* 1, nos. 1–2 (2014): 176.

11. Suzanne J, Kessler and Wendy McKenna, *Gender: An Ethnomethodological Approach* (New York: John Wiley & Sons, 1978), 113–14.

12. Talia Mae Bettcher, "Evil Deceivers and Make-Believers: On Transphobic Violence and the Politics of Illusion," *Hypatia* 22, no. 3 (2007): 50, 59.

13. Judith (Jack) Halberstam, *In a Queer Time and Place: Transgender Bodies, Subcultural Lives* (New York: New York University Press, 2005), 76–96.

14. See Cáel Keegan, "Revisitation: A Trans Phenomenology of the Media Image," *MedieKultur* 61 (2016): 29.

15. For scholarship that conducts representation analysis, see John Phillips, *Transgender On Screen* (New York: Palgrave Macmillan, 2006) on transgender characters in film; and Marjorie B. Garber, *Vested Interests: Cross-Dressing and Cultural Anxiety* (New York: Routledge, 1992) on cross-dressing in popular culture. Recent PhD dissertations by Joelle Ruby Ryan, "Reel Gender: Examining the Politics of Trans Images in Film and Media" (PhD diss., Bowling Green State University, 2009); Jonathan Rachel Williams, "Trans Cinema, Trans Viewers" (PhD diss., University of Melbourne, 2011); Wibke Straube, "Trans Cinema and Its Exit Scapes. A Transfeminist Reading of Utopian Sensibility and Gender Dissidence in Contemporary Film" (PhD diss., Linköping University, 2014); Anthony Clair Wagner, "(Un)Be(Com)ing Others: A Trans* Film Criticism of the Alien Quadrilogy Movies" (PhD diss., Academy of Fine Arts Vienna, 2015); and Akkadia Ford, "Transliteracy and the Trans New Wave: Independent Trans Cinema Representation, Classification, Exhibition" (PhD diss., Southern Cross University, 2016), also focus on films from the perspective of trans stereotypes, audiences, mainstreaming, monster studies, and independent film, respectively.

16. I was personally involved in organizing Amsterdam trans film festivals from 2003–9 (The Netherlands Transgender Film Festival with director Kam Wai Kui) and again in 2012–13 (TranScreen: Amsterdam Film Festival). The film festival scholar Skadi Loist has an impressive and searchable map of LGBT/Q film festivals from 1977 to the present that provides further information about these locations; it is updated regularly on the Google Maps website "LGBT/Q Film Festivals Global (1977–2015) NEW MAP © Skadi Loist," accessed July 15, 2018, https://www .google.com/maps/d/u/0/viewer?mid=1m-UV5Kpw39u-eLn—Dj6RALd4ks &ll=4.13296470981505%2C0&z=1.

17. I thank Tobaron Waxman for suggesting this film for analysis, and for offering ideas about how the erotic ambiguity of Anybodys interrelates to gender

ambiguity, in conversation and during our co-presentation "GenderfluXXXors Uncoded: A FTM Su*pornova*" at Le Petite Versailles Garden Projects in New York City in September 2005. I respectfully acknowledge that I have integrated some of Waxman's own ideas here, and I am grateful for our continuing, enriching conversations on trans art and living.

18. The intersex and trans author of *Aus eines Mannes Mädchenjahren* (*Man's Years as a Young Girl*) (1907) invokes this form of a no body by using the authorial pseudonym N. O. Body. See N. O. Body and Magnus Hirschfeld, *Aus Mannes Mädchenjahren* (Berlin: Gustav Rieckes Buchhandlung, 1907). His legal name was Karl M. Baer, and this personal story was written with Magnus Hirschfeld. Renate Lorenz, Pauline Boudry, and Werner Hirsch more recently created an installation with film and photographs called *N.O.Body* (2008) inspired by Hirschfeld's research and the historical figure Annie Jones (b. 1865) who performed as a bearded lady. "N.O.Body," Pauline Boudry / Renate Lorenz, accessed November 15, 2017, http://www.boudry-lorenz.de/n-o-body/.

19. Sean Cubitt, *The Practice of Light: A Genealogy of Visual Technologies from Prints to Pixels* (Cambridge, MA: MIT Press, 2014).

20. Viviane Namaste, "'Activists Can't Go on Forever Acting in the Abstract': An Interview with Mirha-Soleil Ross," in *Sex Change Social Change: Reflections on Identity, Institutions, and Imperialism* (Toronto, ON: Canadian Scholars Press, 2011), 121. See also Elspeth Brown, "Mirha-Soleil Ross in the Archives: Transsexual Artist, Sex Worker and Activist," LGBTQ *History | Digital Collaboratory* blog, October 3, 2016, http://lgbtqdigitalcollaboratory.org/2016/10/mirha-soleil-ross-transsexual-artist-sex-worker-and-activist/.

21. Gregory Seigworth and Melissa Gregg, "Introduction: An Inventory of Shimmers," in *The Affect Theory Reader*, ed. Gregory Seigworth and Melissa Gregg (Durham, NC: Duke University Press, 2010), 1–28.

22. Roland Barthes, *The Neutral*, trans. Rosalind E. Krauss and Denis Hollier (New York: Columbia University Press, [2002] 2005), 6.

23. Barthes, *Neutral*, 7.

24. Barthes, *Neutral*, 7, 8.

25. Judith Butler, *Undoing Gender* (New York: Routledge, 2004), 4.

26. Barthes, *Neutral*, 51, 191.

27. Barthes, *Neutral*, xv.

28. Barthes, *Neutral*, 48.

29. Barthes, *Neutral*, 51.

30. Barthes, *Neutral*, 51.

31. Sara Ahmed, *The Promise of Happiness* (Durham, NC: Duke University Press, 2010), 41.

32. Barthes, *Neutral*, 73.

33. Barthes, *Neutral*, 73.

34. Barthes, *Neutral*, 77.

35. Barthes, *Neutral*, 75. An inventory of shimmers is perhaps the central scholarly method of Barthes. In his early book *Sade/Fourier/Loyola* (trans. Richard Miller [Berkeley: University of California Press, (1971) 1976]), for example, he is interested in unraveling the fabric of the watered silk moiré pattern in Sade's writing described as "a tapestry of phrases, a changing luster, a fluctuating and glittering surface of styles" (135).

36. Barthes, *Neutral*, 77.

37. Barthes, *Neutral*, 101.

38. Barthes, *Neutral*, 101.

39. Laura Wahlfors, "Resonances and Dissonances: Listening to Waltraud Meier's Envoicing of Isolde," in *On Voice*, ed. Walter Bernhart and Lawrence Kramer (Amsterdam: Rodopi, 2014), 64.

40. Katrina Roen offers a summary of the debates she frames between radical politics of gender transgression and liberal transsexual politics in her article "'Either/Or' and 'Both/Neither': Discursive Tension in Transgender Politics," *Signs: Journal of Women in Culture and Society* 27, no. 2 (2002): 501–22.

41. Alfred North Whitehead, *Adventures of Ideas* (New York: Free Press, 1967); Mieke Bal, *Travelling Concepts in the Humanities: A Rough Guide* (Toronto: Toronto University Press, 2002).

42. Barthes, *Neutral*, 147.

43. Brian Massumi, *Parables for the Virtual: Movement, Affect, Sensation* (Durham, NC: Duke University Press, 2002), 15.

44. Massumi, *Parables for the Virtual*, 15.

45. Eva Hayward, "The Subtle Process of Transformation," *IndyWeek.com*, September 5, 2012, accessed March 18, 2016, http://www.indyweek.com/indyweek /the-subtle-process-of-transformation/Content?oid=3140976.

46. Seigworth and Gregg, "Introduction: An Inventory of Shimmers," 11.

47. Seigworth and Gregg, "Introduction: An Inventory of Shimmers," 4.

48. Barthes, *Neutral*, 42.

49. Elspeth Probyn, "Writing Shame," in *The Affect Theory Reader*, ed. Gregory Seigworth and Melissa Gregg (Durham, NC: Duke University Press, 2010), 74.

50. Eugenie Brinkema, *The Forms of the Affects* (Durham, NC: Duke University Press, 2014), xiii, xv.

51. Massumi, *Parables for the Virtual*, 3.

52. Barthes, *Neutral*, 186–87.

53. Barthes, *Neutral*, 190.

54. Barthes, *Neutral*, 191.

55. Barthes, *Neutral*, 195.

56. Barthes, *Neutral*, 194.

57. Sandy Stone, "The *Empire* Strikes Back: A Posttranssexual Manifesto," in

The Transgender Studies Reader, ed. Stephen Whittle and Susan Stryker (New York: Routledge, [1991] 2006), 221–35. The original copyright dates to 1987, with the history explained in the authorized 4.0 version available through SandyStone .com, April 9, 2014, accessed March 18, 2016, http://sandystone.com/empire-strikes -back.html.

58. Stone, "The *Empire* Strikes Back," 231, emphasis in original.

59. Stone, "The *Empire* Strikes Back," 232.

60. Alan Cholodenko, "'First Principles' of Animation," in *Animating Film Theory*, ed. Karen Beckman (Durham, NC: Duke University Press, 2014), 98, 100. See, for example, Alan Cholodenko, ed., *The Illusion of Life: Essays on Animation* (Sydney: Power Publications, 1991); Alan Cholodenko, ed., *The Illusion of Life 2: More Essays on Animation* (Sydney: Power Publications, 2007).

61. Alan Cholodenko, "The Animation of Cinema," *Semiotic Review of Books* 18, no. 2 (2008): 1.

62. Laura Mulvey, in *Death 24x a Second: Stillness and the Moving Image* (London: Reaktion Books, 2006), argues that digital and digitized films showcase death 24 times a second, accessed by fetishistic spectators who interact with individual still frames by using pause, freeze-frame, slow motion, and other widely available new media effects. Alternatively, Rachel O. Moore, in *Savage Theory: Cinema as Modern Magic* (Durham, NC: Duke University Press, 1999), grasps the magical feature of cinema as a modern incarnation of animism.

63. See, for example, Jay Prosser, *Second Skins: The Body Narratives of Transsexuality* (New York: Columbia University Press, 1998). This narrative has more recently become known as a form of "transnormativity"; see Jasbir Puar, "Bodies with New Organs: Becoming Trans, Becoming Disabled," *Social Text* 33, no. 3 (2015): 45–73, for a critical overview of the concept.

64. Stone, "The *Empire* Strikes Back," 224–25.

65. *Frankenstein*, dir. James Whale, with Colin Clive, Boris Karloff, Mae Clarke, and John Boles (Los Angeles: Universal Pictures, 1931).

66. For people with an intersex diagnosis and who undergo nonconsensual surgeries, this relation to medical treatment is usually in the first place coercive rather than a matter of gatekeeping. See M. Morgan Holmes, ed., *Critical Intersex* (Farnham, UK: Ashgate, 2009). Likewise, "sexual deviants" have been, and in some cases still are, subject to medical treatment including electroshock therapy, lobotomy, and hormonal castration. The shared issue is how any trans-interqueer subjects might be forced to undergo medical treatments in order to have their embodied difference supposedly corrected and to assimilate to the standard set by "normates," a composite identity position held by those unmarked by stigmatized identities (related to ability, sex, race, etc.), coined by Rosemarie Garland Thomson, *Extraordinary Bodies: Figuring Disability in American Culture and Literature* (New York: Columbia University Press, 1997).

67. Susan Stryker, "My Words to Victor Frankenstein Above the Village of Chamounix: Performing Transgender Rage," in *The Transgender Studies Reader*, ed. Susan Stryker and Stephen Whittle (New York: Routledge, [1993] 2006), 248.

68. This phrasing is taken from Susan Stryker, "Christine in the Cutting Room: Cinema, Surgery and Celebrity in the Career of Christine Jorgensen" (paper presented at the Department of Media, Music, Communication and Cultural Studies Public Lecture Series, Macquarie University, Sydney, Australia, May 1, 2013), available from YouTube.com, posted August 16, 2013, accessed March 18, 2016, https://www.youtube.com/watch?v=XlqJ8B9dKCs.

69. Stryker, "Christine in the Cutting Room."

70. Tobias Raun, "Screen-births: Exploring the Transformative Potential in Trans Video Blogs on YouTube," *Graduate Journal of Social Science* 7, no. 2 (2010): 125.

71. Raun, "Screen-births," 126.

72. Peggy Phelan's oft-quoted punch line bears repeating: "If representational visibility equals power, then almost-naked young white women should be running Western culture" (Peggy Phelan, *Unmarked: The Politics of Performance* [New York: Routledge, 1993], 10).

73. Phelan, *Unmarked*, 7.

74. Phelan, *Unmarked*, 6. See also the discussions of trans-specific visibility issues in Reina Gosset, Eric A. Stanley, and Johanna Burton, eds., *Trap Door: Trans Cultural Production and the Politics of Visibility* (Cambridge, MA: MIT Press, 2017).

75. See the work of Édouard Glissant, "For Opacity," in *Poetics of Relation*, trans. Betsy Wing (Ann Arbor: University of Michigan Press, 1997), 189–94. See also the essays in Zach Blas's edited "In Practice: Opacities," *Camera Obscura: Feminism, Culture, and Media Studies* 31, no. 92 (2016): 149–203.

76. Mieke Bal, "Visual Essentialism and the Object of Visual Culture," *Journal of Visual Culture* 2, no. 1 (2003): 8.

77. Bal, "Visual Essentialism," 2, 9. I apply this critique to the particular case of trans porn activism in Eliza Steinbock, "'Look!' but also, 'Touch!': Theorizing Images of Trans-Eroticism Beyond a Politics of Visual Essentialism," in *Porno-Graphics and Porno-Tactics: Desire, Affect, and Representation in Pornography*, ed. Eirini Avramopoulou and Irene Peano (Earth, Milky Way: Punctum Books, 2016), 59–75.

78. Helen Hok-Sze Leung, "Film," *TSQ: Transgender Studies Quarterly* 1, nos. 1–2 (2014): 86.

79. Leung, "Film," 86.

80. I expand on the ways in which trans cinema studies might conduct a revisionist history of the New Queer Cinema in Eliza Steinbock, "Towards Trans

Cinema," in *Routledge Companion to Cinema and Gender*, ed. Kristin Lené Hole, Dijlana Jelača, E. Ann Kaplan, and Patrice Petro (New York: Routledge, 2016), 395–406.

81. Eve Sedgwick, "Gosh, Boy George, You Must Be Awfully Secure in Your Masculinity!," in *Constructing Masculinity*, ed. Maurice Berger, Brian Wallis, and Simon Watson (New York: Routlege, 1995), 17.

82. This point is made more elaborately by Susan Stryker, "Transgender Studies: Queer Theory's Evil Twin," GLQ: *A Journal of Lesbian and Gay Studies* 10, no. 2 (2004): 214.

83. "Saming" is the flipside concept of "othering"; see Naomi Schor, "This Essentialism Which Is Not One: Coming to Grips with Irigaray," *Differences* 1, no. 2 (1988): 38–58.

84. The German website of TrIQ first launched in 2006 and was last modified in 2016; accessed March 18, 2016, http://www.transinterqueer.org.

85. Paisley Currah, Susan Stryker, and Lisa Jean Moore, "Introduction: Trans-, Trans, or Transgender?," WSQ: *Women's Studies Quarterly* 36, nos. 3–4 (2008): 13.

86. Mel Y. Chen, *Animacies: Biopolitics, Racial Mattering, and Queer Affect* (Durham, NC: Duke University Press, 2012).

87. Chen, *Animacies*, 2, 10–11.

ONE Shimmering Phantasmagoria

1. Quoted in Laurent Mannoni, *The Great Art of Light and Shadow* (Exeter: University of Exeter Press, 2000), 144.

2. Here I refer to Laverne Cox playing Sophia Burset on *Orange Is the New Black*, Jamie Clayton playing Nomi on *Sense8*, numerous characters on *Transparent*, Scott Turner Schofield on *The Bold and the Beautiful*, *I Am Cait* about Caitlyn Jenner, *I Am Jazz* on the life of a young trans woman, RuPaul's *Drag Race*, and so on. I mention specific films in the introduction and in this chapter refer to Tom Hooper's 2015 dramatization of *The Danish Girl*.

3. Rita Felski, "*Fin de siècle, Fin de sexe*: Transsexuality, Postmodernism, and the Death of History," *New Literary History* 27 (1996): 338.

4. Elizabeth Freeman, *Time Binds: Queer Temporalities, Queer Histories* (Durham, NC: Duke University Press, 2010), 62–64.

5. He further writes, "I know of no word more complex than 'Phantasmagoria,'" in Tom Gunning, "Illusions Past and Future: The Phantasmagoria and Its Specters" (paper presented at the Refresh! First International Conference on the Histories of Art, Science and Technology, 2004). Consulted via Media Art History accessed March 24, 2016, http://pl02.donau-uni.ac.at/jspui/handle/10002/296/.

6. Terry Castle, "Phantasmagoria: Spectral Technology and the Metaphorics of Modern Reverie," *Critical Inquiry* 15, no. 1 (1988): 29.

7. On surgeries see Dwight Billings and Thomas Urban, "The Socio-Medical Construction of Transsexualism: An Interpretation and Critique," *Social Problems* 29, no. 3 (1982): 266–82; and Bernice Hausman, *Changing Sex: Transsexualism, Technology, and the Idea of Gender* (Durham, NC: Duke University Press, 1995).

On diagnostic categories see Jay Prosser, *Second Skins: The Body Narratives of Transsexuality* (New York: Columbia University Press, 1998); and the provocative R. Nick Gorton, "Transgender as Mental Illness: Nosology, Social Justice, and the Tarnished Golden Mean," in *The Transgender Studies Reader* 2, ed. Susan Stryker and Aren Aizura (New York: Routledge, [2007] 2013), 644–52.

8. Legal and administrative hurdles to gender self-determination in the U.S. context are elaborately discussed in Dean Spade, *Normal Life: Administrative Violence, Critical Trans Politics, and the Limits of Law* (Durham, NC: Duke University Press, 2015).

9. Early examples include Jack (formerly Judith) Halberstam, "F2M: The Making of Female Masculinity," in *The Lesbian Postmodern*, ed. Laura Doan, 210–28 (New York: Columbia University Press, 1994); and Susan Stryker, "My Words to Victor Frankenstein Above the Village of Chamounix: Performing Transgender Rage" [1994], in *The Transgender Studies Reader*, ed. Susan Stryker and Stephen Whittle, 244–56 (New York: Routledge, 2006).

10. On the neoliberal undercurrents to a grossly dividing transnormativity see Jasbir Puar, "Bodies with New Organs: Becoming Trans, Becoming Disabled," *Social Text* 33, no. 3 (2015): 45–75.

11. The first in a series on liquidity is Zygmunt Bauman, *Liquid Life* (London: Polity Press, 2005).

12. Karen Barad, *Meeting the Universe Halfway: Quantum Physics and the Entanglement of Matter and Meaning* (Durham, NC: Duke University Press, 2007).

13. Prosser, *Second Skins*, 211.

14. Susan Stryker, *Transgender History* (Berkeley: Seal Press, 2008), 1.

15. Prosser, *Second Skins*, 211.

16. André Gaudreault, *Film and Attraction: From Kinematography to Cinema*, trans. Timothy Barnard (Chicago: University of Illinois Press, [2008] 2011), 68. Gaudreault acknowledges that Eric de Kuyper articulates ideas similar to his "intermedial meshing" to describe the hodgepodge of technologies among kinematographic phenomena.

17. Vern L. Bullough, "Magnus Hirschfeld, An Often Over-looked Pioneer," *Sexuality and Culture* 7, no. 1 (2003): 62–72. See commentary on the role of Hirschfeld in Merl Storr and Jay Prosser, "Introduction to Part III Transsexuality and Bisexuality," in *Sexology Uncensored: The Documents of Sexual Sci-*

ence, ed. Lucy Bland and Laura Doan (Chicago: Chicago University Press, 1998), 75–77. Sexology today differentiates cross-gender identification from intersex conditions. Conceptualization of trans identification evolved into a psychic cross-gender desire aligned with requested bodily modifications, whereas intersex was kept from becoming an identity by framing bodies as atypical through diagnosis and (nonconsensual) treatment. Hence, both involve hormonal and surgical practices but deployed in one case to treat the psyche and in the other case, the physical irregularity. Today intersex social movements and trans rights organizations both use the language of self-determination and informed consent models to enable people access to voluntary treatment that is seen from a more holistic perspective.

18. See Stryker, *Transgender History*, 95–98; Ulrike Klöppel, "Who Has the Right to Change Gender Status? Drawing Boundaries between Inter- and Trans-sexuality," in *Critical Intersex*, ed. M. Morgan Holmes (Farnham, U.K.: Ashgate, 2009), 171.

19. See Michel Foucault, *The Archaeology of Knowledge*, trans. A. M. Sheridan Smith (New York: Taylor & Francis, [1969] 2013).

20. Gilles Deleuze, *Foucault*, trans. Seán Hand (Minneapolis: University of Minnesota Press, [1986] 1990), 50. In his assessment of Foucault's method, Deleuze places emphasis on the covert literary project entitled *Death and The Labyrinth: The World of Raymond Roussel*, trans. Charles Ruas (London: Athlone Press, [1963] 1987), which Foucault conducts under a pseudonym and which outlines his method of production. In his treatment of Roussel's various kinds of writing, Foucault argues that in his extraction of words selected for a poetic line he reveals the secret meanings of phrases and, similarly, he draws images that show the object's shimmering visibility. Deleuze suggests that Foucault's archaeological method of breaking and extracting may be attributed to becoming inspired by Roussel's various methods to scramble and to decode language and everyday imagery. Deleuze also argues that this (borrowed) method is integral to Foucault's development of the notions of relationality, forces, and power. This work on Roussel anticipates Foucault's Nietzsche-influenced reassessment of power in *Discipline and Punish: The Birth of the Prison* (1975) and was written during the period of *The Birth of the Clinic: An Archaeology of Medical Perception* (1963) that studies power's productive capacity. Upon publication of the book about Roussel, Foucault explained that his analysis was highly personal; he tried to bury the manuscript in his pseudonymously written entry on the work of Foucault (himself!) by not mentioning it. Certainly it stands apart in style and argumentation. See the introduction to the text by John Ashbery for more on the reception of Foucault's Roussel book and its place in his oeuvre (xiii–xxviii).

21. Deleuze, *Foucault*, 52, emphasis mine.

22. Deleuze, *Foucault*, 57–58. In Deleuze's reading of Foucault, the method

of tracing secret statements and the light that makes a thing shimmer underline all of Foucault's historical works. From *The Archaeology of Knowledge* onward, discourse precedes the visible field he designates as "non-discursive." For Foucault, however, this suggests irreducibility, not a reduction. The nonrelation of words and images implies for Foucault an important cultural process of mutual grappling and capture.

23. Foucault tried to locate visibilities in his study of Roussel and isolate them in Manet, tracing an aesthetics of an era in a manner close to that of the French artist Robert Delaunay (1885–1941), argues Deleuze (*Foucault*, 52).

24. Deleuze, *Foucault*, 58.

25. This analysis composes the first chapter of Michel Foucault, *The Order of Things* (New York: Routledge, [1966] 2006).

26. Deleuze, *Foucault*, 53.

27. Jonathan Crary, *Techniques of the Observer: On Vision and Modernity in the Nineteenth Century* (Cambridge, MA: MIT Press, 1990), 132–36.

28. Richard Grusin and Jay David Bolter, *Remediation: Understanding New Media* (Cambridge, MA: MIT Press, 2000), 20.

29. Theodor Adorno quoted in Crary, *Techniques of the Observer*, 132.

30. Karl Marx, "Section 4 The Fetishism of Commodities and the Secret Thereof," in *A Critique of Political Economy: Vol I Part I—The Process of Capitalist Production*, ed. Friedrich Engels (New York: Cosimo Classics, [1867] 2007), 81.

31. Michel Foucault, "Introduction," in *Being the Recently Discovered Memoirs of a Nineteenth-Century French Hermaprodite (1838) by Herculine Barbin*, trans. Richard McDougall (New York: Pantheon, 1980), x. Foucault's study of Barbin's conjectured hermaphroditism recalls and to an extent reproduces the early entanglements of inversion theory relying on the notion of physical and psychic hermaphroditism that enfolds sexological histories of both transsexuality and homosexuality.

32. Foucault, "Introduction," ix, emphasis mine.

33. Foucault "Introduction," xiii.

34. Foucault, "Introduction," xiii. See also Arnold L. Davidson, "Sex and the Emergence of Sexuality," *Critical Inquiry* 14, no. 1 (1987): 16–48 for an extended treatment of Barbin's memoirs.

35. Foucault, "Introduction," xvii.

36. The shifting notion of sexual difference(s) is documented by Joanne Meyerowitz, *How Sex Changed: A History of Transsexuality in the United States* (Cambridge, MA: Harvard University Press, 2002). From the early twentieth century, she writes, "the concepts of sex change and sex-change surgery existed well before the word transsexual entered the medical parlance" (15).

37. Lisa Cartwright, *Screening the Body: Tracing Medicine's Visual Culture* (Minneapolis: University of Minnesota Press, 1995), 9.

38. Following Miriam Hansen and others, I name the essay more generally for brevity and because there are two English versions. I refer to the second version by Walter Benjamin, "The Work of Art in the Age of Its Technological Reproducibility: Second Version (1936)," in *Walter Benjamin: Selected Writings, Vol. 3: 1935–1938*, ed. Howard Eiland and Michael W. Jennings (Cambridge, MA: Belknap Press, 2002), because this was the one Benjamin considered complete. I realize this nomination runs the risk of canonization; I hope the reader can forgive this unintended gesture.

39. W. Benjamin, "Work of Art," 114.

40. W. Benjamin, "Work of Art," 114–19.

41. Susan Buck-Morss, *The Dialectics of Seeing: Walter Benjamin and the Arcades Project* (Cambridge, MA: MIT Press, 1991), 81.

42. André Gaudreault, "Theatricality, Narrativity, and Trickality: Reevaluating the Cinema of Georges Méliès," *Journal of Popular Film and Television* 15, no. 3 (1987): 118.

43. Georges Méliès, "Cinematographic Views," *October* 29 (1984): 30, with additional translation borrowed from André Gaudreault, "Méliès the Magician," trans. Timothy Barnard, *Early Popular Visual Culture* 5, no. 2 (2009): 171.

44. Gaudreault, "Méliès the Magician," 171–73.

45. See Meyerowitz, *How Sex Changed*, 15–20. Beginning with the Austrian physiologist Eugen Steinach in the 1910s, so-called sex transformation experiments were first tried on animals. The successful results were put into practice for humans in the 1920s and 1930s by doctors associated with Hirschfeld's Institute for Sexual Science in Berlin, who reported on their human sex-change surgeries to much acclaim. Meyerowitz notes that Dorchen Richter was the first male-to-female to undergo complete genital transformation, arranged through Hirschfeld's institute. In 1931 Felix Abraham published an article on two such surgeries (one of which was on Richter); in addition, Ludwig Levy Lenz was reputed to have performed several surgeries at this time, the total of which are unknown.

46. Darwin, quoted in Meyerowitz, *How Sex Changed*, 22–23.

47. Méliès, "Cinematographic Views," 30. Méliès calls his produced views "fantastic" because they include transformation scenes of appearance and disappearance like the phantasmagoria, but also effects using theatrical machines, optical illusions, and editing of metamorphosis trick shots.

48. Gaudreault, "Theatricality, Narrativity, and Trickality," 115.

49. Wanda Strauven, "Pour une lecture média-archéologique de l'œuvre de Georges Méliès," in *Méliès, Carrefour des attractions*, ed. André Gaudreault, Laurent Le Forestier, and Stéphane Tralongo (Rennes, France: Presses universitaires de Rennes, 2014), 291–99, 295.

50. Stryker, *Transgender History*, 31–32. From 1848 new city ordinances were made against people appearing "in a dress not belonging to his or her sex," insti-

tutionalizing gender codes in new ways that were patterned on colonial-period laws forbidding people from disguising themselves in public or wearing the clothes of another social rank or profession.

51. Strauven, "Pour une lecture média-archéologique," 296.

52. Darragh O'Donoghue, "Georges Méliès," *Senses of Cinema* 32 (July 2004), accessed March 24, 2016, http://sensesofcinema.com/2004/great-directors/melies/.

53. Gaudreault, "Méliès the Magician," 171–72.

54. Frank Kessler, "Trick Films," in *Encyclopedia of Early Cinema*, ed. Richard Abel (London: Routledge, 2005), 643.

55. Kessler, "Trick Films," 643.

56. André Gaudreault, "From 'Primitive Cinema' to 'Kine-Attractography'" [2004], in *The Cinema of Attractions Reloaded*, ed. Wanda Strauven, trans. Timothy Barnard (Amsterdam: University of Amsterdam Press, 2006), 99, emphasis in original. Gaudreault writes in 104n44 that he first spoke of early cinema's alien quality at a conference held in Paris in 1993.

57. Karen Beckman, *Vanishing Women: Magic, Film, and Feminism* (Durham, NC: Duke University Press, 2003).

58. Walter Benjamin, "On Some Motifs in Baudelaire" [1939], in *Illuminations*, ed. Hannah Arendt (London: Pimlico, 1999), 152–96.

59. W. Benjamin, "On Some Motifs in Baudelaire," 171.

60. Freeman, *Time Binds*, 3.

61. Freeman, *Time Binds*, xvii.

62. Tom Gunning, "Now You See It, Now You Don't! The Temporality of the Cinema of Attractions," *The Velvet Light Trap* 32 (1993): 11.

63. Tom Hooper, dir., *The Danish Girl*, Los Angeles: Working Title Films, 2015, DVD. David Ebershoff, *The Danish Girl* (New York: Penguin Books, 2000). I further develop the transmedial and historical aspect of her figuration in "Lili Elbe's Transmedial Presence and the Politics of Transgender Studies," in *Doing Gender in Media, Art and Culture: A Comprehensive Guide to Gender Studies*, 2nd edition, ed. Rosemarie Buikema, Liedeke Plate, and Kathrin Thiele, 169–81 (New York: Routledge, 2018).

64. For a reading of Gerda's depictions of Lili, see Tobias Raun, "The Trans Woman as Model and Co-Creator: Resistance and Becoming in the Back-Turning Lili Elbe," in *Gerda Wegener* (Arken, Denmark: Arken Museum of Modern Art, 2015), 41–60. For more on Lili's enduring popularity in visual culture, see Eliza Steinbock, "A Pretty Knot of Lilies: Disentangling Lili Elbe's *longue durée* in Pop Culture," in *Comparative Scholarly Edition of* Man into Woman *(1931)*, eds. Pamela L. Caughie and Sabine Meyer (London: Bloomsbury, forthcoming).

65. See Nicholas Chare, "From Landscape into Portrait: Reflections on Lili Elbe and Trans* Aesthetics," *Parallax* 22, no. 3 (2016): 347–65; and my chapter

in *Doing Gender in Media, Art and Culture*, Steinbock, "Lili Elbe's Transmedial Presence," 169–81.

66. Consider the long line from Christine Jorgensen, Renée Richards, Caroline (Tula) Cossey, and Caitlyn Jenner to Janet Mock and most recently Lily Wachowski, sister of fellow trans woman Lana Wachowski.

As part of the forthcoming scholarly edition of *Man into Woman* compiled by editors Pamela Caughie and Sabine Meyer, Caughie has located Lili's intent to publish images in her letter to Maria Garland (the wife of editor Ernst Harthern): (translated from Danish) "The book, or rather the novel, might be released while I am still here. I am sending a handful of photographs from here and will have friends collect some in Paris" (dated June 16, 1931, and sent from Dresden, Germany, when Lili was at the Dresden Municipal Women's Clinic). The research on the different editions also shows that the Danish edition has only two photographs as frontispiece illustrations, one of Einar and one of Lili. The German edition has nine illustrations, but some contain two images side by side. The American publication has sixteen photographs and the British version even more. See Caughie and Meyer, eds., *Comparative Scholarly Edition*.

67. A manuscript existed already in January 1931 when Lili gave an interview for *Politiken* magazine on February 28, 1931. The interviewer was Louise "Loulou" Lassen, one of the book's curators, and the interview's script largely imprinted the main themes of the book and perhaps served to market the book. See Tobias Raun, "The Trans Woman as Model and Co-Creator," 41–42.

68. The original Danish title was *Fra Mand til Kvinde* (1931), translated into German as *Ein mensch wechselt sein geschlecht* (that could be translated as a person changes their sex, or with a masculine or feminine inflection). See Sabine Meyer, "Divine Interventions: Rebirth and Creation Narratives in *Fra mand til kvinder – Lili Elbes bekendelser*," *Kvinder, Køn & Forskning* 3–4 (2011): 68–76.

69. Meyer, "Divine Interventions," 70.

70. Meyer, "Divine Interventions," 70. Sabine Meyer, "Mit dem Puppenwagen in die normative Weiblichkeit. Lili Elbe und die journalistische Inszenierung von Transsexualität in Dänemark," *Nordeuropaforum* 20 (2010): 47–49.

71. Niels Hoyer, ed., *Man into Woman: The First Sex Change, A Portrait of Lili Elbe* (London: Blue Boat Books, [1933] 2004), 23. For context on the discovery of hormones, see Chandak Sengoopta, *The Most Secret Quintessence of Life: Sex, Glands, and Hormones, 1850–1950* (Chicago: Chicago University Press, 2006). And for an overview about the history of medicine in Germany at the beginning of the twentieth century read Paul Weindling, *Health, Race and German Politics between National Unification and Nazism, 1870–1945* (Cambridge: Cambridge University Press, 1989). I thank Heiko Stoff for bringing these references to my attention.

72. Sandy Stone, "The *Empire* Strikes Back: A Posttranssexual Manifesto," in *The Transgender Studies Reader*, ed. Stephen Whittle and Susan Stryker (New York: Routledge, [1991] 2006), 225, 226.

73. Minnie Bruce Pratt, *S/He* (Ithaca, NY: Firebrand, 1995). The title indicates that Pratt details her love relationship with Leslie Feinberg, the well-known American transgender activist, communist, and writer, who died November 15, 2014. This formulation of s/he when applied to transgender people underlines the pervasiveness of dividing trans experience before or after sex change surgery. In fact, gender-affirmative surgeries can involve any number of procedures, making this assumption of the one moment of crossing over highly illogical.

74. Stone's analysis of *Man into Woman* draws a similar conclusion. See Stone, "The *Empire* Strikes Back," 225. *Second Serve: The Renée Richards Story* (New York: Stein & Day, 1983) cites Richards's discovery of Lili's narrative of becoming a woman during college, which she describes as a moment in a shop perusing some books when "Dick's eyes became Renée's eyes. The book was called *Man into Woman*. . . . I had hit the jackpot. It was an account of the life of a Danish painter named Einar Wegener who was the first recorded case of transsexualism. He had been a married man who felt much as I felt. It had seemed to him that his identity was misplaced. Somehow the personality of a woman had been trapped in the body of a man" (55). The way that *Second Serve* (cowritten by John Ames) presents the flickering of Renée/Richard seems patterned on Lili/Andreas-Einar.

75. Hoyer, *Man into Woman*, 266.

76. Hoyer, *Man into Woman*, 255.

77. Prosser, *Second Skins*, 207–23.

78. On Lili presenting herself as a happier person in interviews following her surgery, see Meyer, "Mit dem Puppenwagen," 31, 39, 45–46.

79. The terms *transsexual* or *psychic transsexualism* at no time appear in the English versions. Although *Man into Woman* presents Lili as the first to receive a male-to-female sex change, this posture is not historically accurate, as Dorchen Richter underwent surgical castration (excision of both testes, an orchiectomy) arranged through Hirschfeld's institute in 1922, well before Lili had the same procedure arranged through the institute in 1930. See Meyerowitz, *How Sex Changed*, 17–21. Lili's five operations were among the earliest that German and Danish doctors had conducted with the goal of transforming a human's gonadal, genital, and hormonal sex. Because of the dearth of information available at the time of the hormonal and surgical "treatments" for sexual indeterminacy, *Man into Woman* shows great awareness of the need to authorize the powers of science in order to help others gain access to this treatment. The first chapters explain how damaging it was for Lili to see doctors who discounted her experiences as psychological disturbances, or worse, something that radiation therapy

could cure. The book presents the gynecologist as her life-saving "helper" with God-like powers. See Meyer, "Divine Interventions," 71–76.

80. Hoyer, *Man into Woman*, 255.

81. Hoyer, *Man into Woman*, 19.

82. Meyer, "Divine Interventions," 70.

83. Meyer, "Mit dem Puppenwagen," 33–36.

84. W. Benjamin, "Work of Art," 115.

85. Hoyer, *Man into Woman*, 128.

86. Hoyer, *Man into Woman*, 128. The German edition includes illustrations of her handwriting before and after the surgery at the start of chapter 1.

87. Hoyer, *Man into Woman*, 125–26.

88. Stone, "The *Empire* Strikes Back," 225.

89. Jack (Judith) Halberstam, *In a Queer Time and Place: Transgender Bodies, Subcultural Lives* (New York: New York University Press, 2005), 74.

90. Hoyer, *Man into Woman*, 111.

91. Hoyer, *Man into Woman*, 111.

92. Prosser, *Second Skins*, 4.

93. On voicing suspicion of the veracity of the tales see Stone, "The *Empire* Strikes Back," 227. On the "conventional"—and therefore not truly informative of a trans-temporality—narrative structure of the tale see Pamela L. Caughie, "The Temporality of Modernist Life Writing in the Era of Transsexuality: Virginia Woolf's *Orlando* and Einar Wegener's *Man into Woman*," *MFS: Modern Fiction Studies* 59, no. 3 (2013): 501–25.

94. Prosser, *Second Skins*, 7.

95. Gaudreault, "Méliès the Magician," 172.

96. For the debate about stigma attached to biological diversity see Gorton, "Transgender as Mental Illness"; and Riki Lane, "Trans as Bodily Becoming: Rethinking the Biological as Diversity, Not Dichotomy," *Hypatia* 24, no. 3 (2009): 136–57. Gorton believes in an organic or chemical cause, whereas Lane refutes a single causal mode of thinking from neurology or brain science.

97. On the relationship of filmic form to content, see Scott C. Richmond, "The Persistence of Formalism," *Open Set: Arts, Humanities, Culture*, October 1, 2015, accessed December 1, 2017, http://www.open-set.com/s-richmond/essay -clusters/o-s-form-issue/the-persistence-of-formalism/.

98. Edward Branigan, *Narrative Comprehension and Film* (New York: Routledge, 1992), 64–66.

99. Branigan, *Narrative Comprehension and Film*, 66.

100. Silvan Tomkins, "Surprise—Startle," in *Shame and Its Sisters: A Silvan Tomkins Reader*, ed. Eve Kosofsky Sedgwick and Adam Frank (Durham, NC: Duke University Press, 1995), 108.

101. Tomkins, "Surprise—Startle," 107–8.

102. Viva Paci, "The Attraction of the Intelligent Eye: Obsessions with the Vision Machine in Early Film Theories," in *The Cinema of Attractions Reloaded*, ed. Wanda Strauven (Amsterdam: Amsterdam University Press, 2006), 121–22.

103. Wanda Strauven, "Introduction to an Attractive Concept," in Strauven, ed., *The Cinema of Attractions Reloaded*, 17.

104. Hoyer, *Man into Woman*, 18.

105. Hoyer, *Man into Woman*, 152.

106. I first published on Lili's affinity with the water and the bridge in Eliza Steinbock, "The Violence of the Cut: Transgender Homeopathy and Cinematic Aesthetics," in *Violence and Agency: Queer and Feminist Perspectives* (Gewalt und Handlungsmacht: Queer_Feministische Perspektiven), ed. Gender Initiativkolleg Wien, 154–71 (Frankfurt: Campus Publications, 2012).

107. Hoyer rallies Lili to come forward with her writing, destined for print, about "the remarkable thing about your fate, the unique thing that slumbers within you, namely the emotional bond between the two sexes" (Hoyer, *Man into Woman*, 246). Adopting a warning tone, he says, "this new country, Lili, this new country of the soul, is lying dormant within you, and whether you like it not, it will go on expanding" (246).

108. Katherine Singer Kovács, "Georges Méliès and the 'Féerie,'" *Cinema Journal* 16, no. 1 (1976): 11.

109. Gunning, "Illusions Past and Future," 16.

110. "The purveyors of magical illusions learned that attributing their tricks to explainable scientific process did not make them any less astounding, because the visual illusion still loomed before the viewer, however demystified by rational knowledge that illusion might be," writes Tom Gunning, "Animated Pictures: Tales of Cinema's Forgotten Future After 100 Years of Film," in *The Nineteenth-Century Visual Culture Reader*, ed. Vanessa R. Schwartz and Jeannene M. Przyblyski (New York: Routledge, 2004), 104.

111. Zackary Drucker has eight images from the series on her website, accessed March 24, 2016, http://zackarydrucker.com/photography/b4-after/. A. L. Steiner has nine images from the series on her website, accessed March 24, 2016, http://www.hellomynameissteiner.com/filter/collaborations/BEFORE-AFTER-1. More images can be found in the digital essay version of the installation that includes some eighty statements, to which one can answer either true or false, ironically typical of an intake form given to people who try to access medical treatment for gender "dysphoria." A. L. Steiner and Z. Drucker, "IMG MGMT: Before/After 2009-present," *Art F City* website, May 16, 2011, accessed March 24, 2016, http://artfcity.com/2011/05/16/img-mgmt-z-drucker-a-l-steiner-beforeafter-2009-present/.

112. Prosser, *Second Skins*, 211.

113. Yishay Garbasz, *Becoming: A Gender Flipbook* (New York: Mark Batty, 2010), 180.

114. Vivian Sobchack remarks on the potential for playfulness in her essay in the book, "On *Becoming*," in Garbasz, *Becoming*, 183–84.

115. A video documentation of the "Becoming" zoetrope installation can be viewed on YouTube, published September 25, 2010, accessed February 20, 2016, https://www.youtube.com/watch?v=F5diBtcul_4.

116. Yishay Garbasz, personal communication with author, April 18, 2015.

117. Sobchack, "On *Becoming*," 185.

118. Richmond, "The Persistence of Formalism."

119. Richmond, "The Persistence of Formalism."

120. Eve Kosofsky Sedgwick, "Paranoid Reading and Reparative Reading, Or, You're So Paranoid, You Probably Think This Essay Is about You," in *Touching Feeling: Affect, Pedagogy, Performativity* (Durham, NC: Duke University Press, 2003), 132–33.

121. Sedgwick, "Paranoid Reading and Reparative Reading," 131, emphasis in original.

122. Sedgwick, "Paranoid Reading and Reparative Reading," 146

123. Laura Marks, *The Skin of the Film: Intercultural Cinema, Embodiment, and the Senses* (Durham, NC: Duke University Press, 2000), 30–31.

124. Sean Cubitt, *The Practice of Light: A Genealogy of Visual Technologies from Prints to Pixels* (Cambridge, MA: MIT Press, 2014), 10–11.

125. Gilles Deleuze and Claire Parnet, *Dialogues II*, trans. Hugh Tomlinson and Barbara Habberjam (London: Continuum, 1997), 126–27.

126. Gunning, "Illusions Past and Future," 14.

127. I expand on how to theorize trans art historical and visual culture hirstories in "Collecting Creative Transcestors: Trans* Portraiture Hirstory, from Snapshots to Sculpture," in *Companion to Feminist Art Practice and Theory*, ed. Maria Buszek and Hilary Robinson (Hoboken, NJ: Wiley-Blackwell Publishing, forthcoming).

128. Freeman, *Time Binds*, 63.

129. Link to official website for *Happy Birthday, Marsha!*, posted February 19, 2015, accessed March 24, 2016, http://www.happybirthdaymarsha.com/. This factual element of the historical narrative of the Stonewall riots has been erased in the Hollywood version, *Stonewall* (dir. Roland Emmerich, 2015), which was released to poor reviews.

130. Annalise Ophelian, dir., *Major!*, Floating Ophelia Productions, USA, 2016, accessed March 16, 2016, http://www.missmajorfilm.com/; Sam Feder, dir., *Kate Bornstein Is a Queer and Pleasant Danger*, produced by Sam Feder and Karin Winslow, USA, 2014, accessed March 16, 2016, http://katebornsteinthemovie .com/. The Flawless Sabrina Archive, a nonprofit organization founded by Flawless Sabrina, Zackary Drucker, and Diana Tourjee in 2014 (accessed March 16, 2016, http://www.flawless-sabrina.com/flawless-sabrina-archive/). Mother Flawless Sabrina/Jack Doroshow passed away November 18, 2017.

1. The conference took place at Indiana University, Bloomington, April 8–9, 2011. I participated as an invited speaker during the proceedings. See the editors' introduction to Sandy Stone's "The *Empire* Strikes Back: A Posttranssexual Manifesto," in *The Transgender Studies Reader*, ed. Stephen Whittle and Susan Stryker (Routledge: New York, 2006), 221; and their introduction to Kate Bornstein, "Gender Terror, Gender Rage" in the same volume. Kate Bornstein, *Gender Outlaw: On Men, Women, and the Rest of Us* (Routledge: New York, 1994).

2. Kate Bornstein, "A Conversation Between Sandy Stone and Kate Bornstein Moderated by Susan Stryker" (presentation at the Postposttranssexual: Transgender Studies and Feminism Conference, Bloomington, Indiana, April 8–9, 2011).

3. Susan Stryker, "A Conversation Between Sandy Stone and Kate Bornstein Moderated by Susan Stryker" (presentation at the Postposttranssexual: Transgender Studies and Feminism Conference, Bloomington, Indiana, April 8–9, 2011).

4. Sandy Stone, "The *Empire* Strikes Back: A Posttranssexual Manifesto" [1991], in *The Transgender Studies Reader*, ed. Stephen Whittle and Susan Stryker (New York: Routledge, 2006), 222, 227, 228.

5. Harry Benjamin, *The Transsexual Phenomenon* (New York: Warner, 1966).

6. In medical parlance, the "true transsexual" has a history in the sexology of the 1960s and '70s. The Harry Benjamin International Gender Dysphoria Association's *Standards of Care for Gender Identity Disorders* (sixth version) includes the following history in the section on "Diagnostic Nomenclature": "The true transsexual was thought to be a person with a characteristic path of atypical gender identity development that predicted an improved life from a treatment sequence that culminated in genital surgery. True transsexuals were thought to have: (1) cross-gender identifications that were consistently expressed behaviorally in childhood, adolescence, and adulthood; (2) minimal or no sexual arousal to cross-dressing; and (3) no heterosexual interest, relative to their anatomic sex. True transsexuals could be of either sex. True transsexual males were distinguished from males who arrived at the desire to change sex and gender via a reasonably masculine behavioral developmental pathway. Belief in the true transsexual concept for males dissipated when it was realized that such patients were rarely encountered, and that some of the original true transsexuals had falsified their histories to make their stories match the earliest theories about the disorder. The concept of true transsexual females never created diagnostic uncertainties, largely because patient histories were relatively consistent and gender variant behaviors such as female cross-dressing remained unseen by clinicians. The term 'gender dysphoria syndrome' was later adopted to designate the presence

of a gender problem in either sex until psychiatry developed an official nomenclature" (5). The World Professional Association for Transgender Health, *The Harry Benjamin International Gender Dysphoria Association's Standards of Care for Gender Identity Disorders*, 6th edition, February 2001, accessed November 25, 2017, no longer available on the WPATH site, http://www.wpath.org/Documents2 /socv6.pdf. The seventh version of the *Standards of Care* was adopted in August 2016 and removed this historical overview and replaced it with a glossary, accessed July 15, 2018, https://www.wpath.org/publications/soc.

7. H. Benjamin, *Transsexual Phenomenon*, 27. The full quote describes true transsexualism (exclusively of the male to female variety) in this way: "True transsexuals feel that they belong to the other sex, they want to be and function as members of the opposite sex, not only to appear as such. For them, their sex organs, the primary (testes) as well as the secondary (penis and others) are *disgusting deformities* that must be changed by the surgeon's knife" (27, emphasis mine).

8. J. R. Latham, "Trans Men's Sexual Narrative Practices: Introducing STS to Trans and Sexuality Studies," *Sexualities* 19, no. 3 (2016): 348.

9. Stone, "The *Empire* Strikes Back," 231.

10. He writes, "his sex organs are sources of disgust and hate" (H. Benjamin, *Transsexual Phenomenon*, 33). Again, Benjamin's terms and scale that differentiate the true (male-to-female) transsexual from transvestism and homosexuality rely on the rejection of male sexuality before surgery, whereas after surgery, she may safely embrace a female heterosexual orientation. In addition, some surgeons determine the success of a vaginoplasty according to the ability of the neo-vagina to accommodate a "regularly-sized" penis, rather than sensitivity, revealing a strong heterosexual penetration bias.

11. Stone, "The *Empire* Strikes Back," 232.

12. See Dwight Billings and Thomas Urban, "The Socio-Medical Construction of Transsexualism: An Interpretation and Critique," *Social Problems* 29, no. 3 (1982): 266–82. This article's collection of clinical evidence is further critiqued in Dean Spade, "Mutilating Gender," in *The Transgender Studies Reader*, ed. Stephen Whittle and Susan Stryker (Routledge: New York, 2006), 317–19.

13. Gayle S. Rubin, "Thinking Sex: Notes for a Radical Theory of the Politics of Sexuality" [1984], in *The Lesbian and Gay Studies Reader*, ed. Henry Abelove, Michèle Aina Barale, and David M. Halperin (New York: Routledge, 1993), 3, 13.

14. Rubin, "Thinking Sex," 14.

15. Michel Foucault, *The History of Sexuality*, Vol. 1: *An Introduction [Will to Knowledge]* [1976], trans. Robert Hurley (New York: Vintage, 1978).

16. Spade, "Mutilating Gender," 18.

17. See Spade, "Mutilating Gender," 18–19.

18. For a recent example, see Kai Cheng Thom, "How Trans Women Are Reclaim-

ing their Orgasms," Buzzfeed.com, April 17, 2016, accessed May 20, 2016, https://www.buzzfeed.com/kaichengthom/the-search-for-trans-womens-orgasms?utm_term=.reeKJ8oje#.lrPoOynKe. The opening anecdote details how Thom's doctor told her "most transsexuals" find it disturbing to have sexual drive and even orgasms, which set Thom off on a transfeminist quest to learn about her right to sexual pleasure.

19. Brian McNair, *Striptease Culture: Sex, Media and the Democratisation of Desire* (London: Routledge, 2002), 81.

20. Similar to striptease culture, the neologism "pornification" aims to re-think the common understanding of pornography as contained within a sepa-rated, marginal space; see Susanna Paasonen, Kaarina Nikunen, Laura Saaren-maa, "Introduction: Pornification and the Education of Desire," in *Pornification: Sex and Sexuality in Media Culture* (Oxford: Berg, 2007), 1–22.

21. For a targeted overview of trans porn within this context of the clinical and also queer sexual communities, see Eliza Steinbock, "Representing Trans* Sexualities," in *Routledge Companion to Media, Sex and Sexuality*, ed. Feona Attwood, R. Danielle Egan, Brian McNair, and Clarissa Smith (New York: Rout-ledge, 2017), 27–37.

22. Foucault, *History of Sexuality*, Vol. 1, 35, emphasis in original.

23. Foucault, *History of Sexuality*, Vol. 1, 59.

24. Foucault, *History of Sexuality*, Vol. 1, 42–43.

25. Foucault, *History of Sexuality*, Vol. 1, 43.

26. Foucault, *History of Sexuality*, Vol. 1, 44. The histories of nomenclature for homosexuality and transsexuality in the *Diagnostic and Statistical Manual of Mental Disorders* (DSM) published by the American Psychiatric Association also relate interconnections in how these experiences are conceptualized as patholo-gies. As homosexuality was slowly removed from the DSM in new versions from 1980 ("ego-dystonic sexual orientation") and 1987 ("sexual orientation distur-bance"), transsexualism became introduced as a "gender identity disorder," and in the fifth and most current edition from 2013 is listed as "gender dysphoria," with distress a key symptom.

27. micha cárdenas, *The Transreal: Political Aesthetics of Crossing Realities*, ed. Zach Blas and Wolfgang Schirmacher (New York: Atropos Press, 2011), 39.

28. cárdenas, *Transreal*, 30.

29. cárdenas, *Transreal*, 28–31.

30. Samuel R. Delany, *The Motion of Light in Water: Sex and Science Fiction Writing in the East Village 1960–1965* (Minneapolis: University of Minnesota Press, [1988] 2004).

31. Delany, *Motion of Light in Water*, 84–85.

32. Delany, *Motion of Light in Water*, 104.

33. Delany, *Motion of Light in Water*, 226.

34. Delany, *Motion of Light in Water*, 122.

35. Delany, *Motion of Light in Water*, 570.

36. Delany, *Motion of Light in Water*, 356.

37. Delany, *Motion of Light in Water*, 356.

38. Delany, *Motion of Light in Water*, 253.

39. Joan Scott, "The Evidence of Experience," *Critical Inquiry* 17, no. 4 (1991): 773–97. Delany quoted in Scott, "Evidence of Experience," 774.

40. Scott, "Evidence of Experience," 777.

41. Delany, *Motion of Light in Water*, 292, emphasis in original.

42. Delany, *Motion of Light in Water*, 293–94.

43. Scott, "Evidence of Experience," 778.

44. See Annie Sprinkle's extensive career detailed on her website, www.annie sprinkle.org. Sprinkle began work in commercial porn during the 1970s and in the 1990s launched her sex performance artworks. Her current art practice with partner Beth Stephens explores sexecology, or ecosexuality. This video hails from the very beginning of her self-produced, and often experimental, video porn era. Sprinkle's direct address technique was developed in her first directorial debut, a pornographic bio-pic called, *Deep Inside Annie Sprinkle* (1981). This format became hugely popular, boasting more than a hundred knock-off titles. She elaborated the concept to create a performance called "Deep Inside Porn Stars," which premiered at the Franklin Furnace Art Space, New York (1984). It staged the conversations held between members of the women's porn star support group "Club 90." Stars such as Veronica Vera and Candida Royalle spoke about their careers and about being mothers, daughters, and generally women with concerns and compassion. This "reality" porn was ostensibly a forerunner of the gonzo porn format, consisting of sexual encounters with nonprofessional actors, staged to appear random and filmed with a handheld camera.

45. The story is available on Sprinkle's personal website, listed as "My First Female-to-Male Lover," accessed November 25, 2017, http://anniesprinkle.org /my-first-female-to-male-transsexual-lover/. It was first published as an article with accompanying photographs in *Hustler* 16, no. 8 (February 1990): 7–12. The article describes the "wild" reality of transsexual embodiment, including surgeries, neo-phallus, and Les Nichols's physical fulfillment of what every bisexual wants. Sprinkle construes Nichols's gender identity as "a woman with a cock" and occasionally refers to Les as "she," although this pronoun and gender affiliation is not correlated by Les in the video, who affirms a macho-male identification. In Louis Sullivan's widely circulated *FtM Newsletter*, Sullivan wrote a short notice in the December 1989 issue about the upcoming *Hustler* story. He praises Sprinkle's sex-positivity and is glad the pictures are available to see the results of a phalloplasty, but also he is critical of Sprinkle's "annoying insistence" on getting Nichols's gender wrong, as quoted in Jamison Green, *Becoming a Vis-*

ible Man (Nashville: Vanderbilt University Press, 2004), 172–73. Although arranged differently, the content of the voice-over in the video is largely identical to Sprinkle's text in *Hustler*. The close of the credit sequence also explains that the film was based on an original story by Annie Sprinkle.

46. Les Nichols's genitalia is described as hermaphroditic on the video cover, which wrongly conflates trans surgical adjustments with a genetic intersex embodiment and feeds the misconception that trans medical histories always lead back to an original or eventual intersex condition. Les asserts in the video that he chose to retain his vaginal opening to preserve this route to sexual sensation, so Sprinkle invents vocabulary like "gender-flexible" and "dual-genitalia" to describe his anatomy.

47. This information was communicated to the author via email on May 20, 2011. Sprinkle coined the term *post-porn modernist* to describe her first one-woman theatre piece that she toured starting in this moment from 1989–95. See also Annie Sprinkle, *Post Porn Modernist: My 25 Years as a Multimedia Whore* (San Francisco: Cleis, 1989).

48. Linda Williams, *Hard Core: Power, Pleasure, and the "Frenzy of the Visible"* (Berkeley: University of California Press, 1999), 282–87.

49. The notion of ontological (and later indexical) realism is most often identified with André Bazin's 1945 essay "The Ontology of the Photographic Image," in *What Is the Pornographic Image?* Vol. 1, ed. and trans. Hugh Gray (Berkeley: University of California Press, 1967). Thomas Elsaesser notes that long before "digitalization seemingly did away with the material 'ground' for this indexicality of the optic-chemical imprint or trace, ontological realism had already been challenged, critiqued, and denounced as an ideological fiction," most prominently by the schools of apparatus theory, the society of the spectacle writers Debord and Baudrillard, and feminist film criticism (5). The epistemic critiques of realism, however, assume that "there is such a thing as 'correct representation,' or at least that 'reality' can be distinguished from 'illusion' and that a 'truth' can be meaningfully opposed to 'mere appearance'" (5). As I intend to argue, neither pure ontological truth nor a notion of pure illusion is satisfactory for explaining the confluence of fantasy and realism in this video.

50. It also recalls the British genre of "kitchen sink" documentary that depicts the real lives of people in the most domestic of spaces in the home, the workspace of the kitchen. The hyperreal space of the kitchen lends further truth-effects to the scene depicted. For more on the characteristics of this documentary movement, see Samantha Lay, "1950s and 1960s: Social Problems and Kitchen Sinks," in *British Social Realism: From Documentary to Brit-Grit* (London: Wallflower, 2002), 55–76.

51. Bill Nichols, "The Voice of Documentary," *Film Quarterly* 36, no. 3 (1993): 17–18.

52. Nichols, "The Voice of Documentary," 18.

53. Julie Levin Russo, "'The Real Thing': Reframing Queer Pornography for Virtual Spaces," in *C'Lick Me: A Netporn Studies Reader*, ed. Katrien Jacobs, Marije Janssen, and Matteo Pasquinelli (Amsterdam: Institute of Network Cultures, 2007), 239.

54. Russo, "'The Real Thing,'" 239–40.

55. Russo, "'The Real Thing,'" 239–40.

56. Nichols, "The Voice of Documentary," 20.

57. Nichols, "The Voice of Documentary," 30n3.

58. See Russo, "'The Real Thing,'" 240, 243.

59. Judith Butler, "The Force of Fantasy: Feminism, Mapplethorp, and Discursive Excess," in *Feminism and Pornography*, ed. Drucilla Cornell (Oxford: Oxford University Press, 2000), 489.

60. Butler, "The Force of Fantasy," 487.

61. Butler, "The Force of Fantasy," 487.

62. The idea for making the video came out of Sprinkle's experience of hosting an "F2M support group" at her New York apartment for four years prior. During that time she was often the first person who had ever expressed sexual attraction toward or flirted with some of the participants (A. Sprinkle, personal communication with the author, May 20, 2011). In this way, Sprinkle offers the first on-screen role models for (would-be) partners of trans guys.

63. Green, *Becoming a Visible Man*, 172. For a recent consideration of trans male visibility in terms of genital optics, see Tobias Raun and Cáel M. Keegan, "Nothing to Hide: Selfies, Sex, and the Visibility Dilemma in Trans Male Online Cultures," in *Sex in the Digital Age*, ed. Paul G. Nixon and Isabel K. Düsterhöft (New York: Routledge, 2017), 89–100.

64. This is the context in which Stone calls for a mass coming-out of the transsexual population. On the building momentum of trans organizing in the United States from the late 1970s to the 2000s see Joanne Meyerowitz, *How Sex Changed: A History of Transsexuality in the United States* (Cambridge, MA: Harvard University Press, 2002); Susan Stryker and Jim van Buskirk, *Gay by the Bay: A History of Queer Culture in the San Francisco Bay Area* (San Francisco: Chronicle, 1996); and Susan Stryker, *Transgender History* (Berkeley: Seal Press, 2008).

65. Green, *Becoming a Visible Man*, 172.

66. Green, *Becoming a Visible Man*, 173.

67. Green, *Becoming a Visible Man*, 173.

68. Green, *Becoming a Visible Man*, 173. Sprinkle has since spoken about Les's struggle with living with schizophrenia and about his later suicide (A. Sprinkle, personal communication with the author, May 20, 2011).

69. In the late 1990s, the likely FtM transsexual porn talent "Chance Ryder" performed in videos for Totally Tasteless Productions, of which I have been able

to locate and view four scenes. He is marketed as a "hermaphrodite" and explains on-screen that he was "born this way" (a masculinized body except for a large clitoris and a vulva), though visible scars from a chest surgery suggest otherwise. Ryder unfortunately committed suicide, and no interview or other research has been found to confirm or contest whether he was in fact a person with transsexual history. A trans-produced exception is Christopher Lee's *Alley of the Tranny Boys* (1998) and other trans pornographic films he made during 1996–99, all shot in San Francisco, whose various scenes riff on both gay male and lesbian alternative pornographies.

70. Raven Kaldera and Hanne Blank, eds., "Introduction," in *Best Transgender Erotica* (Cambridge, MA: Circlet, 2002), 8–9.

71. Kaldera and Blank, "Introduction," 9.

72. The member-only site generated enough market interest for Angel to be signed in 2005 by Robert Hill Releasing, which produced videos starring "Buck Angel, the man with a pussy™." Angel broke the contract for unknown reasons, and thereafter set up his production team as Buck Angel Entertainment that continues as of February 2018, http://buckangel.com/. A trademark is a distinctive sign used by an individual or other legal entity to identify that the products or services originate from a unique source, and to distinguish them from those of other entities. It identifies intellectual property, typically a name, word, phrase, logo, symbol, design, image, or a combination. The term *trademark* is also used informally to refer to any distinguishing attribute by which an individual is readily identified, such as the characteristics of celebrities.

73. Since Angel's fame, another FtM (without chest surgery) who goes by "van Diesel" has also made, on a commercial scale, pornographic videos produced by Robert Hill Releasing and marketed to gay men. Titles include *Man with a Pussy*, *Diesel's Double Vision*, and *Diesel Exposed*, all of which play on the popularity of Buck Angel's titles, such as *Buck Naked*, *More Bang for Your Buck*, *Buck's Beaver*. More recently in 2012 James Darling launched FTMFUCKER.com as a portal site for a range of transmasculine porn (categories are straight, gay, queer, and everything) (accessed May 20, 2016).

74. Also, in accordance with the capitalist model of trade, Angel's availability for purchase displays great flexibility: in addition to the various image formats he was regularly booked for sexual performances (for instance, at the club "Torture Garden" in London or Club FUXXX in Amsterdam).

75. The other serious health risks include fissures, bleeding, and infection, among others. For an analysis dated to Buck Angel's moment of FtM transition choices with regard to genital reconstruction see Katherine Rachlin's "Factors Which Influence Individual's Decisions When Considering Female-To-Male Genital Reconstructive Surgery," *International Journal of Transgenderism* 3, no. 3 (July–September 1999), accessed February 2, 2018, https://www.atria.nl/ezines

/web/IJT/97–03/numbers/symposion/ijt990302.htm. Rachlin draws the follow-ing implications from her research results: "It is crucial to be realistic and allow that many FTMs will choose not to have surgery not because they do not want a penis, but because we can not offer them an affordable, realistic, and fully functioning penis" (np.). FtM sources that expand on the possibilities for sur-gical changes mainly through firsthand accounts include *Man Tool: The Nuts and Bolts of Female-to-Male Surgery* (World Wide Web: Zero EBooks, 2001) by Loren Rex Cameron; Dean Kotula's *The Phallus Palace: Female-to-Male Trans-sexuals* (New York: Alyson Books, 2002); and Trystan T. Cotten's edited collec-tions *Hung Jury: Testimonies of Genital Surgery by Transsexual Men* (Stockton Center, CA: Transgress Press, 2012) and *Below the Belt: Genital Talk by Men of Trans Experience* (Stockton Center, CA: Transgress Press, 2016), both of which offer recent satisfactory surgical stories.

76. Foucault, *History of Sexuality*, Vol. 1, 48; the emphasis is mine. The first volume is committed to medicine and psychiatry, whereas the industries of pros-titution and pornography are largely left by the wayside. The writings of de Sade and other confessional texts are taken to be paradigmatic, but no visual pornog-raphies are discussed.

77. Nina Power's chapter on pornography and capitalism in *One Dimensional Woman* (Winchester, UK: Zero Books, 2009) quotes figures similar to those in Linda Williams's introduction to *Porn Studies* (Durham, NC: Duke University Press, 2004), 1–2. Power also places this figure into the context that this is more money than Hollywood and all major league sports make together. In addition, she writes that 300,000 porn sites are available with a click of the mouse, and 200 new films are estimated to be in production each week (56).

78. Although now retired from porn performance, Angel continues to direct docu-porns with other trans men in the *Sexing the Transman* series of four vol-umes in xxx and non–sexually explicit versions (2010–12), and he gives lectures as a sex educator, sex toy designer, advocate, and inspirational speaker.

79. See Bornstein, *Gender Outlaw*; Riki Anne Wilchins, *Read My Lips: Sex-ual Subversions and the End of Gender* (Ithaca, NY: Firebrand Books, 1997); Spade, "Mutilating Gender," 315–32; C. Jacob Hale, "Leatherdyke Boys and Their Daddies: How to Have Sex without Women or Men," *Social Text* 52/53 (1997): 223–36; Jordy Jones, "Gender without Genitals: Hedwig's Six Inches," in Whittle and Stryker, eds., *The Transgender Studies Reader*, 449–68.

80. Freud, "On Fetishism" [1927], in *On Sexuality: Three Essays on the Theory of Sexuality, and other Works*, ed. Angela Richards, trans. James Strachey (New York: Penguin, 1977), 354–58, 357.

81. Angel starred in season 4 of the reality television show WeTV *Secret Lives of Women: Porn Stars* (2008).

82. The "clinical force" is evidenced by the *need* for a potential transsexual

candidate to demonstrate a fetishistic obsession with genitals. This tends to be a part of the diagnostic process: "It was deemed appropriate and even necessary for pre-operative transsexuals to demonstrate a fetishistic obsession with genitals: to be rid of the ones they had, and to obtain the ones they wanted," writes Nikki Sullivan in *A Critical Introduction to Queer Theory* (New York: New York University Press, 2003), 105.

83. Judith Shapiro, "Transsexualism: Reflections on the Persistence of Gender and the Mutability of Sex," in *Body Guards: The Cultural Politics of Gender Ambiguity*, ed. Julia Epstein and Kristina Straub, 248–79 (New York: Routledge, 1991), 260, emphasis mine.

84. See his development of the main terms of fetishism in terms of sexual distinction in Sigmund Freud, "Some Psychical Consequences of the Anatomical Distinction between the Sexes" [1925], in Richards, ed., *On Sexuality*, 323–44, which was published some two years before his essay "On Fetishism" (1927).

85. Freud, "On Fetishism," 353.

86. Freud, "On Fetishism," 354.

87. Freud, "On Fetishism," 353.

88. Freud, "On Fetishism," 353.

89. Williams, *Hard Core*, 104, my emphasis.

90. Freud, "On Fetishism," 353. Because of limitations of space, I am only able to speculate the extent to which this token is a fetish substitute for a phallus for the largest consumer market of his material, gay men, who presumably would be most interested in the penis. This line of thought might be usefully followed with Freud's own inquiry into homosexual men and the castration complex and the analysis of the interchangeability of the phallus and gold in Jean-Joseph Goux, *Symbolic Economies: After Marx and Freud*, trans. Jennifer Curtiss Gage (Ithaca, NY: Cornell University Press, 1990).

91. The phrase *triumphant token* might be taken in an additional sense. Because Buck Angel was the first and for a long time only professional FtM porn star, he also became a "token" or symbolic representative of FtM sexuality in commercial porn, particularly with regard to his nominations and awards from the Adult Video News (2007), in which he was the first trans man to be considered or named and also in consecutive years (2008–10).

92. Freud, "On Fetishism," 351, emphasis in original.

93. In German, as in English, Glans denotes the head or tip of the penis; by synecdoche (part for whole) it extends to the whole penis. Hence Freud puns his way through the entire argument of fetishism and its structure of slippery substitution in which the German Glanz becomes Glans, which allows for the shine in English to convert to a penis. I thank Murat Aydemir for sharing the joke with me.

94. Foucault, *History of Sexuality*, Vol. 1, 152–53. Fetishism is discussed, albeit

briefly, as contributing to a modern notion of sex, the networked dispositif of sexuality. The fetishism model of perversion contributed to a conceptualization of sex and its deviations "governed by the interplay of whole and part, principle and lack, absence and presence, excess and deficiency" (153–54).

95. Foucault, *History of Sexuality*, Vol. 1, 19. A change in the mid–sixteenth century to the Catholic sacrament of penance devolved the moment of trans-gression "from the act itself to the stirrings—so difficult to perceive and formu-late—of desire," writes Foucault (*History of Sexuality*, Vol. 1, 19–20, emphasis in original). Foucault writes, "It was here, perhaps, that the injunction, so peculiar to the West, was laid down for the first time [. . .] the nearly infinite task of telling—telling oneself and another, as often as possible everything that might concern the interplay of innumerable pleasures, sensations, and thoughts which, through the body and the soul, had some affinity with sex" (20).

96. Originally produced by V-Tape, this video is available for viewing online: Mirah-Soleil Ross and Mark Karbusicky, "The Centre for Contemporary Ca-nadian Art: The Canadian Art Database," York University, accessed March 10, 2010, http://www.ccca.ca/.

97. Foucault, *History of Sexuality*, Vol. 1, 61–62. Foucault's planned volumes on the modern formations of Western sexuality and confessing attitudes would have begun with the Christian practices of confession that understood flesh as distinct from the body (*La Chair et le corps* [The Flesh and the Body]). Following this volume, he planned a study of four types of sexual subjects, who constitute breeds of "confessing animals," as the foci of the last volumes. In the French edi-tion, Foucault projected a fifth volume, *Pouvoir de la vérité* (The Power of Truth), that would deal with the coupling of torture and confession in Greek and Roman times. The subsequent volumes, however, proceeded differently. Stuart Elden proposes that the theme of confession had led Foucault back to ancient Latin and Greek texts, to earlier manifestations of techniques of the self (aesthetic prac-tices) that were not necessarily tied into sexuality. Stuart Elden, "The Problem of Confession: The Productive Failure of Foucault's History of Sexuality," *Journal for Cultural Research* 9, no. 1 (2005): 23–41, 36–39.

98. Confession nevertheless remained integral to the arrangement and re-arrangement of the whole Sexuality series, with the title *Les Aveux de la Chair* (The Confessions of the Flesh) announced in volume 2 as the fourth and final in the series. Foucault's death arrived before its publication, and the mostly fin-ished manuscript languishes per his wish. His literary executors have recently announced that Gallimard Press will finally publish "Confessions of the Flesh," the fourth and final in the volume series *History of Sexuality*, in 2018. Elden ar-gues that although the projected and unfinished volumes on confession may have failed in a certain sense, Foucault's working through the interest and con-fusion it posed to him was highly productive for developing new horizons. In

particular, confession held together the divergent articulations of a modality of power and played a role in the production of truth. He cites Foucault in a 1981 interview: "I constantly come up against confession and I wonder whether to write the history of confession as a sort of technique, or to treat this question in the context of studies of the different domains where it seems to play a role, that is in the domain of sexuality and that of penal psychiatry" (Foucault quoted in Elden, "The Problem of Confession," 39). The careful wording of *Les Aveux de la Chair* reflects this proposal for confession, which is not simply the practice *les confession*, but *les aveux*, the word for avowal that suggests that the unconstrained admission or declaration of the flesh's truth is at stake.

99. Michel Foucault, *Ethics: Essential Works of Foucault 1954–1984*, Vol. 1, ed. Paul Rabinow (London: Penguin, 1997), 253.

100. For evidence of interest in (trans) genitals and their function, see Riki Anne Wilchins on "17 Things you DON'T Say" in *Read My Lips* (1997), especially numbers 6 and 7; 8 is the question, "Can you have an orgasm?," reflecting the prurient interest directed toward trans-sexuality in general (27–33). Another humorous retort can be found in the video by Calperina Addams, "Bad Questions to Ask a Transsexual," YouTube.com, last accessed May 25, 2010, http://www .youtube.com/watch?v=BOjeZnjKlpo&feature=channel.

101. Stone, "The *Empire* Strikes Back," 228.

102. Foucault, *History of Sexuality*, Vol. 1, 156–57.

103. Alice Walker writes: "unless the question of Colorism—in my definition, prejudicial or preferential treatment of same-race people based solely on their color—is addressed in our communities and definitely in our black 'sisterhoods' we cannot, as a people, progress. For colorism, like colonialism, sexism, and racism, impedes us," in Alice Walker, *In Search of our Mothers' Gardens: Womanist Prose* (New York: Harcourt Brace Jovanovich, 1983), 291.

104. I follow the film's language in using *trans* (and not *trans** or *transgender*) as an umbrella term for gender variance, genderfuck, and transitioning genders, including transsexual-identified people. *Kinky* refers to those sexual proclivities, desires, and practices that are not "straight," but are experienced with a "kink." It is a shorthand community term that also refers to the recently coined term BDSM. BDSM and SM refer to "a diverse community that includes aficionados of bondage, [D]omination/submission, pain or sensation play, power exchange, leathersex, role-playing and fetishes," writes Margot Weiss in *Techniques of Pleasures: BDSM and the Circuits of Sexuality* (Durham, NC: Duke University Press, 2012), vii. Formally, it is an acronym for bondage/discipline, dominance/submission, and sadomasochism. *Polyamory* is a term for "many loves" and is widely used to refer to practices and theories of nonmonogamy or nonexclusive partnering.

105. During the fifth Netherlands Transgender Film Festival (2009), I selected

this film for our "Sex Positive" program and facilitated after the screening the discussion with director Morty Diamond and Judy Minx, a trans partner and French porn star. It was a sold-out screening (90+ attendees) and was evaluated very highly in the festival survey.

106. Diamond describes himself as a "Jewish, transsexual, writer, artist and filmmaker" (personal webpage, no longer available). The documentation of trans POC in New York City by nontrans and white people includes *"Paris Is Burning"* (dir. Jennie Livingston, 1990) and *The Aggressives* (dir. Daniel Peddle, 2005). Trans and queer POC documentary makers recently produced *Still Black: A Portrait of Black Trans Men* (dir. Kortney Ryan Ziegler, 2008) and *U People* (dir. Hanifah Walidah and Olive Demetrius, 2009). Nevertheless, the intersection of POC, trans, and kink has not been documented before, at least not from *within* these communities.

107. Tristan Taormino, "The New Wave of Trans Cinema: The Latest Transporn Breaks Down Both Boundaries and Inhibitions," *Village Voice*, April 8, 2008, accessed February 2, 2018, http://www.villagevoice. com/2008–04–08/columns /the-new-wave-of-trans-cinema/.

108. Taormino, "The New Wave of Trans Cinema."

109. Linda Williams, "Skin Flicks on the Racial Border: Pornography, Exploitation, and Interracial Lust," in *Porn Studies*, ed. Linda Williams, 271–308 (Durham, NC: Duke University Press, 2004), 272.

110. While Black scholars such as Henry Louis Gates Jr. defended their artistry in court, Black feminists heard in the sexual content of the lyrics intracommunity sexism; see Kimberlé Crenshaw, "Beyond Racism and Misogyny: Black Feminism and 2 Live Crew," *Boston Review* 16, no. 6 (1991): 6–33.

111. For popular coverage of race play see Daisy Hernandez's post "Playing with Race," Colorlines.com, December 21, 2004, accessed November 25, 2017, http://colorlines.com/archives/2004/12/playing_with_race.html.

112. Williams, "Skin Flicks on the Racial Border," 275.

113. Williams, "Skin Flicks on the Racial Border," 285.

114. Mireille Miller-Young, "Hip-Hop Honeys and Da Hustlaz: Black Sexualities in the New Hip-Hop Pornography," *Meridians* 8, no. 1 (2008): 261–92, 266. Williams, "Skin Flicks on the Racial Border," 285.

115. Williams, "Skin Flicks on the Racial Border," 285.

116. Mireille Miller-Young, "Putting Hypersexuality to Work: Black Women and Illicit Eroticism in Pornography," *Sexualities* 13, no. 2 (2010): 219–35, 222–33.

117. Miller-Young, "Hip-Hop Honeys and Da Hustlaz," 223.

118. Sara Ahmed, "Happy Objects," in *The Affect Theory Reader*, ed. Melissa Gregg and Gregory J. Seigworth, 29–51 (Durham, NC: Duke University Press, 2010), 30.

119. Ahmed, "Happy Objects," 29.

120. Ahmed, "Happy Objects," 37.

121. José Esteban Muñoz, "Feeling Brown: Ethnicity and Affect in Ricardo Bracho's 'The Sweetest Hangover (and Other STDs),'" *Theatre Journal* 52, no. 1 (2000): 67–79. Latinx has come to replace Latino/a inscriptions of gender difference marked in Spanish, as Muñoz uses in his text, with the "x" also specifying trans variations on gender identity. See coverage by Tanisha Love Ramirez, "Why People Are Using the Term 'Latinx,'" HuffingtonPost.com, "Latino Voices," August 5, 2016, accessed November 25, 2017, http://www.huffingtonpost.com/entry/why-people-are-using-the-termlatinx_us_57753328e4b0ccofa136a159.

122. Muñoz, "Feeling Brown," 70.

123. Muñoz, "Feeling Brown," 70.

124. Muñoz, "Feeling Brown," 70.

125. Expanding on Michele Wallace's 1990 essay "Variations of Negation" in *Invisibility Blues*, among other Black Feminist scholarship, the problems of reading the distorting effects of Black sexuality are explained by Evelynn Hammonds, "Black (W)holes and the Geometry of Black Female Sexuality," in *Differences: Feminism Meets Queer Theory*, ed. Elizabeth Weed and Naomi Schor, 136–56 (Bloomington: Indiana University Press, 1997), 149.

126. Susan Stryker, "Transgender Studies: Queer Theory's Evil Twin," GLQ: *A Journal of Lesbian and Gay Studies* 10, no. 2 (2004): 212–15, 215.

127. This point has also been made by J. R. Latham, "Trans Men's Sexual Narrative-Practices," 346–68.

128. By refuting the sex-based categories of sexuality, this is not to say that trans people cannot have a lesbian, gay, bi, or other sexual identifications. My point is to stress that binary sex organized sexuality excludes nonbinary genders, but moreover it occludes the conceptualization of sexuality in which gender is not genitally organized. New sexual identity categories such as tranny fag or trans lesbian are important "nonce taxonomies" that Sedgwick suggests is evidence of the inventiveness of desire, and the tactical expression of navigating the social field of sexualities; see Eve Kosofsky Sedgwick, *Epistemology of the Closet* (Berkeley: University of California Press, 1990), 23.

129. Zowie Davy, *Recognizing Transsexuals: Personal, Political, and Medico-legal Embodiment* (New York: Routledge, 2011).

130. Davy, *Recognizing Transsexuals*, 10.

131. Jay Prosser, *Second Skins: The Body Narratives of Transsexuality* (New York: Columbia University Press, 1998), 66.

132. Davy, *Recognizing Transsexuals*, 10–11.

133. Jacques Lacan, *The Four Fundamental Concepts of Psychoanalysis*, ed. Richard Feldstein, Bruce Fink, and Maire Jaanus (London: Penguin, 1979), 117, 118.

134. Unhindered suturing is a status that many nontranssexual and binary-

identified people may take for granted. For instance, someone who can check the male or female box on an institutional form without qualms would be successfully, if fictionally, sutured.

135. Kaja Silverman, *The Threshold of the Visible World* (New York: Routledge, 1996).

136. Silverman, *Threshold of the Visible World*, 14–16.

137. Silverman, *Threshold of the Visible World*, 17.

138. Robin Bauer, "Transgressive and Transformative Gendered Sexual Practices and White Privileges: The Case of the Dyke/Trans BDSM Communities," *WSQ: Women's Studies Quarterly* 36, nos. 3–4 (2008): 233–53, 241–44.

139. Hale, "Leatherdyke Boys and Their Daddies," 226.

140. Hale, "Leatherdyke Boys and Their Daddies," 227, my emphasis.

141. Hale, "Leatherdyke Boys and Their Daddies," 230.

142. Hale, "Leatherdyke Boys and Their Daddies," 230.

143. Together with Zowie Davy, I have explored how bodily aesthetics and different kinds of sexual interaction can serve as a transgender practice to transform corporality in Eliza Steinbock and Zowie Davy, "'Sexing Up' Bodily Aesthetics: Notes towards Theorizing Trans Sexuality," in *Sexualities: Past Reflections and Future Directions*, ed. Sally Hines and Yvette Taylor, 266–85 (Basingstoke: Palgrave Macmillan, 2012).

144. Hale, "Leatherdyke Boys and Their Daddies," 233.

145. Silverman, *Threshold of the Visible World*, 17.

146. Silverman, *Threshold of the Visible World*, 18.

147. Silverman, *Threshold of the Visible World*, 45.

148. Silverman, *Threshold of the Visible World*, 40–41.

149. Silverman, *Threshold of the Visible World*, 23–24.

150. Mieke Bal, "Looking at Love: An Ethics of Vision," review of *The Threshold of the Visible World*, by Kaja Silverman, *Diacritics* 27, no. 1 (1997): 59–72, 62.

151. Jean-Pierre Oudart, "Cinema and Suture," *Screen Dossier on Suture* 18, no. 4 (1977–88): 35–47.

152. Silverman, *Threshold of the Visible World*, 96.

153. Kaja Silverman, *Male Subjectivity at the Margins* (New York: Routledge, 1992), 150.

154. Silverman, *Threshold of the Visible World*, 19.

155. Silverman, *Threshold of the Visible World*, 78–9.

156. José Esteban Muñoz, *Disidentifications: Queers of Color and the Performance of Politics* (Minneapolis: University of Minnesota Press, 1999), 12.

1. Donna Haraway, "A Cyborg Manifesto: Science, Technology, and Socialist-Feminism in the Late Twentieth Century," in *Simians, Cyborgs, and Women: The Reinvention of Nature* (New York: Routledge, 1991), 149–81.

2. Haraway, "Cyborg Manifesto," 150.

3. Sandy Stone, "Keynote Lecture" (Trans*Studies: An International Transdisciplinary Conference on Gender, Embodiment, and Sexuality, Tucson, Arizona, September 7, 2016).

4. Of the media in information society, one in particular holds sway as deeply ambivalent, writes Marita Sturken: "This [video] is a medium in which the ongoing developments in electronic technology, and their relationship to the power of technology in our culture—as it is manifested in the transmission of images on television, the storage of information in computers, and the mass media—cannot be ignored. But we are ambivalent about technology in Western culture. On one hand we see it as a panacea for global problems, on the other hand we feel we have little control over it"; see Marita Sturken, "Paradox in the Evolution of an Art Form: Great Expectations and the Making of a History" [1988], in *Illuminating Video: An Essential Guide to Video Art*, ed. Doug Hall and Sally Jo Fifer, 101–21 (New York: Aperture, 1990), 120–21.

5. Paul (formally Beatriz) Preciado suggests the term *sex-design* in the context of this history in "Pharmaco-pornographic Politics: Towards a New Gender Ecology," *Parallax* 46 (2008): 105–17.

6. On the relation between digital and analog, see Wendy Hui Kyong Chun, *Programmed Visions: Software and Memory* (Cambridge, MA: MIT Press, 2013). Also, Eugene Thacker gives an overview of the literature on virtual bodies and cyberculture in "What Is Biomedia?" *Configurations* 11 (2003): 47–79. He includes Anne Balsamo, *Technologies of the Gendered Body* (Durham, NC: Duke University Press, 1997); Mike Featherstone and Roger Burrows, eds., *Cyberspace / Cyberbodies / Cyberpunk* (London: Sage, 1995); Arthur Kroker and Marilouise Kroker, *Hacking the Future* (New York: St. Martin's, 1996); Allucquère Rosanne Stone, *The War of Desire and Technology at the Close of the Mechanical Age* (Cambridge, MA: MIT Press, 1996). The work produced under the banner of FemTechNet represents some of the most current and exciting sources for hacking cyberculture: femtechnet.org/publications/.

7. Kara Keeling, *The Witch's Flight: The Cinematic, the Black Femme, and the Image of Common Sense* (Durham, NC: Duke University Press, 2007).

8. Keeling, *Witch's Flight*, 12.

9. Henri Bergson, *Matter and Memory* [1908], trans. N. M. Paul and W. S. Palmer (New York: Zone Books, 1988).

10. Keeling, *Witch's Flight*, 13.

11. Keeling, *Witch's Flight*, 14, 18.

12. Keeling, *Witch's Flight*, 14. Keeling cites in-text a quotation from Deleuze's *Cinema 2* (54) about the potential of the time-image to break with motor-action into thought. Also 160–161n5 contains an extended quote on the "floating images" of anonymous clichés that form sound and visual slogans taken from *Cinema 1* (208–09).

13. This misguided cyborg figuration of trans subjects arises in gender and media theories, some of which I discuss below. A paradigmatic example of charging transsexuality with artificiality is Jean Baudrillard, *The Transparency of Evil: Essays on Extreme Phenomena* (New York: Verso, 2009), 20–25.

14. Hans Scheirl, dir., *Dandy Dust* (London: Millivres Multimedia, 1998); Cheang Shu Lea, dir., *I.K.U.* (Tokyo: UPLINK Co., 2000).

15. B. Ruby Rich reports that according to Cheang, at *I.K.U.*'s premier at Sundance (Park City, Utah) approximately 40 percent of viewers left the cinema. See B. Ruby Rich, "'Bodies Are Packages Made to be Opened': Shu Lea Cheang's 'I.K.U.' (2000)," Rhizome blog, May 26, 2005, accessed March 14, 2017, rhizome .org/editorial/2015/may/26/iku-experience-shu-lea-cheang-phenomenon/. *Dandy Dust* premiered at the London Gay and Lesbian Film Festival in 1998 and went on to show at many midnight screenings, where it was "grabbing international film audiences by the throat and hurling them headfirst into the nearest available human orifice," leading to journalists storming out of the screening and branding it pornography, relates the dust cover on the VHS release.

16. I refer here to the work of, for example, Laura Mulvey, Vivian Sobchack, and David Bordwell.

17. Eve Kosofsky Sedgwick and Adam Frank, "Shame in the Cybernetic Fold: Reading Silvan Tomkins," in *Shame and its Sisters: A Silvan Tomkins Reader* (Durham, NC: Duke University Press, 1995), 12.

18. Eva Hayward and Jami Weinstein, "Introduction: Tranimalities in the Age of Trans* Life," TSQ: *Transgender Studies Quarterly* 2, no. 2 (2015): 196–97.

19. Jonathan Roffe, "Multiplicity," in *The Deleuze Dictionary*, ed. Adrian Parr, 176–77 (New York: Columbia University Press, 2005), 176.

20. Gilles Deleuze, *Bergsonism*, trans. Hugh Tomlinson and Barbara Habberjam (New York: Zone Books, [1966] 1991).

21. John Mullarkey, "Gilles Deleuze," in *Film, Theory, and Philosophy: The Key Thinkers*, ed. Felicity Colman (New York: Routledge, 2014), 187.

22. Quoted in Mullarkey, "Gilles Deleuze," 187.

23. Roffe, "Multiplicity," 176–77.

24. Deleuze quoted in Mullarkey, "Gilles Deleuze," 188.

25. Eva Hayward discusses the reach of the asterisk in her text cowritten with

Jami Weinstein, "Introduction: Tranimalities," 199; see also an extension of her theorizing in Eva Hayward and Che Gossett, "The Impossibility of *That*," *Angelaki: Journal for Theoretical Humanities* 22, no. 2 (2017): 15–24.

26. I refer to the research of Tobias Raun, *Out Online: Trans Self-Representation and Community Building on YouTube* (New York: Routledge, 2016); and Laura Horak, "Trans on YouTube: Intimacy, Visibility, Temporality," *TSQ: Transgender Studies Quarterly* 1, no. 4 (2014): 572–85.

27. They are missing in the major writings on the New Queer Cinema by B. Ruby Rich, *New Queer Cinema: The Director's Cut* (Durham, NC: Duke University Press, 2013) and in the edited collection by Michelle Aaron, *New Queer Cinema: A Critical Reader* (New Brunswick, NJ: Rutgers University Press, 2004). Rich has written a brief review of *I.K.U.*, as mentioned in note 15. In her volume *The Queer German Cinema* (Stanford, CA: Stanford University Press, 2000), Alice A. Kuzniar includes *Dandy Dust* in a chapter on "Experimental Visions" that mainly examines the film for how it relates to the thematics of short Super-8 films and video Scheirl made with Ursula Pürrer in decades prior (224). Although other chapters focus on feature-length films or major filmmakers, Kuzniar groups Scheirl and *Dandy Dust* together with many other works.

28. Denise Riley, "Am I That Name? Feminism and the Category of 'Women' in History," in *Bodies, Identities, Feminisms* (Basingstoke, U.K.: Palgrave Macmillan, 1988), 96, emphasis in original.

29. For a critical history of experimental video projection, including theorizing its technical evanescence and changing technical support, see Liz Kotz, "Video Projection: The Space Between Screens," in *Art and the Moving Image: A Critical Reader*, ed. Tanya Leighton (London: Afterall, 2008), 371–85.

30. Hans Scheirl, "I Am Opposed to the Practice of Not Showing the Horrible Things," interview by Andrea Braidt, in *[Cyborg.Nets/z] Catalogue on* Dandy Dust *(Hans Scheirl, 1998)*, ed. Andrea B. Braidt (Vienna: BKA Filmbeirat, 1999), 19.

31. Scheirl, "I Am Opposed," 19.

32. William Kaizen, "Live on Tape: Video, Liveness and the Immediate," in *Art and the Moving Image: A Critical Reader*, ed. Tanya Leighton (London: Afterall, 2008), 265.

33. Scheirl, "I Am Opposed," 19.

34. Eugenie Brinkema, *The Forms of the Affects* (Durham, NC: Duke University Press, 2014), 31–36.

35. Steven Shaviro, *The Cinematic Body* (Minneapolis: University of Minnesota Press, 1993).

36. Shaviro, *Cinematic Body*, 47.

37. Roland Barthes, *The Neutral* [2002], trans. Rosalind E. Krauss and Denis Hollier (New York: Columbia University Press, 2005), 101.

38. Barthes, *Neutral*, 101.

39. Barthes, *Neutral*, 73.

40. Roland Barthes, *The Rustle of Language* [1984], trans. Richard Howard (Berkeley: University of California, 1989), 178.

41. Hans Scheirl, "Manifesto for the Dada of the Cyborg-Embrio," in *The Eight Technologies of Otherness*, ed. Sue Golding (London: Routledge, 1997), 56. Scheirl announces this chimeric aesthetic as hermaphroditic, which calls on the allegory of intersex in a way that problematically metaphorizes actual intersex bodies and also conflates transgender embodiment with historical renderings of hermaphrodite bodies. I suggest instead focusing on how Scheirl's cinema develops through trans*forming, in his words, "a cinematic language that liquefies the hierarchies of the body: blood speaks through the light projection, skin through a certain flimmering of the film grain, the psyche in the harmony of exaggeration and disguise—which to me means drag: parody, simulation" (quoted in Kuzniar, *Queer German Cinema*, 229).

42. Keeling, *Witch's Flight*, 38; Brinkema, *Forms of the Affects*, 37.

43. I follow David Getsy's refusal to nominate an object (or form or structure) ambiguous, which he calls a resignation and avoidance to learn about "all that does not fit into our categories" and therefore is written off as unknowable. See David J. Getsy, "Refusing Ambiguity" (paper presented at the Renaissance Society symposium Ambiguity Forum, University of Chicago, January 14, 2017).

44. A shimmer might be that insurrection of form, shape, pattern and its uses that Getsy describes as central to a queer formalism's belief in the politics of form, in the politics of relationality and intercourse. See David J. Getsy, "Queer Relations," *ASAP/Journal* 2, no. 2 (May 2017): 254–57.

45. For an extensive analysis of how *I.K.U.* loops back to the closing romantic relationship of *Blade Runner* and restarts it as sex (work), not love exchange, with particular attention to the critique of nostalgia for analog Hollywood film and white victimhood complexes, see the insightful chapter by Jian Chen, "TRANScoding the Transnational Digital Economy," in *Trans Studies: The Challenge to Hetero/Homo Normativities*, ed. Yolanda Martinez-San Miguel and Sarah Tobiaso (New Brunswick, NJ: Rutgers University Press, 2016), 83–100.

46. Katrien Jacobs, "Queer Voyeurism and the Pussy-Matrix in Shu Lea Cheang's Japanese Pornography," in *Mobile Cultures: New Media in Queer Asia*, ed. Chris Berry, Fran Martin, and Audrey Yue (Durham, NC: Duke University Press, 2003), 208.

47. Chen describes this as the "flat yet live feel of viewing an information feed that becomes interactive," which I note might be found within game space or RSS feeds within a website (Chen, TRANScoding, 91).

48. This film project was made on the tail of the first new-media art project, "BRANDON: A One-Year Narrative Project in Installments" (1998–99), which was explicitly concerned with the dangerous act of scanning for a transgender

embodiment that led to the rape and murder of Brandon/Teena Brandon (December 1993). It consisted of four interfaces for artists' participation that deploy Brandon into cyberspace through multilayered narratives accessed by a field of options. One click on a detail thrusts the user's visual experience down a portal. See "Brandon" on The Guggenheim Museum's website, accessed March 15, 2017, http://brandon.guggenheim.org/credits/.

49. Chen, "TRANScoding," 87–89. On the central new-media concept of transcoding (the translation of computer code to cultural code that is intrinsic to all new media, like the internet), see Lev Manovitch, *The Language of New Media* (Cambridge, MA: MIT Press, 2001).

50. Sue Golding [as Johnny de Philo], "To Tremble the Ejaculate," in Braidt, ed., *[Cyborg. Nets/z]*, 69–70.

51. Golding [de Philo], "To Tremble the Ejaculate," 69.

52. Jaap Kooijman writes about zapping channels as a mode of cruising, highlighting the erotic dimension of interest and the queerness of what one finds interesting, qua television studies; see Jaap Kooijman, "Cruising the Channels: The Queerness of Zapping," in *Queer TV: Theories, Histories, Politics*, ed. Glyn Davis and Gary Needham (New York: Routledge, 2009), 159–71.

53. Scheirl, "Manifesto for the Dada," 46

54. Scheirl, "Manifesto for the Dada," 48.

55. Scheirl, "Manifesto for the Dada," 50. In Scheirl's artist statement for a 2004 solo show of paintings, "Hans in Transition," he writes: "The term 'transition' is used in the transsexual and transgender community for the stretch of time it takes a person to change into the other gender. Now, i'm [sic] not going from A to B, but rather zigzagging my way through a large, open space of possibilities." See Hans Scheirl, "Hans in Transition: Paintings by Hans Scheirl," press release and artist's statement, Transition Gallery Press, 2004, accessed March 15, 2017, www.transitiongallery.co.uk/htmlpages/hans/hans_pr.html.

56. Roland Barthes, *The Preparation of the Novel: Lecture Courses and Seminars at the Collège de France (1978–1979 and 1979–1980)*, trans. Kate Briggs (New York: Columbia University Press, 2010), 45.

57. Scheirl, "Manifesto for the Dada," 51.

58. Pornographic actress Mai Hoshino was hired for the lead role of Reiko but disappeared three days before shooting began. Of the subsequent actresses auditioned, Cheang was unable to find one who was both able to act and willing to perform all of the sexual acts outlined in the script. Instead, seven (erotic) actresses were selected and the lead role modified to incorporate the shapeshifting element, allowing the contentious hardcore scenes to be meted out between the seven. Even so, the hardcore acts were continually renegotiated throughout filming. See Johannes Schönherr, "Shu Lea Cheang: Sex Art Aborigine," in *Fleshpot:*

Cinema's Sexual Myth Makers & Taboo Breakers, ed. Jack Stevenson (New York: Critical Vision, 2000), 197–200.

59. Karen Barad, "TransMaterialities: Trans*/Matter/Realities and Queer Political Imaginings," GLQ: *A Journal of Lesbian and Gay Studies* 21, nos. 2–3 (2015): 410–12.

60. Sedgwick and Frank, "Shame in the Cybernetic Fold," 5.

61. Sedgwick and Frank, "Shame in the Cybernetic Fold," 7.

62. Tomkins quoted in Sedgwick and Frank, "Shame in the Cybernetic Fold," 7.

63. Michel Foucault, *The History of Sexuality*, Vol. 2: *The Use of Pleasure* [1984], trans. Robert Hurley (New York: Vintage, 1990), 8–9.

64. Scheirl, "Manifesto for the Dada," 55.

65. Laura Mulvey theorizes the figure of Pandora as a feminist investigator in "Pandora's Box: Topographies of Curiosity," in *Fetishism and Curiosity* (Bloomington: Indiana University Press, 1996), 53–55.

66. David J. Getsy, *Abstract Bodies: Sixties Sculpture in the Expanded Field of Gender* (New Haven, CT: Yale University Press, 2015), 34–36.

67. Guy Hocquenghem, *Homosexual Desire* [1972], trans. Daniella Dangoor (Durham, NC: Duke University Press, 1993), 101.

68. Getsy, *Abstract Bodies*, xv.

69. A detailed transgender studies reading of the Wachowski siblings' filmography in the context of cultural and media history is conducted by Cáel M. Keegan, *Lana and Lilli Wachowski: Sensing Transgender* (Chicago: University of Illinois Press, 2018).

70. Cheang makes this remark in an interview with Geert Lovink through an email exchange that was archived December 29, 2000, on the nettime.org listserv, but it is no longer available. It is quoted by Timothy Murray, "Time @ Cinema's Future: New Media Art and the Thought of Temporality," in *After-images of Gilles Deleuze's Film Philosophy*, ed. David N. Rodowick (Minneapolis: University of Minnesota Press, 2010), 364.

71. Linda Williams, *Hard Core: Power, Pleasure, and the "Frenzy of the Visible"* (Berkeley: California University Press, 1999), 94. See also the deconstruction of ejaculation as an involuntary, unperformed act in Murat Aydemir, *Images of Bliss: Ejaculation, Masculinity, and Meaning* (Minneapolis: University of Minnesota Press, 2007).

72. Jacobs, "Queer Voyeurism," 217.

73. Brinkema, *Forms of the Affects*, xvi.

74. Eve Oishi, "'Collective Orgasm': The Eco-Cyber-Pornography of Shu Lea Cheang," WSQ: *Women's Study Quarterly* 35, nos. 1–2 (2007): 31.

75. Cheang quoted in Dominic Pettman, *Love and Other Technologies: Retrofitting Eros for an Information Age* (New York: Fordham University Press, 2006), 120.

76. The "data rape" reading of *I.K.U.* is introduced very briefly by reviewer Giovanni Fazio in "Artcore: In the Realm of the Explicit," *Japan Times* Culture section, May 2, 2001, accessed March 15, 2017, www.japantimes.co.jp/culture /2001/05/02/films/film-reviews/artcore/#.WEAkECMrKCQ.

77. Gilles Deleuze and Claire Parnet, *Dialogues II*, trans. Hugh Tomlinson and Barbara Habberjam (New York: Columbia University Press, [1987] 2007), 96.

78. By inducing hallucinatory effects, *Dandy Dust* borrows from the historical expanded cinema that wanted to expand the field of cinematic projection, overloading spectators with image and sound, married to the political ideology for expanding consciousness. In Gene Youngblood's (1970) words, "the intermedia network of cinema and television, which now functions as nothing less than the nervous system of mankind," could facilitate new forms of subjectivity, so that "when we say expanded cinema we actually mean expanded consciousness" (quoted in Kotz, "Video Projection," 379).

79. Dennis Harvey, "Review: 'Dandy Dust,'" *Variety*, July 13, 1998, accessed March 15, 2017, variety.com/1998/film/reviews/dandy-dust-1200454459/.

80. Harvey, "Review," n.p.

81. James Gibson, *The Ecological Approach to Visual Perception* (Hillsdale, NJ: Lawrence Erlbaum, 1987), 183.

82. Anne Rutherford, "Cinema and Embodied Affect," *Senses of Cinema* 25 (2003), accessed February 2, 2018, http://sensesofcinema.com/2003/feature -articles/embodied_affect/. Another cinema scholar who develops spectatorship theory with Gibson's framework but in the direction of phenomenology is Scott C. Richmond, *Cinema's Bodily Illusions: Flying, Floating, and Hallucinating* (Minneapolis: University of Minnesota Press, 2016).

83. Next to identifying with/as a cyborg, "I identify myself as boy, dragking, transvestite, and transgender. Insect. That's the truly new word: insect." Scheirl quoted in Kuzniar, *Queer German Cinema*, 224 (from an interactive email interview published in *Rundbrief Film* in 1996).

84. Scheirl, "Manifesto for the Dada," 55.

85. Scheirl, "Manifesto for the Dada," 55.

86. Scheirl, "Manifesto for the Dada," 51.

87. Paul Willemen uses this term in claiming that the avant-garde develops a repertory of techniques for "critical adversariness"; see Paul Willemen, "An Avant-Garde for the 1990s," in *Looks and Frictions: Essays in Cultural Studies and Film Theory*, ed. Paul Willemen (London: British Film Institute, 1994), 144.

88. Rudolf Kuenzli, "Introduction," in *Dada and Surrealist Film* [1987] (Cambridge, MA: MIT Press, 1996), 1–12.

89. Janco quoted in Kuenzli, "Introduction," 2.

90. Thomas Elsaesser, "Dada/Cinema?," in *Dada and Surrealist Film* [1987], ed. Rudolf Kuenzli (Cambridge, MA: MIT Press, 1996), 17.

91. Kotz, "Video Projection," 383–84.

92. Elsaesser, "Dada/Cinema?," 17.

93. Scheirl, "Manifesto for the Dada," 51.

94. Getsy, *Abstract Bodies*, 127.

95. Elsaesser, "Dada/Cinema?," 14.

96. Gilles Deleuze, *Francis Bacon: The Logic of Sense* [2002], trans. Daniel W. Smith (London: Continuum, 2005), 3–4, 16.

97. Chen argues that Nataf symbolizes the militant, masculine American imperialism that infringes on Japanese sovereignty and mixes uneasily with the specter of Black power; see Chen, "TRANScoding," 92.

98. See Peter Wollen, "Two Avant-Gardes" [1975], in *Readings and Writings: Semiotic Counter-Strategies* (London: Verso Press, 1982), 92–104.

99. Julian Carter reads gender transitions in light of choreographic transitions that link to any number of steps; see Julian Carter, "Embracing Transition, or Dancing in the Folds of Time," in *The Transgender Studies Reader 2*, eds. Susan Stryker and Aren Z. Aizura (New York: Routledge, 2013), 131.

100. Haraway, "Cyborg Manifesto," 149.

101. Eugenie Brinkema, "Afterword: Of Bodies, Changed to Different Bodies, Changed to Other Forms," *Somatechnics* 8, no. 1 (2018): 125, emphasis in original.

102. These thoughts are developed in the cowritten introduction to the special issue "Tranimacies: Intimate Links Between Animal and Trans* Studies"; see Eliza Steinbock, Marianna Szczygielska, and Anthony Wagner, "Introduction: Thinking Linking," *Angelaki: Journal of Theoretical Humanities* 22, no. 2 (2017): 4. We expanded on the critique of Zakiyyah Iman Jackson, "Animal: New Directions in the Theorization of Race and Posthumanism," *Feminist Studies* 39, no. 3 (2013): 669–85.

103. bell hooks, "Postmodern Blackness," in *The Norton Anthology: Theory and Criticism*, ed. Vincent B. Leitch (New York: W. W. Norton, 2001), 2482.

104. Zakiyyah Iman Jackson, "Outer Worlds: The Persistence of Race in Movement 'Beyond the Human,'" *GLQ: A Journal of Lesbian and Gay Studies* 21, no. 2 (2015): 215.

105. Susan Stryker, *Transgender History* (Berkeley: Seal Press, 2008), 6.

106. Nicolas Gane, "When We Have Never Been Human, What Is to Be Done? Interview with Donna Haraway," *Theory, Culture, and Society* 23, nos. 7–8 (2006): 156.

107. Jackie Orr, "Materializing a Cyborg's Manifesto," *WSQ: Women's Studies Quarterly* 40, nos. 1–2 (2012): 277.

108. Gane, "When We Have Never Been Human," 156.

109. Gane, "When We Have Never Been Human," 138.

110. Joanna Zylinska, "A Bit(e) of the Other: An Interview with Sue Golding," *Parallax* 5, no. 4 (1999): 154.

111. Keeling, *Witch's Flight*, 14.

112. Keeling, *Witch's Flight*, 137.

113. Susan Stryker, "My Words to Victor Frankenstein above the Village of Chamounix: Performing Transgender Rage" [1994], in *A Transgender Studies Reader*, ed. Susan Stryker and Stephen Whittle (New York: Routledge, 2006), 253.

114. Stryker, "My Words to Victor Frankenstein," 253.

115. Stryker, "My Words to Victor Frankenstein," 251.

116. Stryker, "My Words to Victor Frankenstein," 251.

117. Stryker, "My Words to Victor Frankenstein," 251.

118. Stryker, "My Words to Victor Frankenstein," 251.

119. Stryker, "My Words to Victor Frankenstein," 252.

120. Gordene O. Mackenzie, "50 Billion Galaxies of Gender: Transgendering the Millennium," in *Reclaiming Genders: Transsexual Grammars at the Fin de Siècle*, ed. Kate More and Stephen Whittle (London: Cassell, 1999), 204.

121. Brinkema, *Forms of the Affects*, 261.

122. Barad, "TransMaterialities," 396, emphasis in original.

123. Barad, "TransMaterialities," 415, emphasis in original.

Conclusion

1. *103 Shots*, dir. Cassils, 2016, last accessed July 15, 2018, https://www.youtube .com/watch?v=cpEyQVKif_k.

2. The number of critically wounded was later established as being fifty-eight. See "Pulse Nightclub," Wikipedia, accessed December 1, 2017, https://en .wikipedia.org/wiki/Pulse_nightclub.

3. See the video link embedded at Julia Steinmetz, "103 Shots: Listening to Orlando," *Huffington Post*, "Queer Voices" blog, last updated June 27, 2016, accessed December 1, 2017, https://www.huffingtonpost.com/entry/103-shots-listening-to -orlando_us_57714cd9e4b0fa01a1405b42.

4. Gilles Deleuze, *Foucault* [1986], trans. Seán Hand (Minneapolis: University of Minnesota Press, 2000), 64.

5. Cassils, "About," personal website, accessed December 1, 2017, http://cassils .net/.

6. See Katie Mettler, "Orlando's Club Pulse Owes Its Name and Its Spirit to 'Loving Brother' Who Died from AIDS," *Washington Post*, June 13, 2016, accessed December 1, 2017, https://www.washingtonpost.com/news/morning-mix /wp/2016/06/13/more-than-just-another-gay-club-pulse-was-founded-in-her -brothers-memory-and-named-for-his-beating-heart/?utm_term=.bf4b91a6d969.

7. Ann Cvetkovitch, "Public Feelings," *South Atlantic Quarterly* 106, no. 3 (summer 2007): 465.

8. Elijah Adiv Edelman, "Why We Forget the Pulse Nightclub Murders: Bodies that (Never) Matter and a Call for Coalitional Models of Queer and Trans Social Justice," GLQ: A Journal of Gay and Lesbian Studies 24, no. 1 (2018): 31–35, 34.

9. Heather Love, *Feeling Backward: Loss and the Politics of Queer History* (Cambridge, MA: Harvard University Press, 2007), 18.

10. Williams cited in Love, *Feeling Backward*, 12.

11. See documentary images of the series at Creative Time, accessed December 1, 2017, http://creativetime.org/projects/kissing-doesnt-kill-greed-and -indifference-do/.

12. Sandy Stone, "The *Empire* Strikes Back: A Posttranssexual Manifesto" [1991], in *The Transgender Studies Reader*, ed. Stephen Whittle and Susan Stryker (New York: Routledge, 2006), 232.

13. Jian Chen and Lissette Olivares, "Transmedia," TSQ: *Transgender Studies Quarterly* 1, nos. 1–2 (2014): 246.

14. S. Stone, "The *Empire* Strikes Back," 231, emphasis in original.

15. Shannon Bell, "Fast Feminism," *Journal of Contemporary Thought* 14 (2001): 93–112.

16. Susan Stryker, "Dungeon Intimacies: The Poetics of Transsexual Sadomasochism," *Parallax* 46 (2008): 39.

17. Eliza Steinbock, "Interview: A Conversation with Cassils on Propagating Collective Resilience in Times of War." Forthcoming.

18. This view is shared with expanded cinema proponents; see Andrew V. Uroski, *Between the Black Box and the White Cube: Expanded Cinema and Postwar Art* (Chicago: University of Chicago Press, 2014), 38.

19. Robert Hayden, "Monet's Waterlillies," AllPoetry.com, accessed December 1, 2017, https://allpoetry.com/Monet's-Waterlilies. See L. H. Stallings, *Funk the Erotic: Transaesthetics and Black Sexual Cultures* (Chicago: University of Illinois Press, 2015), 206.

20. Stallings, *Funk the Erotic*, 2016.

21. Stallings invokes the precise concept of transworld identity from Alvin Plantinga: "the notion of transworld identity [. . .] is the notion that the same object exists in more than one possible world (with the actual world treated as one of the possible worlds)"; see Stallings, *Funk the Erotic*, 209.

22. Alexander Weheliye, *Habeas Viscus: Racializing Assemblages, Biopolitics, and Black Feminist Theories of the Human* (Durham, NC: Duke University Press, 2014). Stallings, *Funk the Erotic*, 206.

BIBLIOGRAPHY

Aaron, Michelle, ed. *New Queer Cinema: A Critical Reader*. New Brunswick, NJ [ea]: Rutgers University Press, 2004.

Addams, Calperina. "Bad Questions to Ask a Transsexual." Accessed May 25, 2010. https://www.youtube.com/watch?v=BOjeZnjKlp0&feature=channel.

Ahmed, Sara. "Happy Objects." In *The Affect Theory Reader*, edited by Melissa Gregg and Gregory J. Seigworth, 29–51. Durham, NC: Duke University Press, 2010.

Ahmed, Sara. *The Promise of Happiness*. Durham, NC: Duke University Press, 2010.

Aydemir, Murat. *Images of Bliss: Ejaculation, Masculinity, and Meaning*. Minneapolis: University of Minnesota Press, 2007.

Bal, Mieke. "Looking at Love: An Ethics of Vision." Review of *The Threshold of the Visible World*, by Kaja Silverman. *Diacritics* 27, no. 1 (1997): 58–72.

Bal, Mieke. *Travelling Concepts in the Humanities: A Rough Guide*. Toronto: Toronto University Press, 2002.

Bal, Mieke. "Visual Essentialism and the Object of Visual Culture." *Journal of Visual Culture* 2, no. 1 (2003): 5–32.

Balsamo, Anne. *Technologies of the Gendered Body*. Durham, NC: Duke University Press, 1997.

Barad, Karen. *Meeting the Universe Halfway: Quantum Physics and the Entanglement of Matter and Meaning*. Durham, NC: Duke University Press, 2007.

Barad, Karen. "TransMaterialities: Trans*/Matter/Realities and Queer Political Imaginings." *GLQ: A Journal of Lesbian and Gay Studies* 21, nos. 2–3 (2015): 387–422.

Barthes, Roland. *The Neutral*. Translated by Rosalind E. Krauss and Denis Hollier. New York: Columbia University Press, [2002] 2005.

Barthes, Roland. *The Preparation of the Novel: Lecture Courses and Seminars at the Collège de France (1978–1979 and 1979–1980)*. Translated by Kate Briggs. New York: Columbia University Press, 2010.

Barthes, Roland. *The Rustle of Language*. Translated by Richard Howard. Berkeley: University of California Press, [1984] 1989.

Barthes, Roland. *Sade/Fourier/Loyola*. Translated by Richard Miller. Berkeley: University of California Press, [1971] 1976.

Baudrillard, Jean. *The Transparency of Evil: Essays on Extreme Phenomena*. New York: Verso, 2009.

Bauer, Robin. "Transgressive and Transformative Gendered Sexual Practices and White Privileges: The Case of the Dyke/Trans BDSM Communities." *WSQ: Women's Studies Quarterly* 36, nos. 3–4 (2008): 233–53.

Bauman, Zygmunt. *Liquid Life*. London: Polity Press, 2005.

Bazin, André. "The Ontology of the Photographic Image." In *What Is Cinema?* Vol. 1, edited and translated by Hugh Gray, 9–16. Berkeley: University of California Press, 1967.

Beckman, Karen. *Vanishing Women: Magic, Film, and Feminism*. Durham, NC: Duke University Press, 2003.

Benjamin, Harry. *The Transsexual Phenomenon*. New York: Warner, 1966.

Benjamin, Walter. "On Some Motifs in Baudelaire" [1939]. In *Illuminations*, edited by Hannah Arendt, 152–96. London: Pimlico, 1999.

Benjamin, Walter. "The Work of Art in the Age of Its Technological Reproducibility: Second Version (1936)." In *Walter Benjamin: Selected Writings, Volume 3: 1935–1938*, edited by Howard Eiland and Michael W. Jennings. Cambridge, MA: Belknap Press, 2002.

Bell, Shannon. "Fast Feminism." *Journal of Contemporary Thought* 14 (2001): 93–112.

Bergson, Henri. *Matter and Memory*. Translated by N. M. Paul and W. S. Palmer. New York: Zone Books, [1908] 1988.

Bettcher, Talia Mae. "Evil Deceivers and Make-Believers: On Transphobic Violence and the Politics of Illusion." *Hypatia* 22, no. 3 (2007): 43–65.

Billings, Dwight, and Thomas Urban. "The Socio-Medical Construction of Transsexualism: An Interpretation and Critique." *Social Problems* 29, no. 3 (1982): 266–82.

Blas, Zach, ed. "In Practice: Opacities." *Camera Obscura: Feminism, Culture, and Media Studies* 31, no. 2.92 (2016): 149–203.

Body, N. O., and Magnus Hirschfeld. *Aus Mannes Mädchenjahren*. Berlin: Gustav Rieckes Buchhandlung, 1907.

Bornstein, Kate. "A Conversation Between Sandy Stone and Kate Bornstein Moderated by Susan Stryker." Presentation at *Postposttranssexual: Transgender Studies and Feminism Conference*. Bloomington, Indiana, April 8–9, 2011.

Bornstein, Kate. *Gender Outlaw: On Men, Women, and the Rest of Us*. New York: Vintage, 1994.

Bornstein, Kate. "Gender Terror, Gender Rage." In *The Transgender Studies Reader*, edited by Stephen Whittle and Susan Stryker, 236–43. New York: Routledge, 2006.

"Brandon." Guggenheim Museum. Accessed March 15, 2017. http://brandon .guggenheim.org/credits/.

Branigan, Edward. *Narrative Comprehension and Film*. New York: Routledge, 1992.

Brinkema, Eugenie. "Afterword: Of Bodies, Changed to Different Bodies, Changed to Other Forms." *Somatechnics* 8, no. 1 (2018): 125–36.

Brinkema, Eugenie. *The Forms of the Affects*. Durham, NC: Duke University Press, 2014.

Buck-Morss, Susan. *The Dialectics of Seeing: Walter Benjamin and the Arcades Project*. Cambridge, MA: MIT Press, 1991.

Bullough, Vern L. "Magnus Hirschfeld, An Often Over-looked Pioneer." *Sexuality and Culture* 7, no. 1 (2003): 62–72.

Butler, Judith. "The Force of Fantasy: Feminism, Mapplethorp, and Discursive Excess." In *Feminism and Pornography*, edited by Drucilla Cornell, 487–508. Oxford: Oxford University Press, 2000.

Butler, Judith. *Undoing Gender*. New York: Routledge, 2004.

Cameron, Loren Rex. *Man Tool: The Nuts and Bolts of Female-to-Male Surgery*. World Wide Web: Zero EBooks, 2001.

cárdenas, micha. *The Transreal: Political Aesthetics of Crossing Realities*. Edited by Zach Blas and Wolfgang Schirmacher. New York: Atropos Press, 2011.

Carter, Julian. "Embracing Transition, or Dancing in the Folds of Time." In *The Transgender Studies Reader 2*, edited by Susan Stryker and Aren Z. Aizura, 130–44. New York: Routledge, 2013.

Cartwright, Lisa. *Screening the Body: Tracing Medicine's Visual Culture*. Minneapolis: University of Minnesota Press, 1995.

Cassils, dir. *103 Shots*, 2016. Accessed July 15, 2018. https://www.youtube.com /watch?v=cpEyQVKif_k.

Castle, Terry. "Phantasmagoria: Spectral Technology and the Metaphorics of Modern Reverie." *Critical Inquiry* 15, no. 1 (1988): 26–61.

Caughie, Pamela L. "The Temporality of Modernist Life Writing in the Era of Transsexuality: Virginia Woolf's *Orlando* and Einar Wegener's *Man into Woman*." *MFS: Modern Fiction Studies* 59, no. 3 (2013): 501–25.

Caughie, Pamela L., and Sabine Meyer, eds. Forthcoming. *Comparative Scholarly Edition of Man into Woman (1931)*. Bloomsbury Publishing's Modernist Archives series. London: Bloomsbury.

Chare, Nicholas. "From Landscape into Portrait: Reflections on Lili Elbe and Trans* Aesthetics." *Parallax* 22, no. 3 (2016): 347–65.

Cheang, Shu-Lea, dir. *I.K.U.* Tokyo: UPLINK Co., 2000.

Chen, Jian. "TRANScoding the Transnational Digital Economy." In *Trans Studies: The Challenge to Hetero/Homo Normativities*, ed. Yolanda Martinez-San Miguel and Sarah Tobias, 83–100. New Brunswick, NJ: Rutgers University Press, 2016.

Chen, Jian, and Lissette Olivares, "Transmedia." *TSQ: Transgender Studies Quarterly* 1, nos. 1–2 (2014): 245–48.

Chen, Mel Y. *Animacies: Biopolitics, Racial Mattering, and Queer Affect*. Durham, NC: Duke University Press, 2012.

Cholodenko, Alan. "The Animation of Cinema." *Semiotic Review of Books* 18, no. 2 (2008): 1–10.

Cholodenko, Alan. "'First Principles' of Animation." In *Animating Film Theory*, edited by Karen Beckman, 98–110. Durham, NC: Duke University Press, 2014.

Cholodenko, Alan, ed. *The Illusion of Life: Essays on Animation*. Sydney: Power Publications, 1991.

Cholodenko, Alan, ed. *The Illusion of Life 2: More Essays on Animation*. Sydney: Power Publications, 2007.

Chun, Wendy Hui Kyong. *Programmed Visions: Software and Memory*. Cambridge, MA: MIT Press, 2013.

Cotten, Trystan T., ed. *Below the Belt: Genital Talk by Men of Trans Experience*. Stockton Center, CA: Transgress Press, 2016.

Cotten, Trystan T., ed. *Hung Jury: Testimonies of Genital Surgery by Transsexual Men*. Stockton Center, CA: Transgress Press, 2012.

Crary, Jonathan. *Techniques of the Observer: On Vision and Modernity in the Nineteenth Century*. Cambridge, MA: MIT Press, 1990.

Crenshaw, Kimberlé. "Beyond Racism and Misogyny: Black Feminism and 2 Live Crew." *Boston Review* 16, no. 6 (1991): 6–33. Accessed Feburary 2, 2018. http://bostonreview.net/archives/BR16.6/crenshaw.html.

Cubitt, Sean. *The Practice of Light: A Genealogy of Visual Technologies from Prints to Pixels*. Cambridge, MA: MIT Press, 2014.

Currah, Paisley, Susan Stryker, and Lisa Jean Moore. "Introduction: Trans-, Trans, or Transgender?" *WSQ: Women's Studies Quarterly* 36, nos. 3–4 (2008): 11–22.

Cvetkovitch, Ann. "Public Feelings." *South Atlantic Quarterly* 106, no. 3 (Summer 2007): 459–68.

Darling, James. "FTMFUCKER." Launched in 2012. Accessed May 20, 2016. ftmfucker.com.

Davidson, Arnold L. "Sex and the Emergence of Sexuality." *Critical Inquiry* 14, no. 1 (1987): 16–48.

Davy, Zowie. *Recognizing Transsexuals: Personal, Political, and Medicolegal Embodiment*. New York: Routledge, 2011.

Delany, Samuel R. *The Motion of Light in Water: Sex and Science Fiction Writing in the East Village 1960–1965*. Minneapolis: University of Minnesota Press, [1988] 2004.

Deleuze, Gilles. *Bergsonism*. New York: Zone Books, [1966] 1991.

Deleuze, Gilles. *Cinema 2: The Time-Image*. Translated by Hugh Tomlinson and Robert Galeta. Minneapolis: University of Minnesota Press, [1985] 1994.

Deleuze, Gilles. *Foucault*. Translated by Seán Hand. Minneapolis: University of Minnesota Press, [1986] 2000.

Deleuze, Gilles. *Francis Bacon: The Logic of Sense*. Translated by Daniel W. Smith. London: Continuum, [2002] 2005.

Deleuze, Gilles, and Claire Parnet. *Dialogues II*. Translated by Hugh Tomlinson and Barbara Habberjam. London: Continuum, 1997.

Drucker, Zackary. "03 BEFORE/AFTER | Zackary Drucker." Accessed March 24, 2016. http://zackarydrucker.com/photography/b4-after/.

Drucker, Zackary, and A. L. Steiner. "Before/After 2009-Present." *Art F City* website, Section IMG MGMT, May 16, 2011. Accessed March 24, 2016. http://artfcity.com/2011/05/16/img-mgmt-z-drucker-a-l-steiner-beforeafter-2009-present/.

Ebershoff, David. *The Danish Girl*. New York: Penguin Books, 2000.

Edelman, Elijah Adiv. "Why We Forget the Pulse Nightclub Murders: Bodies that (Never) Matter and a Call for Coalitional Models of Queer and Trans Social Justice." GLQ: *A Journal of Gay and Lesbian Studies* 24, no. 1 (2018): 31–56.

Elden, Stuart. "The Problem of Confession: The Productive Failure of Foucault's History of Sexuality." *Journal for Cultural Research* 9, no. 1 (2005): 23–41.

Elsaesser, Thomas. "Dada/Cinema?" In *Dada and Surrealist Film*, edited by Rudolf Kuenzli, 13–27. Cambridge, MA: MIT Press, [1987] 1996.

Emmerich, Roland. *Stonewall*, 2015, Berlin and Los Angeles: Centropolis Entertainment.

Fazio, Giovanni. "Artcore: In the Realm of the Explicit." *Japan Times* Culture section, May 2, 2001. Accessed March 15, 2017, www.japantimes.co.jp/culture/2001/05/02/films/film-reviews/artcore/#.WEAkECMrKCQ.

Featherstone, Mike, and Roger Burrows, eds. *Cyberspace / Cyberbodies / Cyberpunk*. Londen: Sage, 1995.

Feder, Sam. *Kate Bornstein Is a Queer and Pleasant Danger*, 2014. Accessed March 16, 2016. http://katebornsteinthemovie.com/.

Felski, Rita. "*Fin de Siècle, Fin de Sexe*: Transsexuality, Postmodernism, and the Death of History." *New Literary History* 27 (1996): 337–49.

"Flawless Sabrina Archive." *Flawless Sabrina*. Accessed March 16, 2016. http://www.flawless-sabrina.com/flawless-sabrina-archive/.

Florez, StormMiguel, and Annalise Ophelian. *Major!*, 2016. Accessed March 1, 2016. http://www.missmajorfilm.com/.

Ford, Akkadia. "Transliteracy and the Trans New Wave: Independent Trans Cinema Representation, Classification, Exhibition." PhD diss., Southern Cross University, 2016.

Foucault, Michel. *The Archaeology of Knowledge*. Translated by A. M. Sheridan Smith. New York: Taylor & Francis, [1969] 2013.

Foucault, Michel. *The Birth of the Clinic: An Archaeology of Medical Perception*. Translated by A. M. Sheridan Smith. New York: Vintage, [1963] 1973.

Foucault, Michel. *Death and the Labyrinth: The World of Raymond Roussel*. Translated by Charles Ruas. London: Athlone Press, [1963] 1987.

Foucault, Michel. *Discipline and Punish: The Birth of the Prison*. Translated by Alan Sheridan. New York: Pantheon, 1977.

Foucault, Michel. *Ethics: Essential Works of Foucault 1954–1984*, Vol. 1. Edited by Paul Rabinow. London: Penguin, 1997.

Foucault, Michel. *The History of Sexuality, Vol. 1: An Introduction [Will to Knowledge]*. Translated by Robert Hurley. New York: Vintage, [1976] 1978.

Foucault, Michel. *The History of Sexuality, Vol. 2: The Use of Pleasure*. Translated by Robert Hurley. New York: Vintage, [1984] 1990.

Foucault, Michel. "Introduction." In *Being the Recently Discovered Memoirs of a Nineteenth-Century French Hermaprodite (1838) by Herculine Barbin*, translated by Richard McDougall, vi–xvii. New York: Pantheon, 1980.

Foucault, Michel. *The Order of Things*. New York: Routledge, [1966] 2006.

Freeman, Elizabeth. *Time Binds: Queer Temporalities, Queer Histories*. Durham, NC: Duke University Press, 2010.

Freud, Sigmund. "On Fetishism." In *On Sexuality: Three Essays on the Theory of Sexuality, and Other Works*, edited by Angela Richards, translated by James Strachey, 345–57. New York: Penguin, [1927] 1977.

Freud, Sigmund. "Some Psychical Consequences of the Anatomical Distinction between the Sexes." In *On Sexuality: Three Essays on the Theory of Sexuality, and Other Works*, edited by Angela Richards, translated by James Strachey, 331–43. New York: Penguin, [1925] 1977.

Gane, Nicolas. "When We Have Never Been Human, What Is to Be Done? Interview with Donna Haraway." *Theory, Culture, and Society* 23, nos. 7–8 (2006): 135–58.

Garbasz, Yishay. *Becoming: A Gender Flipbook*. New York: Mark Batty, 2010.

Garbasz, Yishay. "Installation Process of Becoming at the Busan Biennale 2010." YouTube. Accessed February 20, 2016. https://www.youtube.com/watch?v=F5diBtcul_4.

Garber, Marjorie B. *Vested Interests: Cross-Dressing and Cultural Anxiety*. New York: Routledge, 1992.

Garland Thomson, Rosemarie. *Extraordinary Bodies: Figuring Disability in American Culture and Literature*. New York: Columbia University Press, 1997.

Gaudreault, André. *Film and Attraction: From Kinematography to Cinema.* Translated by Timothy Barnard. Chicago: University of Illinois Press, [2008] 2011.

Gaudreault, André. "From 'Primitive Cinema' to 'Kine-Attractography'" [2004]. In *The Cinema of Attractions Reloaded,* edited by Wanda Strauven, translated by Timothy Barnard, 85–104. Amsterdam: University of Amsterdam Press, 2006.

Gaudreault, André. "Méliès the Magician." Translated by Timothy Barnard. *Early Popular Visual Culture* 5, no. 2 (2009): 167–74.

Gaudreault, André. "Theatricality, Narrativity, and Trickality: Reevaluating the Cinema of Georges Méliès." *Journal of Popular Film and Television* 15, no. 3 (1987): 110–19.

Getsy, David J. *Abstract Bodies: Sixties Sculpture in the Expanded Field of Gender.* New Haven, CT: Yale University Press, 2015.

Getsy, David J. "Queer Relations." *ASAP/Journal* 2, no. 2 (2017): 254–57.

Getsy, David J. "Refusing Ambiguity." Paper presented at the Renaissance Society symposium Ambiguity Forum, University of Chicago, January 14, 2017.

Gibson, James. *The Ecological Approach to Visual Perception.* Hillsdale, NJ: Lawrence Erlbaum, 1987.

Glissant, Édouard. "For Opacity." In *Poetics of Relation,* translated by Betsy Wing, 189–94. Ann Arbor: University of Michigan Press, 1997.

Golding, Sue [as Johnny de Philo]. "To Tremble the Ejaculate." In *[Cyborg. Nets/z] Catalogue on* Dandy Dust *(Hans Scheirl, 1998),* edited by Andrea B. Braidt, 68–73. Vienna: BKA Filmbeirat, 1999.

Gorton, R. Nick. "Transgender as Mental Illness: Nosology, Social Justice, and the Tarnished Golden Mean." In *The Transgender Studies Reader 2,* edited by Susan Stryker and Aren Aizura, 644–52. New York: Routledge, [2007] 2013.

Gossett, Reina, Eric A. Stanley, and Johanna Burton, ed. *Trap Door: Trans Cultural Production and the Politics of Visibility.* Cambridge, MA: MIT Press, 2017.

Goux, Jean-Joseph. *Symbolic Economies: After Marx and Freud.* Translated by Jennifer Curtiss Gage. Ithaca, NY: Cornell University Press, 1990.

Green, Jamison. *Becoming a Visible Man.* Nashville: Vanderbuilt University Press, 2004.

Grusin, Richard, and Jay David Bolter. *Remediation: Understanding New Media.* Cambridge, MA: MIT Press, 2000.

Gunning, Tom. "Animated Pictures: Tales of Cinema's Forgotten Future After 100 Years of Film." In *The Nineteenth-Century Visual Culture Reader,* edited by Vanessa R. Schwartz and Jeannene M. Przyblyski, 100–113. New York: Routledge, 2004.

Gunning, Tom. "Illusions Past and Future: The Phantasmagoria and Its Specters." Paper presented at the Refresh! First International Conference on the Histories of Art, Science and Technology, 2004. Consulted via Media Art History. Accessed March 24, 2016. http://plo2.donau-uni.ac.at/jspui/handle /10002/296.

Gunning, Tom. "Now You See It, Now You Don't! The Temporality of the Cinema of Attractions." *The Velvet Light Trap* 32 (1993): 3–12.

Halberstam, Judith. "F2M: The Making of Female Masculinity." In *The Lesbian Postmodern*, edited by Laura Doan, 210–28. New York: Columbia University Press, 1994.

Halberstam, Judith (Jack). *In a Queer Time and Place: Transgender Bodies, Subcultural Lives.* New York: New York University Press, 2005.

Hale, C. Jacob. "Leatherdyke Boys and Their Daddies: How to Have Sex without Women or Men." *Social Text* 52/53 (1997): 223–36.

Hammonds, Evelynn. "Black (W)holes and the Geometry of Black Female Sexuality." In *Differences: Feminism Meets Queer Theory*, edited by Elizabeth Weed and Naomi Schor, 136–56. Bloomington: Indiana University Press, 1997.

Haraway, Donna. "A Cyborg Manifesto: Science, Technology, and Socialist-Feminism in the Late Twentieth Century." In *Simians, Cyborgs and Women: The Reinvention of Nature*, 149–81. New York: Routledge, 1991.

Harvey, Dennis. "Review: 'Dandy Dust.'" *Variety*, July 13, 1998. Accessed March 15, 2017. variety.com/1998/film/reviews/dandy-dust-1200454459/.

Hausman, Bernice. *Changing Sex: Transsexualism, Technology, and the Idea of Gender.* Durham, NC: Duke University Press, 1995.

Hayward, Eva. "The Subtle Process of Transformation." IndyWeek.com, September 5, 2012. Accessed March 18, 2016. http://www.indyweek.com /indyweek/the-subtle-process-of-transformation/Content?oid=3140976.

Hayward, Eva, and Che Gossett. "The Impossibility of *That*." *Angelaki: Journal for Theoretical Humanities* 22, no. 2 (2017): 15–24.

Hayward, Eva, and Jami Weinstein. "Introduction: Tranimalities in the Age of Trans* Life." *TSQ: Transgender Studies Quarterly* 2, no. 2 (2015): 195–208.

Hernandez, Daisy. "Playing with Race." Colorlines.com, December 21, 2004. Accessed Feburary 2, 2018. http://colorlines.com/ archives/2004/12/playing _with_race.html.

Hocquenghem, Guy. *Homosexual Desire.* Translated by Daniella Dangoor. Durham, NC: Duke University Press, [1972] 1993.

Holmes, M. Morgan, ed. *Critical Intersex.* Farnham, U.K.: Ashgate, 2009.

hooks, bell. "Postmodern Blackness." In *The Norton Anthology: Theory and Criticism*, edited by Vincent B. Leitch, 2478–84. New York: W. W. Norton, 2001.

Hooper, Tom, dir. *The Danish Girl.* Los Angeles, Working Title Films, 2015.

Horak, Laura. "Trans on YouTube: Intimacy, Visibility, Temporality." *TSQ: Transgender Studies Quarterly* 1, no. 4 (2014): 572–85.

Hoyer, Niels, ed. *Man into Woman: The First Sex Change, A Portrait of Lili Elbe.* London: Blue Boat Books, [1933] 2004.

Jacobs, Katrien. "Queer Voyeurism and the Pussy-Matrix in Shu Lea Cheang's Japanese Pornography." In *Mobile Cultures: New Media in Queer Asia*, edited by Chris Berry, Fran Martin, and Audrey Yue, 201–21. Durham, NC: Duke University Press, 2003.

Jackson, Zakiyyah Iman. "Animal: New Directions in the Theorization of Race and Posthumanism," *Feminist Studies* 39, no. 3 (2013): 669–85.

Jackson, Zakiyyah Iman. "Outer Worlds: The Persistence of Race in Movement 'Beyond the Human,'" *GLQ: A Journal of Lesbian and Gay Studies* 21.2 (2015): 215–18.

Jones, Jordy. "Gender without Genitals: Hedwig's Six Inches." In *The Transgender Studies Reader*, edited by Stephen Whittle and Susan Stryker, 449–68. New York: Routledge, 2006.

Kaizen, William. "Live on Tape: Video, Liveness and the Immediate." In *Art and the Moving Image: A Critical Reader*, edited by Tanya Leighton, 258–74. London: Afterall, 2008.

Kaldera, Raven, and Hanne Blank, eds. "Introduction." In *Best Transgender Erotica*. Cambridge, MA: Circlet, 2002.

Kuzniar, Alice A. *The Queer German Cinema*, Stanford, CA: Stanford University Press, 2000.

Keegan, Cáel M. *Lana and Lilly Wachowski: Sensing Transgender.* Chicago: University of Illinois Press, 2018.

Keegan, Cáel M. "Revisitation: A Trans Phenomenology of the Media Image." *MedieKultur* 61 (2016): 26–41.

Keeling, Kara. *The Witch's Flight: The Cinematic, the Black Femme, and the Image of Common Sense.* Durham, NC: Duke University Press, 2007.

Kessler, Frank. "Trick Films." In *Encyclopedia of Early Cinema*, edited by Richard Abel, 643–45. London: Routledge, 2005.

Kessler, Suzanne J., and Wendy McKenna. *Gender: An Ethnomethodological Approach.* New York: John Wiley & Sons, 1978.

Klöppel, Ulrike. "Who Has the Right to Change Gender Status? Drawing Boundaries between Inter- and Transsexuality." In *Critical Intersex*, edited by M. Morgan Holmes, 171–90. Farnham, U.K.: Ashgate, 2009.

Kooijman, Jaap. "Cruising the Channels: The Queerness of Zapping." In *Queer TV: Theories, Histories, Politics*, edited by Glyn Davis and Gary Needham, 159–71. New York: Routledge, 2009.

Kotula, Dean. *The Phallus Palace: Female-to-Male Transsexuals.* New York: Alyson Books, 2002.

Kotz, Liz. "Video Projection: The Space Between Screens," in *Art and the Moving Image: A Critical Reader*, edited by Tanya Leighton, 371–85. London: Afterall, 2008.

Kovács, Katherine Singer. "Georges Méliès and the 'Féerie.'" *Cinema Journal* 16, no. 1 (1976): 1–13.

Kroker, Arthur, and Marilouise Kroker. *Hacking the Future*. New York: St. Martin's, 1996.

Kuenzli, Rudolf. "Introduction." In *Dada and Surrealist Film*, 1–12. Cambridge, MA: MIT Press, [1987] 1996.

Lacan, Jacques. *The Four Fundamental Concepts of Psychoanalysis*. Edited by Richard Feldstein, Bruce Fink, and Maire Jaanus. London: Penguin, 1979.

Lacan, Jacques. "Some Reflections on the Ego." *Psychoanalytic Quarterly* 23 (1954): 11–17.

Lane, Riki. "Trans as Bodily Becoming: Rethinking the Biological as Diversity, Not Dichotomy." *Hypatia* 24, no. 3 (2009): 136–57.

Latham, J. R. "Trans Men's Sexual Narrative-Practices: Introducing STS to Trans and Sexuality Studies." *Sexualities* 19, no. 3 (2016): 347–68.

Lay, Samantha. "1950s and 1960s: Social Problems and Kitchen Sinks." In *British Social Realism: From Documentary to Brit-Grit*, 55–76. London: Wallflower, 2002.

Leung, Helen Hok-Sze. "Film." *TSQ: Transgender Studies Quarterly* 1, nos. 1–2 (2014): 86–9.

Livingston, Jennie, dir. *Paris Is Burning*. Miramax, 1990.

Loist, Skadi. "LGBT/Q Film Festivals Global (1977–2015) NEW MAP © Skadi Loist." Accessed July 15, 2018, https://www.google.com/maps/d/u/0/viewer?mid=1m-UV5Kpw39u-eLn—Dj6RALd4ks&ll=4.13296470981505%2C0&z=1.

Lorenz, Renate, Pauline Boudry, and Werner Hirsch. *N.O.Body*, 2008. Installation with film and photographs. Accessed Feburary 2, 2018. http://www.boudry-lorenz.de/n-o-body/.

Love, Heather. *Feeling Backward: Loss and the Politics of Queer History*. Cambridge, MA: Harvard University Press, 2007.

MacCormack, Patricia. *Cinesexuality*. Farnham, UK: Ashgate, 2008.

Mackenzie, Gordene O. "50 Billion Galaxies of Gender: Transgendering the Millennium." In *Reclaiming Genders: Transsexual Grammars at the Fin de Siècle*, edited by Kate More and Stephen Whittle, 193–218. London: Cassell, 1999.

Mannoni, Laurent. *The Great Art of Light and Shadow*. Exeter, UK: University of Exeter Press, 2000.

Manovitch, Lev. *The Language of New Media*. Cambridge, MA: MIT Press, 2001.

Marks, Laura. *The Skin of the Film: Intercultural Cinema, Embodiment, and the Senses*. Durham, NC: Duke University Press, 2000.

Marx, Karl. "Section 4 The Fetishism of Commodities and the Secret Thereof."

In *A Critique of Political Economy: Vol. I Part I—The Process of Capitalist Production*, translated by Friedrich Engels. New York: Cosimo Classics, [1867] 2007.

Massumi, Brian. *Parables for the Virtual: Movement, Affect, Sensation*. Durham, NC: Duke University Press, 2002.

McNair, Brian. *Striptease Culture: Sex, Media and the Democratisation of Desire*. London: Routledge, 2002.

Méliès, Georges. "Cinematographic Views." *October* 29 (1984): 24–34.

Meyer, Sabine. "Divine Interventions: Rebirth and Creation Narratives in *Fra Mand Til Kvinder – Lili Elbes Bekendelser*." *Kvinder, Køn & Forskning* 3–4 (2011): 68–76.

Meyer, Sabine. "Mit Dem Puppenwagen in Die Normative Weiblichkeit. Lili Elbe Und Die Journalistische Inszenierung von Transsexualität in Dänemark." *Nordeuropaforum* 20 (2010): 33–61.

Meyerowitz, Joanne. *How Sex Changed: A History of Transsexuality in the United States*. Cambridge, MA: Harvard University Press, 2002.

Miller-Young, Mireille. "Hip-Hop Honeys and Da Hustlaz: Black Sexualities in the New Hip-Hop Pornography." *Meridians* 8, no. 1 (2008): 261–92.

Miller-Young, Mireille. "Putting Hypersexuality to Work: Black Women and Illicit Eroticism in Pornography." *Sexualities* 13, no. 2 (2010): 219–35.

Moore, Rachel O. *Savage Theory: Cinema as Modern Magic*. Durham, NC: Duke University Press, 1999.

Mullarkey, John. "Gilles Deleuze." In *Film, Theory, and Philosophy: The Key Thinkers*, edited by Felicity Colman, 179–89. New York: Routledge, 2014.

Mulvey, Laura. "Afterthoughts on 'Visual Pleasure and Narrative Cinema' Inspired by King Vidor's *Duel in the Sun* (1946)." In *Visual and Other Pleasures*, 29–38. London: Macmillan, 1989.

Mulvey, Laura. *Death 24x a Second: Stillness and the Moving Image*. London: Reaktion Books, 2006.

Mulvey, Laura. "Pandora's Box: Topographies of Curiosity." In *Fetishism and Curiosity*, 53–64. Bloomington: Indiana University Press, 1996.

Muñoz, José Esteban. *Disidentifications: Queers of Color and the Performance of Politics*. Minneapolis: University of Minnesota Press, 1999.

Muñoz, José Esteban. "Feeling Brown: Ethnicity and Affect in Ricardo Bracho's 'The Sweetest Hangover (and Other STDs).'" *Theatre Journal* 52, no. 1 (2000): 67–79.

Murray, Timothy. "Time @ Cinema's Future: New Media Art and the Thought of Temporality." In *Afterimages of Gilles Deleuze's Film Philosophy*, edited by David N. Rodowick, 351–72. Minneapolis: University of Minnesota Press, 2010.

Namaste, Viviane. "'Activists Can't Go on Forever Acting in the Abstract': An

Interview with Mirha-Soleil Ross." In *Sex Change Social Change: Reflections on Identity, Institutions, and Imperialism*. Toronto, ON: Canadian Scholars Press, 2011, 117–38.

Namaste, Vivian. *Invisible Lives: The Erasure of Transsexual and Transgendered People*. Chicago: University of Chicago Press, 2000.

Nichols, Bill. "The Voice of Documentary." *Film Quarterly* 36, no. 3 (1993): 17–30.

O'Donoghue, Darragh. "Georges Méliès." *Senses of Cinema* 32 (July 2004). Accessed March 24, 2016. http://sensesofcinema.com/2004/great-directors /melies/.

Oishi, Eve. "'Collective Orgasm': The Eco-Cyber-Pornography of She Lea Cheang." wsq: *Women's Studies Quarterly* 35, nos. 1–2 (2007): 20–44.

Orr, Jackie. "Materializing a Cyborg's Manifesto." wsq: *Women's Studies Quarterly* 40, nos. 1–2 (2012): 273–80.

Oudart, Jean-Pierre. "Cinema and Suture." *Screen Dossier on Suture* 18, no. 4 (1977–88): 35–47.

Paasonen, Susanna, Kaarina Nikunen, and Laura Saarenmaa, eds. "Introduction: Pornification and the Education of Desire." In *Pornification: Sex and Sexuality in Media Culture*, 1–22. Oxford: Berg, 2007.

Paci, Viva. "The Attraction of the Intelligent Eye: Obsessions with the Vision Machine in Early Film Theories." In *The Cinema of Attractions Reloaded*, edited by Wanda Strauven, 121–38. Amsterdam: Amsterdam University Press, 2006.

Peddle, Daniel, dir. *The Aggressives*. Los Angeles: Seventh Art Releasing, 2005.

Pettman, Dominic. *Love and Other Technologies: Retrofitting Eros for an Information Age*. New York: Fordham University Press, 2006.

Phelan, Peggy. *Unmarked: The Politics of Performance*. New York: Routledge, 1993.

Phillips, John. *Transgender On Screen*. New York: Palgrave Macmillan, 2006.

Power, Nina. *One Dimensional Woman*. Winchester, UK: Zero Books, 2009.

Pratt, Minnie Bruce. *S/He*. Ithaca, NY: Firebrand, 1995.

Preciado, Paul (Beatriz). "Pharmaco-Pornographic Politics: Towards a New Gender Ecology." *Parallax* 46 (2008): 105–17.

Probyn, Elspeth. "Writing Shame." In *The Affect Theory Reader*, edited by Gregory Seigworth and Melissa Gregg, 71–92. Durham, NC: Duke University Press, 2010.

Prosser, Jay. *Second Skins: The Body Narratives of Transsexuality*. New York: Columbia University Press, 1998.

Puar, Jasbir K. "Bodies with New Organs: Becoming Trans, Becoming Disabled." *Social Text* 33, no. 3 (2015): 45–73.

Rachlin, Katherine. "Factors Which Influence Individual's Decisions When

Considering Female-to-Male Genital Reconstructive Surgery." *International Journal of Transgenderism* 3, no. 3 (July–September 1999). Accessed February 2, 2018. https://www.atria.nl/ezines/web/IJT/97–03/numbers/symposion/ijt990302.htm

Ramirez, Tanisha Love. "Why People Are Using the Term 'Latinx.'" HuffingtonPost.com, August 5, 2016. Accessed February 2, 2018. www.huffingtonpost.com/entry/why-people-are-using-the-term-latinx_us_57753328e4b0ccofa136a159.

Raun, Tobias. *Out Online: Trans Self-Representation and Community Building on YouTube.* New York: Routledge, 2016.

Raun, Tobias. "Screen-births: Exploring the Transformative Potential in Trans Video Blogs on YouTube." *Graduate Journal of Social Science* 7, no. 2 (2010): 113–30.

Raun, Tobias. "The Trans Woman as Model and Co-Creator: Resistance and Becoming in the Back-Turning Lili Elbe." In *Gerda Wegener Catalog*, 41–60. Arken, Denmark: Arken Museum of Modern Art, 2015.

Raun, Tobias, and Cáel M. Keegan, "Nothing to Hide: Selfies, Sex, and the Visibility Dilemma in Trans Male Online Cultures," in *Sex in the Digital Age*, ed. Paul G. Nixon and Isabel K. Düsterhöft, 89–100. New York: Routledge, 2017.

Rich, B. Ruby. "'Bodies Are Packages Made to be Opened': Shu Lea Cheang's 'I.K.U.' (2000)." *Rhizome* blog, May 26, 2005. Accessed March 14, 2017. rhizome.org/editorial/2015/may/26/iku-experience-shu-lea-cheang-phenomenon/.

Rich, B. Ruby. *New Queer Cinema: The Director's Cut.* Durham, NC: Duke University Press, 2013.

Richards, Rashna Wadia. *Cinematic Flashes: Cinephilia and Classical Hollywood.* Bloomington: Indiana University Press, 2013.

Richards, Renée, and John Ames. *Second Serve: The Renée Richards Story.* New York: Stein & Day, 1983.

Richmond, Scott C. *Cinema's Bodily Illusions: Flying, Floating, and Hallucinating.* Minneapolis: University of Minnesota Press, 2016.

Richmond, Scott C. "The Persistence of Formalism." *Open Set: Arts, Humanities, Culture.* October 1, 2015. Accessed December 1, 2017. http://www.open-set.com/s-richmond/essay-clusters/o-s-form-issue/the-persistence-of-formalism/.

Riley, Denise. "Am I That Name? Feminism and the Category of 'Women' in History." In *Bodies, Identities, Feminisms.* Basingstoke, U.K.: Palgrave Macmillan, 1988.

Roen, Katrina. "'Either/Or' and 'Both/Neither': Discursive Tension in Transgender Politics." *Signs* 27, no. 2 (2002): 501–22.

Roffe, Jonathan. "Multiplicity." In *The Deleuze Dictionary*, edited by Adrian Parr, 76–77. New York: Columbia University Press, 2005.

Ross, Mirah-Soleil, and Mark Karbusicky. *Tremblement de Chair*. V-Tape, 2001. Accessed March 10, 2010. http://www.ccca.ca/.

Rubin, Gayle S. "Thinking Sex: Notes for a Radical Theory of the Politics of Sexuality." In *The Lesbian and Gay Studies Reader*, edited by Henry Abelove, Michèle Aina Barale, and David M. Halperin, 3–44. New York: Routledge, 1993.

Russo, Julie Levin. "'The Real Thing': Reframing Queer Pornography for Virtual Spaces." In *C'Lick Me: A Netporn Studies Reader*, edited by Katrien Jacobs, Marije Janssen, and Matteo Pasquinelli, 239–51. Amsterdam: Institute of Network Cultures, 2007.

Rutherford, Anne. "Cinema and Embodied Affect." *Senses of Cinema* 25 (2003). Accessed February 2, 2018. http://www.sensesofcinema.com/2003/feature-articles/embodied_affect/.

Ryan, Joelle Ruby. "Reel Gender: Examining the Politics of Trans Images in Film and Media." PhD diss., Bowling Green State University, 2009.

Scheirl, Hans, dir. *Dandy Dust*. London: Millivres Multimedia, 1998.

Scheirl, Hans. "Hans in Transition: Paintings by Hans Scheirl." Press release and artist's statement. Transition Gallery Press, 2004. Accessed March 15, 2017. www.transitiongallery.co.uk/htmlpages/hans/hans_pr.html.

Scheirl, Hans. "I Am Opposed to the Practice of Not Showing the Horrible Things." Interview by Andrea Braidt. In *[Cybord.Nets/z] Catalogue on* Dandy Dust *(Hans Scheirl, 1998)*, edited by Andrea B. Braidt, 18–23. Vienna: BKA Filmbeirat, 1999.

Scheirl, Hans. "Manifesto for the Dada of the Cyborg-Embrio." In *The Eight Technologies of Otherness*, edited by Sue Golding, 45–57. London: Routledge, 1997.

Schönherr, Johannes. "Shu Lea Cheang: Sex Art Aborigine." In *Fleshpot: Cinema's Sexual Myth Makers & Taboo Breakers*, edited by Jack Stevenson, 197–200. New York: Critical Vision, 2000.

Schor, Naomi. "This Essentialism Which Is Not One: Coming to Grips with Irigaray." *Differences* 1, no. 2 (1988): 38–58.

Scott, Joan. "The Evidence of Experience." *Critical Inquiry* 17, no. 4 (1991): 773–97.

Sedgwick, Eve Kosofsky. *Epistemology of the Closet*. Berkeley: University of California Press, 1990.

Sedgwick, Eve Kosofsky. "Gosh, Boy George, You Must Be Awfully Secure in Your Masculinity!" In *Constructing Masculinity*, edited by Maurice Berger, Brian Wallis, and Simon Watson, 11–20. New York: Routledge, 1995.

Sedgwick, Eve Kosofsky. "Paranoid Reading and Reparative Reading, Or, You're So Paranoid, You Probably Think This Essay Is about You." In *Touching Feeling: Affect, Pedagogy, Performativity*, 121–52. Durham, NC: Duke University Press, 2003.

Sedgwick, Eve Kosofsky, and Adam Frank. "Shame in the Cybernetic Fold: Reading Silvan Tomkins." In *Shame and Its Sisters: A Silvan Tomkins Reader,* 1–28. Durham, NC: Duke University Press, 1995.

Seid, Danielle M. "Reveal." *TSQ: Transgender Studies Quarterly* 1, nos. 1–2 (2014): 176–77.

Seigworth, Gregory, and Melissa Gregg. "Introduction: An Inventory of Shimmers." In *The Affect Theory Reader,* edited by Gregory Seigworth and Melissa Gregg, 1–28. Durham, NC: Duke University Press, 2010.

Sengoopta, Chandak. *The Most Secret Quintessence of Life: Sex, Glands, and Hormones, 1850–1950.* Chicago: Chicago University Press, 2006.

Shapiro, Judith. "Transsexualism: Reflections on the Persistence of Gender and the Mutability of Sex." In *Body Guards: The Cultural Politics of Gender Ambiguity,* edited by Julia Epstein and Kristina Straub, 248–79. New York: Routledge, 1991.

Shaviro, Steven. *The Cinematic Body.* Minneapolis: University of Minnesota Press, 1993.

Silverman, Kaja. *Male Subjectivity at the Margins.* New York: Routledge, 1992.

Silverman, Kaja. *The Threshold of the Visible World.* New York: Routledge, 1996.

Sobchack, Vivian. "On *Becoming.*" In *Becoming: A Gender Flipbook,* edited by Yishay Gabasz, 182–87. New York: Mark Batty Publisher, 2010.

Spade, Dean. "Mutilating Gender." In *The Transgender Studies Reader,* edited by Stephen Whittle and Susan Stryker, 315–32. New York: Routledge, 2006.

Spade, Dean. *Normal Life: Administrative Violence, Critical Trans Politics and the Limits of Law.* Durham, NC: Duke University Press, 2015.

Sprinkle, Annie. "My First Female-to-Male Lover." *Hustler* 16, no. 8 (February 1990): 7–12. Accessed February 2, 2018. http://anniesprinkle.org/my-first-female-to-male-transsexual-lover/.

Sprinkle, Annie. *Post Porn Modernist: My 25 Years as a Multimedia Whore.* San Francisco: Cleis, 1989.

Sprinkle, Annie, Albert Jaccoma, and John Armstrong, dir. *Linda/Les and Annie: The First Female-to-Male Transsexual Love Story.* 1989.

Stallings, L. H. *Funk the Erotic: Transaesthetics and Black Sexual Cultures.* Chicago: University of Illinois Press, 2015.

Star People LLC. "Happy Birthday Marsha!," February 19, 2015. Accessed March 24, 2016. http://www.happybirthdaymarsha.com.

Steinbock, Eliza. "Collecting Creative Transcestors: Trans* Portraiture Hirstory, from Snapshots to Sculpture." In *Companion to Feminist Art,* edited by Maria Buszek and Hilary Robinson. Hoboken, NJ: Wiley-Blackwell Publishing. Forthcoming.

Steinbock, Eliza. "Interview: A Conversation with Cassils on Propagating Collective Resilience in Times of War," *Performance Matters,* 4 no. 2 (2018).

Steinbock, Eliza. "Lili Elbe's Transmedial Presence and the Politics of Transgender Studies." In *Doing Gender in Media, Art and Culture*, 2nd ed., edited by Rosemarie Buikema, Liedeke Plate, and Kathrin Thiele, 169–81. New York: Routledge, 2018.

Steinbock, Eliza. "'Look!' but also, 'Touch!': Theorizing Images of Trans-Eroticism Beyond a Politics of Visual Essentialism." In *Porno-Graphics and Porno-Tactics: Desire, Affect, and Representation in Pornography*, edited by Eirini Avramopoulou and Irene Peano, 59–75. Earth, Milky Way: Punctum Books, 2016.

Steinbock, Eliza. "Parsing Affective Economies of Race, Sexuality, and Gender: The Case of 'Nasty Love.'" In *Structures of Feeling: Affectivity and the Study of Culture,* edited by Devika Sharma and Frederik Tygstrup, 40–9. Berlin and Boston: de Gruyter, 2015.

Steinbock, Eliza. "A Pretty Knot of Lilies: Disentangling Lili Elbe's *longue durée* in Pop Culture." In *Comparative Scholarly Edition of* Man into Woman *(1931),* edited by Pamela L. Caughie and Sabine Meyer. London: Bloomsbury. Forthcoming.

Steinbock, Eliza. "Representing Trans* Sexualities." In *Routledge Companion to Media, Sex and Sexuality,* edited by Feona Attwood, R. Danielle Egan, Brian McNair, and Clarissa Smith, 27–37. New York: Routledge, 2017.

Steinbock, Eliza. "Towards Trans Cinema." In *Routledge Companion to Cinema and Gender,* edited by Kristin Lené Hole, Dijlana Jelača, E. Ann Kaplan, and Patrice Petro, 395–406. New York: Routledge, 2016.

Steinbock, Eliza. "The Violence of the Cut: Transgender Homeopathy and Cinematic Aesthetics." In *Violence and Agency: Queer and Feminist Perspectives* (Gewalt und Handlungsmacht: Queer_Feministische Perspektiven), edited by Gender Initiativkolleg Wien, 154–71. Frankfurt: Campus Publications, 2012.

Steinbock, Eliza, and Zowie Davy. "'Sexing Up' Bodily Aesthetics: Notes towards Theorizing Trans Sexuality." In *Sexualities: Past Reflections and Future Directions*, edited by Sally Hines and Yvette Taylor, 266–85. Basingstoke, U.K.: Palgrave Macmillan, 2012.

Steinbock, Eliza, Marianna Szczygielska, and Anthony Wagner. "Introduction: Thinking Linking," *Angelaki: Journal of Theoretical Humanities* 22, no. 2 (2017): 1–10.

Steiner, A. L. "BEFORE/AFTER A. L. Steiner." Accessed March 24, 2016. http://www.hellomynameissteiner.com/filter/collaborations/BEFORE-AFTER-1.

Steiner, A. L., and Z. Drucker. "IMG MGMT: Before/After 2009-Present." *Art F City* website. May 16, 2011. Accessed March 24, 2016. http://artfcity.com/2011/05/16/img-mgmt-z-drucker-a-l-steiner-beforeafter-2009-present/.

Steinmetz, Julia. "103 Shots: Listening to Orlando." *Huffington Post,* "Queer

Voices" blog, last updated June 27, 2016. Accessed December 1, 2017. https://www.huffingtonpost.com/entry/103-shots-listening-to-orlando_us_57714cd9e4b0fa01a1405b42.

Stone, Allucquère Rosanne. *The War of Desire and Technology at the Close of the Mechanical Age*. Cambridge, MA: MIT Press, 1996.

Stone, Sandy. "The *Empire* Strikes Back: A Posttranssexual Manifesto" [1991]. In *The Transgender Studies Reader*, edited by Stephen Whittle and Susan Stryker, 221–35. New York: Routledge, 2006.

Stone, Sandy. "Keynote Lecture." Presented at the Trans*Studies: An International Transdisciplinary Conference on Gender, Embodiment, and Sexuality, Tucson, Arizona, September 7, 2016.

Stone, Sandy, and Kate Bornstein. "A Conversation Between Sandy Stone and Kate Bornstein Moderated by Susan Stryker." Presentation at the Postposttranssexual: Transgender Studies and Feminism Conference. Bloomington, Indiana, April 8–9, 2011.

Storr, Merl, and Jay Prosser. "Introduction to Part III Transsexuality and Bisexuality." In *Sexology Uncensored: The Documents of Sexual Science*, edited by Lucy Bland and Laura Doan, 75–77. Chicago: Chicago University Press, 1998.

Straube, Wibke. "Trans Cinema and Its Exit Scapes. A Transfeminist Reading of Utopian Sensibility and Gender Dissidence in Contemporary Film." PhD diss., Linköping University, 2014.

Strauven, Wanda. "Introduction to an Attractive Concept." In *The Cinema of Attractions Reloaded*, edited by Wanda Strauven, 11–30. Amsterdam: Amsterdam University Press, 2006.

Strauven, Wanda. "Pour Une Lecture Média-Archéologique de L'œuvre de Georges Méliès." In *Méliès, Carrefour Des Attractions*, edited by André Gaudreault, Laurent Le Forestier, and Stéphane Tralongo, 291–99. Rennes, France: Presses universitaires de Rennes, 2014.

Stryker, Susan. "Christine in the Cutting Room: Cinema, Surgery and Celebrity in the Career of Christine Jorgensen." Paper presented at the Department of Media, Music, Communication and Cultural Studies Public Lecture Series, Macquarie University, Sydney, Australia, May 1, 2013. Available on *YouTube.com*, posted August 16, 2013. Accessed March 18, 2016. https://www.youtube.com/watch?v=XlqJ8B9dKCs.

Stryker, Susan. "A Conversation Between Sandy Stone and Kate Bornstein Moderated by Susan Stryker." Presentation at the Postposttranssexual: Transgender Studies and Feminism Conference. Bloomington, Indiana, April 8–9, 2011.

Stryker, Susan. "Dungeon Intimacies: The Poetics of Transsexual Sadomasochism." *Parallax* 46 (2008): 36–47.

Stryker, Susan. "My Words to Victor Frankenstein Above the Village of Cham-

ounix: Performing Transgender Rage." In *The Transgender Studies Reader*,
edited by Susan Stryker and Stephen Whittle, 244–56. New York: Routledge,
[1994] 2006.

Stryker, Susan. *Transgender History*. Berkeley: Seal Press, 2008.

Stryker, Susan. "The Transgender Issue: An Introduction." GLQ: *Journal of Lesbian and Gay Studies* 4, no. 2 (1998): 145–58.

Stryker, Susan. "Transgender Studies: Queer Theory's Evil Twin." GLQ: *A Journal of Lesbian and Gay Studies* 10, no. 2 (2004): 212–15.

Stryker, Susan, and Jim van Buskirk. *Gay by the Bay: A History of Queer Culture in the San Francisco Bay Area*. San Francisco: Chronicle, 1996.

Sturken, Marita. "Paradox in the Evolution of an Art Form: Great Expectations and the Making of a History." In *Illuminating Video: An Essential Guide to Video Art*, edited by Doug Hall and Sally Jo Fifer, 101–21. New York: Aperture, [1988] 1990.

Sullivan, Louis, ed. *FtM Newsletter*, December 1989.

Sullivan, Nikki. *A Critical Introduction to Queer Theory*. New York: New York University Press, 2003.

Taormino, Tristan. "The New Wave of Trans Cinema: The Latest Transporn Breaks Down Both Boundaries and Inhibitions." *The Village Voice*, April 8, 2008. Accessed February 2, 2018. http://www.villagevoice.com/2008–04–08/columns/the-new-wave-of-trans-cinema/.

Thacker, Eugene. "What Is Biomedia?" *Configurations* 11 (2003): 47–79.

Thom, Kai Cheng. "How Trans Women Are Reclaiming Their Orgasms." Buzzfeed.com, April 1, 2016. Accessed May 20, 2016. https://www.buzzfeed.com/kaichengthom/the-search-for-trans-womens-orgasms?utm_term=.reeKJ8oje#.lrPoOynKe.

Tomkins, Silvan. *Shame and Its Sisters: A Silvan Tomkins Reader*. Edited by Eve Kosofsky Sedgwick and Adam Frank. Durham, NC: Duke University Press, 1995.

TrIQ. "TransInterQueer e.V.," 2006. Last updated 2016. Accessed March 18, 2016. http://www.transinterqueer.org.

Uroski, Andrew V. *Between the Black Box and the White Cube: Expanded Cinema and Postwar Art*. Chicago: University of Chicago Press, 2014.

Wagner, Anthony Clair. "(Un)Be(Com)ing Others: A Trans* Film Criticism of the Alien Quadrilogy Movies." PhD diss., Academy of Fine Arts Vienna, 2015.

Wahlfors, Laura. "Resonances and Dissonances: Listening to Waltraud Meier's Envoicing of Isolde." In *On Voice*, edited by Walter Bernhart and Lawrence Kramer, 57–76. Amsterdam: Rodopi, 2014.

Walidah, Hanifah, and Olive Demetrius. *U People*, New York City: U People LLC, 2009.

Walker, Alice. *In Search of Our Mothers' Gardens: Womanist Prose*. New York: Harcourt Brace Jovanovich, 1983.

Wallace, Michele. *Invisibility Blues: From Pop to Theory*. London: Verso, 1990.

Weheliye, Alexander. *Habeas Viscus: Racializing Assemblages, Biopolitics, and Black Feminist Theories of the Human*. Durham, NC: Duke University Press, 2014.

Weindling, Paul. *Health, Race and German Politics between National Unification and Nazism, 1870–1945*. Cambridge, MA: Cambridge University Press, 1989.

Weiss, Margot. *Techniques of Pleasures: BDSM and the Circuits of Sexuality*. Durham, NC: Duke University Press, 2012.

Whale, James, dir. *Frankenstein*. Los Angeles: Universal Pictures Production, 1931.

Whitehead, Alfred North. *Adventures of Ideas*. New York: Free Press, 1967.

Wilchins, Riki Anne. *Read My Lips: Sexual Subversions and the End of Gender*. Ithaca, NY: Firebrand Books, 1997.

Willemen, Paul. "An Avant-Garde for the 1990s." In *Looks and Frictions: Essays in Cultural Studies and Film Theory*, edited by Paul Willemen, 141–61. London: British Film Institute, 1994.

Williams, Jonathan Rachel. "Trans Cinema, Trans Viewers." PhD diss., University of Melbourne, 2011.

Williams, Linda. *Hard Core: Power, Pleasure, and the "Frenzy of the Visible."* Berkeley: California University Press, 1999.

Williams, Linda. "Porn Studies: Proliferating Pornographies On/Scene: An Introduction." In *Porn Studies*, edited by Linda Williams, 1–23. Durham, NC: Duke University Press, 2004.

Williams, Linda. "Skin Flicks on the Racial Border: Pornography, Exploitation, and Interracial Lust." In *Porn Studies*, edited by Linda Williams, 271–307. Durham, NC: Duke University Press, 2004.

Wollen, Peter. "Two Avant-Gardes." In *Readings and Writings: Semiotic Counter-Strategies*, 92–104. London: Verso Press, 1982.

World Professional Association for Transgender Health. *The Harry Benjamin International Gender Dysphoria Association's Standards of Care for Gender Identity Disorders*. 6th ed., February 1, 2001. Accessed February 2, 2018. http://www.cpath.ca/wp-content/uploads/2009/12/WPATHsocv6.pdf.

Ziegler, Kortney Ryan. *Still Black: A Portrait of Black Trans Men*, 2008.

Zylinska, Joanna. "A Bit(e)of the Other: An Interview with Sue Golding." *Parallax* 5, no. 4 (1999): 145–55.

INDEX

Bold page numbers refer to figures

Armstrong, John: *Linda/Les, and Annie: The First Female-to-Male Transsexual Love Story (L/LA)*, 23, 65, 70–79, 99, 178n46
Ashbery, John, 165n20
asterisk, 20–21, 110, 112, 139, 189n25
Australia, 44; Sydney, 6
Austria, 167n45
autobiography, 16, 23, 30, 44
autoethnography, 64
avant-garde films, 15, 20, 37, 106, 109–44, 194n87
Aydemir, Murat, 182n93

Baby Boomers, 60
"bad sex" *vs.* "good sex" binary, 63, 105
Baer, Karl M. *See* Body, N.O.
Bal, Mieke, 11, 18, 104
Barad, Karen, 124
Barbin, Herculine (Adélaîde/Abel), 33–34, 38
Barthes, Roland, 9–14, 30, 54, 57, 112, 117, 123, 146, 149; *The Preparation of the Novel*, 123; *Sade/Fourier/Loyola*, 160n35
bathroom bills, 109
Baudrillard, Jean, 178n49, 189n13
Bauer, Robin, 102
Bauman, Zygmunt, 28
Bazin, André, 178n49
BDSM, 96, 98, 102–3, 184n104. *See also* kink
Beckman, Karen, 41
Bell, Shannon, 154
Benetton, 151
Benjamin, Harry, 174n6; *The Transsexual Phenomenon*, 62, 175n7, 175n10. *See also* Harry Benjamin International Gender Dysphoria Association
Benjamin, Walter, 39, 41, 49, 59; "Work of Art," 35–36, 167n38
Bergson, Henri, 24, 111; *Matter and Memory*, 108
Bergstedt, Spencer, 103

Best Transgender Erotica, 79
Bettcher, Talia Mae, 5
Bindel, Julie, 141
biopolitics, 20
bisexuality, 19, 80, 100, 177n45
bi-trans sexualities, 23
Blade Runner, 118, 191n45
Blanchot, Maurice, 11
Blank, Hanne: *Best Transgender Erotica*, 79
Body, N.O.: *Man's Years as a Young Girl*, 159n18
Bohemia, 42
The Bold and the Beautiful, 163n2
Bolter, Jay David, 33
Bordwell, David, 189n16
Bornstein, Kate, 60, 81, 100; *Gender Outlaw*, 61
Bosch, Hieronymus: *The Garden of Earthly Delights*, 10
Boudry, Pauline: *N.O. Body*, 159n18
Boys Don't Cry, 4
"BRANDON: A One-Year Narrative Project in Installments," 191n48
Branigan, Edward, 51
Brinkema, Eugenie, 13, 115–16, 118, 125, 128, 139, 144
BuckAngel.com, 79–**80**, 180n72
Buck Angel Entertainment, 180n72
Buck-Morss, Susan, 36
Buck Naked, 180n73
Buck's Beaver, 180n73
Busan Biennale, 57
butches, vii, 68
Butler, Judith, 10, 77

Cahiers du cinema, 104
California: Los Angeles, 6; San Francisco, 146, 179n69
Canada: Toronto, 6, 9
cárdenas, micha, 67–68, 156
Carter, Julian, 139, 195n99
Cassils: *103 Shots*, 146–51, 153–55
Castle, Terry, 28

Caughie, Pamela, 50, 169n66

celluloid, 35–36, 41, 114

Cheang, Shu Lea, 193n70; *I.K.U.*, 24, 109, 113, 118–**20**, 124–30, 133–39, 189n15, 190n27, 191n45, 192n58, 194n76

Chen, Jian, 191n45, 191n47, 195n97

Chen, Mel, 20

chirugie filmique, 38

Cholodenko, Alan, 15

choreography studies, 139

Chris: *Trans Entities: The Nasty Love of Papí and Will*, 23, 65, 92–99, 101, 103, 184n105

Christianity, 183n95, 183n97

Chromoscope, 8

chrononormativity, 41, 53

cinema of attractions, 42–43

cinema studies, 3, 8–9, 15, 40, 66, 96; antipsychoanalytic film theory, 116; cognitive film theory, 110; feminist film theory, 3, 110, 113, 178n49

cinematic form, ix

cinematic logic of transsexual embodiment, 17, 21–22, 36

cinematic specificity, 40

cinematography, 6–7, 15, 21, 24, 27, 35–36, 39–40, 85, 114, 131; double exposure, 54, 65, 85, 87–90

cinephiles, 2, 8, 13, 24, 52, 115, 125, 131, 145–46, 153, 157n4

cinesexuality, 131, 157n4

Cipriani, Jana: *Dandy Dust*, 24, 109, 113–18, 120–23, 125–26, 130–39, 152–53, 189n15, 190n27, 194n78

Clair, René: *Entr'acte*, 134

Clayton, Jamie, 163n2

close reading, 13, 112, 117, 122, 141

Club 90, 177n44

Club FUXXX, 180n74

Collège de France, 9

colonialism, 18, 140, 142, 167n50, 184n103. *See also* imperialism

colorism, 65, 92–93, 96, 184n103. *See also* racism

common sense, 5, 108, 112, 117, 140–42, 146, 155

conjunction, 6, 13, 19–20, 101, 113, 147

corporeality, 6, 18, 39, 100, 104, 114, 132, 147. *See also* embodiment

Cossey, Caroline (Tula), 169n66

counter-history, 15, 150

Counting Past 2 film and art festival, 9

Cox, Laverne, 163n2

Coxxx, Papí: *Trans Entities: The Nasty Love of Papí and Will*, 23, 65, 92–99, 101, 103, 184n105

Crary, Jonathan, 33

cross-dressing, 4, 41, 138, 174n6. *See also* transvestism

cross-identification, 4

The Crying Game, 4

Cubitt, Sean, 7, 59

Currah, Paisley, 20

the cut, 6, 17, 40, 52, 57, 70–71, 127, 131, 133, 135; forward slash and, 20–21; irrational, 111–13; surgical/filmic, 21, 35–36, 45, 100, 154; suturing and, 2, 42, 53–60, 100, 153, 155. *See also* editing

Cvetkovitch, Ann, 150

cybernetics, 106–12, 132–33

cyborg, 20, 24, 107–9, 113, 122–23, 126, 134, 140–41, 152, 154, 189n13, 194n83

Cyrus, Miley, 28

dada, 20, 24, 109, 113–14, 122, 133–37

Daly, Mary, 141

Dandy Dust, 24, 109, 113–18, 120–23, 125–26, 130–39, 152–53, 189n15, 190n27, 194n78

The Danish Girl (film), 42–43, 60, 163n2

Darling, James, 180n73

Darwin, Charles, 37

Davy, Zowie, 100–102, 187n143

d@d@, 24, 113, 133–39

d/Deaf communities, 93, 97

Debord, Guy, 178n49

decoloniality, 18

deconstruction, 18, 21, 146

Hi-8, 114
Hirsch, Werner: *N.O. Body*, 159n18
Hirschfeld, Magnus, 44, 159n18, 167n45,
    170n79; "Yearbooks for Sexual Inter-
    mediaries," 31
Hocquenghem, Guy, 126
Hollywood, 40, 42, 81, 173n129, 181n77,
    191n45; Golden Age, 30
homonationalism, 150
homosexuality, 31, 62, 67, 69, 80, 92, 100,
    166n31, 175n10, 176n26, 182n90
hooks, bell, 140
Hooper, Tom: *The Danish Girl* (film),
    42–43, 60, 163n2
Hoshino, Mai, 192n58
Hoyer, Niels. *See* Hathern, Ernst (Niels
    Hoyer)
Hubble telescope, 143–44
Huffington Post, 146
humanism, 20, 140
Hustler, 71, 73, 78, 177n45
hyphen, 20–21, 23

I Am Cait, 163n2
I Am Jazz, 163n2
identification, 58, 100, 105, 110, 125, 132,
    141, 143; anachronistic, 60; erotic,
    21, 186n128; gendered, 2–6, 19, 32,
    42, 92–94, 99, 164n17, 174n6, 177n45,
    184n104, 194n83; heteropathic, 104;
    idiopathic, 104; pseudo-identification,
    101–2. *See also* cross-identification;
    disidentification
ideology of the visible, 18
I.K.U., 24, 109, 113, 118–**20**, 124–30,
    133–39, 189n15, 190n27, 191n45, 192n58,
    194n76
Illdoya, Danny, vii
illusive flesh, 155–56
Imaginary (Lacan), 101–2
imperialism, 18. *See also* colonialism
Indiana University, 61
Institute for Sexual Science, 167n45,
    170n79

intermedial meshing, 30–31, 164n16
intersex people, viii, 10, 17–19, 21, 31, 34,
    43, 159n18, 161n66, 164n17, 178n46,
    191n41
Italy: Bologna, 6

Jaccoma, Albert: *Linda/Les, and Annie:
    The First Female-to-Male Transsexual
    Love Story (L/LA)*, 23, 65, 70–79, 99,
    178n46
Jackson, Zakiyyah Iman, 140
Jacobs, Katrien, 119, 128
Janco, Marcel, 133
Japan, 119, 127, 129–30, 136, 138–39,
    195n97
Jeffries, Sheila, 141
Jenner, Caitlyn, 169n66; *I am Cait*, 163n2
Jewel Box Review, 68
Johnson, Marsha P.: *Happy Birthday
    Marsha!*, 60
Jones, Annie, 159n18
Jorgensen, Christine, 17, 35, 169n66

Kaldera, Raven: *Best Transgender Erot-
    ica*, 79
kaleidoscopes, 8, 31, 126, 131
Kamiyama, Hoppy, 130
Karbusicky, Mark: *Tremblement de Chair
    (Trembling Flesh)*, 84–**91**, 99, 101
Keegan, Cáel M., 193n69
Keeling, Kara, 24, 108, 116, 142, 189n12
Kessler, Frank, 40
kink, 92–95, 184–85, 184n104. *See also*
    BDSM
kitchen sink, 178n50
Klein, Melanie, 58
Knudsen, Poul, 44
Kooijman, Jaap, 192n52
Krueger, Suzi, 122
Kuzniar, Alice A., 190n27

Lacan, Jacques, 4, 104–5
Lane, Riki, 171n96
Lao-tzu, 10

nasty, 65, 151; nasty love, 23, 65, 91–99, 105

Nataf, Zachary, 24, 119, 195n97

neoliberalism, 28

Netherlands, 180n74, 184n105; Amsterdam, 6, 158n16

Netherlands Transgender Film Festival, 158n16, 184n105

the Neutral/Neuter (Barthes), 9–11, 13–14, 25, 51, 112, 117, 144, 146

New Gender Politics, 10

New Queer Cinema, 19, 113

New Woman, 43

New York City, 7, 177n44, 179n62; Brooklyn, 4; Manhattan, 68

Nichols, Bill, 74

Nichols, Les, 177n45; *Linda/Les, and Annie: The First Female-to-Male Transsexual Love Story (L/LA)*, 23, 65, 70–79, 99, 178n46

Nietzsche, Friedrich, 165n20

9/11, 146

nonbinarism, vii–viii, 3, 14, 25, 43, 61, 126, 145, 186n128

nonce taxonomies, 186n128

normates, 161n66

ob/scene, 71

O'Donoghue, Darragh, 39

103 Shots, 146–51, 153–55

onto-epistemologies, 11, 29. *See also* epistemology; ontology

ontology, ix, 6, 11–12, 15, 35, 61, 65, 73, 77, 98–100, 109–11, 139, 149, 152, 178n49

Orange is the New Black, 163n2

Orr, Jackie, 141

Oudart, Jean-Pierre, 104

Ovid: *Metamorphoses*, 139

Paci, Viva, 51

Pandora, 126, 193n65

paradigm, 9–14, 25, 50, 86, 111, 143, 152–53, 181n76

paranoid reading, 58

Paris Is Burning, 185n106

Parnet, Claire, 59

passing, 29, 53, 67

pathos, 10–11, 112, 115

Peddle, Daniel: *The Aggressives*, 185n106

phalloplasty, 71, 80, 177n45

phantasmagoria, 8, 20–22, 26–60, 155, 167n47; new urban, 36

Phelan, Peggy, 18, 162n72

phenomenology, 100–103, 110

Philidor, Philip, 26

philosophy, 2, 9, 19, 24, 28, 104, 111, 131, 154, 156. *See also* pornosophy

photography, 22, 27, 29–30, 37, 40, 42, 45–50, 53–**56**, 81, 85, 133, 159n18, 169n66, 177n45, 178n49; spiritualist, 41

Place de l'Opéra, 36

Plantinga, Alvin, 197n21

Plato, 115; *Symposium*, 50

Poma, Barbara, 149

Poma, John, 149

pornification, 176n20

pornographicity, 154

pornography, 22, 60, 109, 118–19, 128–29, 151, 155, 179n69, 180n73, 181nn76–77, 182n91, 184n105, 189n15, 192n58; docuporn, 15, 22–23, 61–106, 153, 181n78; gonzo, 177n44; net-porn, 134; post-porn modernism, 178n47; reality, 177n44; "she-male," 4, 79; techno-porn, 24, 130

pornosophy, 154

pornosphere, 64

postgender, ix, 107, 140–41

postmodernism, 26, 28, 107, 110, 140

post-Newtonian physics, 143

Postposttranssexual: Transgender Studies and Feminism Conference, 61

posttranssexuality, 14–15, 59, 61, 64, 101, 107, 152

Power, Nina, 181n77

practices of light, 8, 145, 155

Pratt, Minnie Bruce, 1–2, 170n73

Preciado, Paul, 188n5

Probyn, Elspeth, 13
pronouns, vii–viii, 112, 122, 177n45
proprioceptive ego, 102–4
Prosser, Jay, 29–30, 46, 50, 54, 100
psychoanalysis, 4, 18, 65, 101–4, 110, 116.
    See also mirror stage
psychology, viii, 16, 31, 50, 53, 61, 124,
    170n79
Puar, Jasbir, 150
Pulse mass murder (2016), 146–51,
    153–55
Pürrer, Ursula, 190n27
pussy-shot, 113, 128, 130

Queer Nation, 150–**51**
queerness, viii, 17–21, 27–28, 31, 33, 43,
    58, 67, 75, 93–95, 98–99, 126, 146–55,
    161n66, 180n73, 185n106, 192n52; queer
    affect, 110; queer formalism, 191n44.
    See also New Queer Cinema; Queer
    Nation; queer theory; trans-inter-
    queer (concept)
queer theory, 10, 19. *See also* gay and les-
    bian studies

race, 7–8, 20, 24, 69, 91, 108, 150–51,
    156, 161n66, 184n103; color blindness,
    97; embodied, 98; gendered, 19, 65,
    92–96, 99, 108–9, 112, 138–40; race
    play, 65, 93, 96–99; racial essentialism,
    92; racial realism, 23, 92, 99. *See also*
    colorism; racism
Rachlin, Katherine, 180n75
racism, 92–93, 97, 140, 150, 184n103;
    Donald Trump's, 146. *See also*
    colorism
rage, 17, 24–25, 106, 113, 140–43, 142–43,
    155
Raun, Tobias, 18
Raymond, Janice, 141
realism, 54, 58, 70, 72, 74, 77, 180n75;
    antirealism, 39; indexical, 178n49;
    ontological, 178n49; racial, 23, 92, 99;
    social, 73, 178n50

rear projection, 32
Redmayne, Eddie, 42
referent, 30, 34, 54, 81–82, 125
religious right, 141
reparative reading/method, 5, 22, 58, 60
reterritorialization, 103
the reveal, 4–5, 22, 29, 53, 58, 60, 71–72,
    81. *See also* forced disclosure
Rich, B. Ruby, 189n15
Richards, Rashna Wadia, 157n4
Richards, Renée, 169n66; *Second Serve*,
    170n74
Richmond, Scott C., 58
Richter, Dorchen, 167n45, 170n79
Riemann, Georg, 111
Riley, Denise, 113
Rivera, Sylvia, 60
Robert Hill Releasing, 180n72
Roen, Katrina, 160n40
Rogers-Wright, Leonora, 122
Rose, Ruby, 28
Ross, Mirha-Soleil, 9, 23, 65; *Tremble-
    ment de Chair (Trembling Flesh)*,
    84–**91**, 99, 101
Roussel, Raymond, 165n20, 166n23
Royalle, Candida, 177n44
Rubin, Gayle S., 63
RuPaul: *RuPaul's Drag Race*, 163n2
RuPaul's Drag Race, 163n2
Russo, Julie Levin, 75
Rutherford, Anne, 132
Ryder, Chance, 179n69

Sade, Marquis de, 160n35, 181n76
Saint Marks Baths, 69
saming, 19, 163n83
Saussurean linguistics, 9
Scheirl, Hans: *Dandy Dust*, 24, 109,
    113–18, 120–23, 125–26, 130–39,
    152–53, 189n15, 190n27, 194n78; "Hans
    in Transition," 192n55; "Manifesto for
    the Dada of the Cyborg-Embrio," 122,
    191n41
Scheler, Max, 104

the transreal, 66, 68–70, 72, 156
TransScreen: Amsterdam Film Festival,
158n16
trans-sexualities, 21–23, 63–64, 63–66,
70, 78, 94, 99–100, 103, 184n100
transsexual logic of cinematic embodiment, 17, 21–22, 36
Transsexual-man.com, 79
transgender studies, 2–4, 8, 11–12, 17, 19,
28, 50, 61, 143, 145
transvestism, vii, 4, 31, 34, 41, 62, 63,
157n6, 175n10, 194n83; psychic, 42. *See
also* cross-dressing
trans women, 4, 16, 60, 67, 163n2, 169n66
transworld identity, 197n21
transxploitation films, 16
traveling concepts, 11
Tremblement de Chair (Trembling Flesh),
84–**91**, 99, 101
trick films, 15, 22, 30, 36–42, 49, 53–54,
135, 155, 172n110
Trump, Donald: racism of, 146
Tsukamoto, Shinya: *Tetsuo II – Body
Hammer*, 136
Twitter, vii
2 Live Crew: *As Nasty as They Wanna
Be*, 96

U People, 185n106

van Diesel, 101–2; *Diesel Exposed*,
180n73; *Diesel's Double Vision*, 180n73;
Man with a Pussy, 180n73
"The Vanishing Lady" (stage show), 41
Variety, 131
Velázquez, Diego: *Las Meninas*, 32
Vera, Veronica, 177n44
visibilities (Deleuze), 31, 151, 166n23
visual essentialism, 18, 65, 106, 155
vlogs, 17–18
von Kreutz, Werner. *See* Warnekros,
Kurt (Werner von Kreutz)
voyeurism, 18, 155

Wachowski, Lana, 169n66, 193n69;
The Matrix, 128
Wachowski, Lilly, 169n66, 193n69; *The
Matrix*, 128
Wahlfors, Laura, 11
Wai Kui, Kam, 158n16
Walidah, Hanifah: *U People*, 185n106
Walker, Alice, 92, 184n103
Wallace, Michele, 186n125
Wallon, Henri, 102–3
Warnekros, Kurt (Werner von Kreutz),
44
war on terrorism, 146
Washington: Seattle, 6
Waxman, Tobaron, 4, 158n17
Wegener, Einar. *See* Elbe, Lili (Einar
Wegener/Lili Ilse Elvenes)
Wegener, Gerda, 42–44, **47**, 50
Weheliye, Alexander, 156
Weinstein, Jami, 110
West Side Story, 6–8
WeTV, 181n81
Whale, James: *Frankenstein* (film),
16–17
Whitehead, Alfred North, 11
Wilchins, Riki Anne, 81, 184n100
Willemen, Paul, 194n87
Williams, Linda, 71, 82, 96, 128, 181n77
Williams, Raymond, 150
Wishman, Doris: *Let Me Die a Woman*,
16
World War I, 134
World Wide Web, 108
Wortzel, Sasha: *Happy Birthday Mar-
sha!*, 60

Youngblood, Gene, 194n78
YouTube, 17

Ziegler, Kortney Ryan: *Still Black: A Portrait of Black Trans Men*, 185n106
zoetrope, 22, 27, 56–57

www.ingramcontent.com/pod-product-compliance
Lightning Source LLC
Chambersburg PA
CBHW071738270326
41928CB00013B/2721